Microsoft·Press

W9-CQW-932

Microsoft
SQL Server™ 7.0
Administrator's
Pocket
Consultant

William R. Stanek

PUBLISHED BY
Microsoft Press
A Division of Microsoft Corporation
One Microsoft Way
Redmond, Washington 98052-6399

Library of Congress Cataloging-in-Publication Data
Stanek, William R.
    Microsoft SQL Server 7.0 Administrator's Pocket Consultant /
  William R. Stanek.
      p. cm.
   ISBN 0-7356-0596-3
   1. Client/server computing. 2. SQL server.   I. Title.
  QA76.9.C55S79   1999
  005.75'85--dc21   99-33879
                                              CIP

Printed and bound in the United States of America.

2 3 4 5 6 7 8 9   MLML   4 3 2 1 0 9

Distributed in Canada by Penguin Books Canada Limited.

A CIP catalogue record for this book is available from the British Library.

Microsoft Press books are available through booksellers and distributors worldwide. For further information about international editions, contact your local Microsoft Corporation office or contact Microsoft Press International directly at fax (425) 936-7329. Visit our Web site at mspress.microsoft.com.

Acquisitions Editor: Juliana Aldous
Project Editor: Susan Bradley

Contents at a Glance

Table of Contents

Part II
Microsoft SQL Server 7.0 Administration

3 Managing the Enterprise 59

5   **Microsoft SQL Server 7.0 Security   111**

Part III
Microsoft SQL Server 7.0 Data Administration

Part IV
Performance, Optimization, and Maintenance

Tables

Acknowledgments

Wow, writing this book was a great experience that *really* put my years of Microsoft SQL Server administration and consulting knowledge to the test. It is gratifying to see the techniques that I've used time and again to solve problems put into a printed book so that others may benefit from them. But no man is an island, and this book couldn't have been written without help from some very special people.

As I stated in *Microsoft Windows NT 4.0 Server Administrator's Pocket Consultant*, the team at Microsoft Press is top-notch. I owe a huge "Thank You" to Anne Hamilton, as publisher, and Stuart Stuple, as managing editor, both for recognizing the potential of my practical and useful approach to the Pocket Consultant series, and for their willingness to run with the approach. Juliana Aldous handled acquisitions and helped out when possible to keep the project rolling. Maureen Zimmerman and Susan Bradley watched over the editorial process from the Microsoft Press side and Sarah Kimnach headed up the editorial process for nSight, Inc. Their thoroughness and attention to every detail is much appreciated!

As content manager, Tracy Thomsic ensured that everyone involved in the project kept to the schedule. With the extensive author review and editing phases for this book, this was a very difficult feat. Joseph Gustaitis was copy editor for the book and Piotr Prussak was the technical editor for the book. Together, they did a great job of ensuring the copy and content were accurate.

Thanks also to Studio B literary agency and my agents, David Rogelberg and Neil Salkind. Now, if you could just land that commentary column for me I'd be as happy as a cat that swallowed a canary.

Hopefully, I haven't forgotten anyone but, if I have, it was an oversight. *Honest.* ;-)

Introduction

Microsoft SQL Server 7.0 Administrator's Pocket Consultant is designed to be a concise and usable resource for SQL Server administrators. This is the readable resource guide that you'll want on your desktop at all times. It covers everything you need to perform the core administrative tasks for SQL Server. Because the focus is on giving you maximum value in a pocket-sized guide, you don't have to wade through hundreds of pages of extraneous information to find what you're looking for. Instead, you'll find exactly what you need to get the job done.

In short, I hope that *Microsoft SQL Server 7.0 Administrator's Pocket Consultant* will be the resource you turn to when you have questions about SQL Server 7.0 administration. To this end, the book zeroes in on daily administration procedures, frequently performed tasks, documented examples, and options that are representative, though not necessarily inclusive. The goal is to keep content so concise that the book remains compact and easy to navigate while still being as packed with information as possible. Thus, rather than a hefty 1000-page tome or a superficial 100-page quick reference, you get a resource guide that will help you quickly and easily perform tasks, solve problems, and implement advanced SQL Server technologies such as DTS, replication, distributed queries, and multiserver administration.

Who Is This Book For?

Microsoft SQL Server 7.0 Administrator's Pocket Consultant covers the Small Business Server (SBS), Standard, and Enterprise editions of SQL Server. The book is designed for

- Current SQL Server 7.0 database administrators
- Accomplished users who have some administrator responsibilities
- Administrators migrating to SQL Server 7.0 from previous versions
- Administrators shifting from other database architectures

To pack in as much information as possible, I had to assume that you have basic networking skills and a basic understanding of SQL Server, and that SQL Server is installed on your systems. With this in mind, I don't devote entire chapters to understanding SQL Server architecture, installing SQL Server, or running simple SQL queries. I do, however, cover SQL Server configuration, enterprise-wide server management, performance tuning, optimization, maintenance, and much more.

I also assume that you are fairly familiar with SQL commands and stored procedures as well as the standard Microsoft Windows user interface. If you need help learning SQL basics, you should consult other reference books (many of which are available from Microsoft Press).

How Is This Book Organized?

Microsoft SQL Server 7.0 Administrator's Pocket Consultant is designed to be used in the daily administration of SQL Server. As a result, it's organized according to job-related tasks rather than according to SQL Server features. It might help you to know the difference between Pocket Consultants and Administrator's Companions. Although both types of books are designed to be a part of an administrator's library, Pocket Consultants are the down-and-dirty, in-the-trenches books and Administrator's Companions are the comprehensive tutorials and references that cover every aspect of deploying a product or technology.

Speed and ease of reference are essential features of this hands-on guide. The book has an expanded table of contents and an extensive index that will let you find answers quickly. Many other quick reference features have been added to the book as well. These features include step-by-step instructions, lists, tables with fast facts, and extensive cross-references. The book is broken down into both parts and chapters. The parts contain an opening paragraph or two about the chapters contained in that part.

Part I, "Microsoft SQL Server 7.0 Administration Fundamentals," covers the fundamental tasks you need for SQL Server administration. Chapter 1 provides an overview of SQL Server administration tools, techniques, and concepts. Chapter 2 explores configuring and tuning SQL Server. You'll learn about optimizing memory usage, parallel processing, authentication, auditing, and more.

In Part II, "Microsoft SQL Server 7.0 Administration," you'll find the essential tasks for administering SQL Server. Chapter 3 details management techniques for server groups and servers. It also shows you how to control services and server processes. The core administration tasks for creating and managing databases are covered in Chapter 4, with a logical follow-up on SQL Server security in Chapter 5. To manage server security, you'll create user logons, configure logon permissions, and assign roles. The permissions and roles you assign determine the actions that users can perform, as well as what types of data they can access.

Part III, "Microsoft SQL Server 7.0 Data Administration," focuses on managing data. Chapter 6 starts by explaining how to create a backup and recovery plan. Then the chapter dives into common tasks for creating and restoring backups. In Chapter 7 you'll find tasks for importing and exporting data using DTS (data transformation services), as well as the old standby BCP (bulk copy). Chapter 8 focuses on integrating SQL Server databases with other SQL Server databases and with other data sources. You'll find detailed discussions of distributed queries, distributed transactions, MS DTC (Microsoft Distributed Transaction Coordinator), and linking remote servers. The final chapter in this part, Chapter 9, explores data replication. You'll learn all about the latest replication techniques, including merge replication and immediate-updating subscribers.

Part IV, "Performance, Optimization, and Maintenance," covers administration tasks you'll use to enhance and maintain SQL Server. Chapter 10 provides the essentials for working with server logs, monitoring SQL Server performance, and solving performance problems. In Chapter 11 you'll learn techniques for creating, managing, and optimizing tables and indexes. Chapter 12 explores database automation and maintenance and shows you how to create alerts, schedule jobs, handle operator notifications, and more. You'll also learn how to create maintenance plans and resolve database consistency problems.

Conventions Used in This Book

I've used a variety of elements to help keep the text clear and easy to follow. You'll find code terms and listings in monospace type, except when I tell you to actually type a command. In that case, the command appears in **bold** type. When I introduce and define a new term, I put it in *italics*.

Other conventions include

Notes   To provide details on a point that needs emphasis.

Tips   To offer helpful hints or additional information.

Cautions   To warn you when there are potential problems you should look out for.

More Info   To provide more information on the subject.

Best Practice   To provide real-world advice when discussing advanced topics.

I truly hope you find that *Microsoft SQL Server 7.0 Administrator's Pocket Consultant* provides everything you need to perform essential administrative tasks on SQL Server as quickly and efficiently as possible. You are welcome to send your thoughts to me at sql-consulting@tvpress.com. Thank you.

Support

Every effort has been made to ensure the accuracy of this book. Microsoft Press provides corrections for books through the World Wide Web at the following address:

http://mspress.microsoft.com/support/

If you have comments, questions, or ideas about this book, please send them to Microsoft Press using either of the following methods:

Postal Mail:
Microsoft Press
Attn: Microsoft SQL Server 7.0 Administrator's Pocket Consultant Editor

One Microsoft Way
Redmond, WA 98052-6399
E-mail:
MSPINPUT@MICROSOFT.COM

Please note that product support is not offered through the mail addresses. For support information about SQL Server 7.0, go to the following Web address:

http://www.microsoft.com/sql/support.htm

Part I
Microsoft SQL Server 7.0 Administration Fundamentals

The fundamental tasks you need for Microsoft SQL Server 7.0 administration are covered in Part I. Chapter 1 provides an overview of SQL Server administration tools, techniques, and concepts. Chapter 2 explores configuring and tuning SQL Server. You'll learn about optimizing memory usage, parallel processing, authentication, auditing, and more.

Chapter 1

Microsoft SQL Server 7.0 Administration Overview

SQL SERV. ENT. MANAGER

Microsoft SQL Server 7.0 is the most powerful version of SQL Server ever created. It is loaded with new features and new ways of performing database administration. In SQL Server 7.0, you won't find many of the old standby utilities. They've been replaced with easier-to-use tools that are smarter and more intuitively designed. For example:

- ISQL/w has been replaced with SQL Server Query Analyzer. Query Analyzer enhances many of the old ISQL/w features and adds new ones, like graphical execution plans and color-coded queries.

- MS Query has been removed from SQL Server and replaced with the Microsoft Visual Database tools. These tools are integrated into SQL Server Enterprise Manager.

- SQL Server's integrated security is now a part of standard domain authentication and is completely managed within SQL Server Enterprise Manager. As a result, you no longer need SQL Security Manager.

- SQL Server Web Assistant is now a standard wizard and is integrated into the main administration tool, SQL Server Enterprise Manager.

- SQL Trace has been renamed SQL Server Profiler. It has additional features for generating audit trails and tracing user activity.

- SQL Executive has been replaced by SQL Server Agent, which manages scheduling and automation features.

SQL Server 7.0 has been totally re-architectured, so much so that it no longer resembles the SQL 6.5 that was based on Sybase. SQL Server can scale upward to support very large databases and can scale downward to support very small databases running laptop or desktop systems. Server versions of SQL Server 7.0 run on Windows NT and Windows 2000 Server. Desktop versions can run on Windows 95, Windows 98, and Windows 2000 Professional as well.

SQL Server 7.0 has many new features. Some features that you'll want to examine closely are:

- **Data Transformation Services (DTS)** Provides an improved solution for importing and exporting data between heterogeneous data sources. You can use DTS to move data from legacy systems on a one-time basis or to move data back and forth continuously for data warehousing.

- **Online Analytical Processing (OLAP) Services** Provides a multidimensional data model and data aggregation techniques for organizing large amounts of data so that it can be rapidly analyzed. OLAP enables data warehouses to be used effectively in processing real-time transactions.

- **Linked Servers and Distributed Queries** Use linked servers to connect local and remote database servers. Use distributed queries to create queries that span databases on multiple servers.

- **Microsoft English Query** Provides an environment that allows users to make plain-English queries against a database. For example, a user could enter the question, "What were the total sales revenues for the fourth quarter?"

As you get started with Microsoft SQL Server 7.0, you should concentrate on these key areas:

- How SQL Server 7.0 works with your hardware
- Which versions and editions of SQL Server 7.0 are available
- How SQL Server 7.0 works with Microsoft Windows-based operating systems
- Which administration tools are available

SQL Server 7.0 and Your Hardware

Successful database server administration depends on three things:

- Good database administrators
- Strong database architecture
- Appropriate hardware

The first two ingredients are covered: you're the administrator, you're smart enough to buy this book to help you through the rough spots, and you've enlisted Microsoft SQL Server 7.0 to provide your high-performance relational database needs. This brings us to the issue of hardware. Microsoft SQL Server 7.0 should run on a system with adequate memory, processing speed, and disk space. You also need an appropriate data and system protection plan at the hardware level. Key guidelines for choosing hardware for SQL Server are as follows:

- **Memory** A minimum of 64 MB RAM for Small Business Server and Standard editions and 128 MB RAM for Enterprise editions. This is double the minimum memory required by Microsoft; the primary reason for this extra memory is performance. SQL Server 7.0 uses about 4 MB of this as a baseline. User connections consume 24 KB each. Data requests and other SQL Server processes use memory as well, and this memory usage is in addition to all other processes and applications running on the server.

- **CPU** SQL Server 7.0 only runs on Intel x86 and DEC Alpha-AXP. It will not run on Motorola MIPS R4000 or PowerPC processors. SQL Server achieves solid benchmark performance with Intel Pentium II 400 MHz and Alpha 4100

5/600 MHz, achieving a 60 percent improvement over Intel Pentium II 300 MHz and a 70 percent improvement over Alpha 2100A 5/375 MHz, respectively. Both CPUs provide good starting points for the average SQL Server system.

- **SMP** SQL Server 7.0 supports symmetric multiprocessors and can process complex parallel queries. Parallel queries are only valuable when few users are on a system and you are processing large queries. On a dedicated system that runs only SQL Server and supports fewer than 100 simultaneous users, a single CPU should suffice. If the server supports more than 100 users or doesn't run on a dedicated system, you may want to consider adding processors (or using a system that can support additional processors as your needs grow).

- **Disk drives** The amount of data storage capacity you need depends entirely on the number and size of the databases the server supports. You need enough disk space to store all your data plus work space, system files, and virtual memory. I/O throughput is just as important as drive capacity. In most cases SCSI drives are faster than IDE/EIDE and are therefore recommended. Instead of using a single large drive, you should use several smaller drives, which allows you to configure fault tolerance with RAID (redundant array of independent disks). I recommend separating data and logs, and placing them on separate drives.

- **Data protection** You should add protection against unexpected drive failures by using RAID. For data, use RAID 0 or RAID 5. For logs, use RAID 1. RAID 0 (disk striping without parity) offers good read/write performance, but any failed drive means that SQL Server can't continue operation on an affected database until the drive is replaced. RAID 1 (disk mirroring) creates duplicate copies of data on separate drives, but recovery from drive failure usually interrupts operations while you restore the failed drive from transaction logs or database backups. RAID 5 (disk striping with parity) offers good protection against single drive failure but has poor write performance.

- **UPS** SQL Server is designed to maintain database integrity at all times and can recover information using transaction logs. This doesn't protect the server hardware, however, from sudden power loss or power spikes. Both of these can seriously damage hardware. To prevent this, get an uninterruptible power supply. A UPS system gives you time to shut down the system properly in the event of a power outage, and it is also important in maintaining database integrity when the server uses write-back caching controllers.

If you follow these hardware guidelines, you'll be well on your way to success with Microsoft SQL Server 7.0.

SQL Server 7.0 and SQL Server Desktop

SQL Server 7.0 is distributed in three main editions: Small Business Server (SBS), Standard, and Enterprise. In all of these editions, you'll find a server installation and a desktop installation. The server installation includes the full version of SQL

Server. The desktop installation includes a scaled-down version of SQL Server with some limitations.

The most widely deployed edition is the Standard edition, which is designed for the average-sized organization and has a richer feature set than the SBS edition. The Standard edition

- Runs on multiple versions of the Microsoft Windows operating system, including Microsoft BackOffice SBS, Windows NT Server, Windows NT Server Enterprise, and Windows 2000 Server.

- Supports an unlimited database size, 4 CPUs for symmetric multiprocessing, and Microsoft SQL Server OLAP services. (In this edition, the OLAP services don't support user-defined cube partitions.)

While the Standard edition is a strong database server solution, large organizations will want to consider the Enterprise edition. The Enterprise edition adds extended memory and failover support while boosting the number of configurable CPUs to 32. As you might expect, the SQL Server 7.0 Enterprise edition runs only on Enterprise editions of the Windows operating system. In contrast, the Small Business Server edition is designed primarily for small organizations and is a trimmed-down version with fewer features. Fewer features mean more limitations and as a result, the Small Business Server edition

- Runs only on Microsoft BackOffice SBS
- Has a maximum database size of 10 GB
- Supports a maximum of four CPUs
- Lacks extended memory or failover support
- Lacks OLAP services support

All editions of SQL Server 7.0 automatically and dynamically configure user connections. This is different from previous versions where specific limitations were placed on the number of simultaneous user connections. So you don't have to worry about managing user connections as much as you used to. Just keep in mind that as the number of user connections increases, so does the amount of resource usage on the server. The server has to balance the workload among the many user connections, which can result in decreased throughput for user connections and the server as a whole.

Whether you use the Standard, SBS, or Enterprise edition, you have three options for working with SQL Server. You can

- **Work with the full server and tool installation**   Perform a complete installation of SQL Server, choosing the appropriate options. The installation can be performed locally or remotely.

- **Work with only the management or development tools, or both**   Start a normal installation but choose only the tools you need to work with SQL Server remotely. Get the management tools and books online. Add development tools if you plan to do any development. Don't select the server components. (If you use per-server licensing, this is the best option for management and development.)

- **Work with the SQL Server Desktop** Install the SQL Server Desktop edition on any Microsoft Windows workstation or server operating system, including Windows 95, Windows 98, and Windows 2000. For best performance, five or fewer connections are recommended. (If you use per-seat licensing, this is the best option for management and development.)

The desktop version provides a full SQL Server database yet has some limitations. Features not supported by the desktop include

- Parallel queries when multiple CPUs are available
- Failover clusters and extended memory addressing for Enterprise editions
- Transactional replication
- Read-ahead scans
- Hash and merge joins
- Full-text search (normally a custom installation option)
- OLAP services (but you can use the client PivotTable service)

Furthermore, if you install the desktop on Windows 95 or Windows 98, you'll find additional features that aren't supported, such as the SQL Server Performance Monitor and the SQL Server Version Upgrade utility. Other key features not supported include

- Named Pipes, AppleTalk Net-Libraries, and Banyan Vines Net-Libraries
- Windows NT authentication for incoming server connections
- Server encryption with multiprotocol Net-Library
- Components such as event logging and Windows NT services, which aren't installed but can be accessed through alerts and executables

Note As you can see, most of the differences between various editions of SQL Server are below the surface and do not affect the interface. Because of this, I refer to specific editions or differentiate between the full server install and the desktop install only when necessary.

SQL Server and Windows

When you install SQL Server on server operating systems, SQL Server makes several modifications to the environment. These modifications include new system services, additions to the taskbar, integrated authentication, new domain/workgroup accounts, and registry updates.

Services for SQL Server

When you install SQL Server on Windows NT or Windows 2000, several services are installed on the server. These services include

- **MSSQLServer** The SQL Server database service.

- **SQLServerAgent** The SQL Server Agent service used with scheduling. This service replaces SQLExecutive in previous versions of SQL Server.

- **MSDTC** The Distributed Transaction Coordinator coordinates distributed transactions between two or more database servers.

- **Microsoft Search** Used with full-text searches on databases. Only available when full-text search is installed as a custom component. Not available with SQL Server Desktop.

 Note SQL Server Desktop does not use services or service accounts. You'll learn more about managing services and configuring service-related options in Chapter 3, "Managing the Enterprise."

Taskbar Extras for SQL Server

A taskbar shortcut is available for SQL Server. You can use this shortcut to manage services and display service status as follows:

- Double-click the shortcut to start the SQL Server Service Manager.

- Right-click the shortcut and then select the Current Service On \\COMPUTER-NAME option to configure which service's icon is displayed on the taskbar.

- Right-click the shortcut and then select Start, Stop, or Pause to control the active service.

- Right-click the shortcut and then select Options to configure options for SQL Server Service Manager.

- Right-click the shortcut and then select Remove Startup Shortcut to permanently remove the SQL Server shortcut from the taskbar.

- Right-click the shortcut and then select Exit to temporarily remove the SQL Server shortcut from the taskbar.

Authentication Enhancements

SQL Server security is completely integrated with Windows domain security, allowing for authentication based on user and group memberships as well as standard SQL Server user accounts. The authentication enhancements make it much easier to manage logons and security. You can

- Combine domain and SQL Server authentication so users in Windows domains can access the server using a single account and other users can be logged on using a SQL Server login ID. This is the default setting.

- Use authentication based on Windows domain accounts only, so only users with a domain account can access the server.

Service Accounts

On Windows NT Server and Workstation, the MSSQLServer and SQLServerAgent services are configured to use Windows NT logon accounts. Additional SQL Server services can also be configured to use Windows NT logon accounts. Two types of accounts are supported:

- **Local system accounts** Provide administrative privileges to SQL Server on the local system but no privileges on the network. If the server requires resources on the local server only, use the local system account.

- **Domain accounts** Set the service to use a standard domain account with privileges you configure through User Manager or User Manager for Domains. Use domain accounts when the server requires resources across the network, when you need to forward events to the application logs of other systems, and when you want to configure e-mail or pager notification.

Caution With domain accounts, make sure MSSQLServer has Administrator privileges on the local system. If you don't do this, the tasks you can perform with the server are restricted. You'll learn more about accounts and security in Chapter 5, "Microsoft SQL Server 7.0 Security."

SQL Server Administration Tools

SQL Server provides many administration tools. The tools you'll use the most are

- **Graphical administration tools** These are the key tools for managing SQL Server. You can access them by selecting them individually. Select Start, choose Programs, and then use the Microsoft SQL Server 7.0 menu.

- **Administration wizards and the Taskpad** These are tools designed to automate key administration tasks. They are accessed in SQL Server Enterprise Manager.

- **Command-line utilities** These are additional utilities designed to be run at the command line or accessed in scripts.

The following sections provide brief introductions to these administration tools. Additional details for key tools are provided throughout the book. Keep in mind that you may need administration access to SQL Server to use these utilities.

Graphical Administration Tools

SQL Server 7.0 provides several types of tools for administration. The graphical administration tools are the ones you'll use the most. You can access these tools by selecting Start, choosing Programs, and then using the Microsoft SQL Server 7.0 menu.

SQL Server 7.0 is designed for local and remote management. You can use most of the tools to manage local resources as well as remote resources. For example, in SQL Server Enterprise Manager, you can register a new server and then connect to it. Afterward, the server and all its databases can be remotely managed from your system.

Table 1-1 provides a list of the key graphical administration tools and their uses.

Table 1-1. Quick Reference for Key SQL Server 7.0 Administration Tools

Administration Tool	Purpose
Client Network Utility	Configures the client network libraries and DB library. Covered in Chapter 2.
MSDTC Administrative Console	Manages the Microsoft Distributed Transaction Coordinator (MSDTC). See Chapter 8.
Performance Monitor	A customized version of the standard performance monitor, featuring special objects and counters for SQL Server. (Not available with Windows 95/98 desktop installations.) See Chapter 10.
SQL Server Enterprise Manager	The main administration tool for SQL Server 7.0. Manages SQL servers, databases, security, and more. Key aspects discussed in Chapter 3.
SQL Server Network Utility	Configures server network libraries. Covered in Chapter 2.
SQL Server Profiler	Allows you to analyze user activity and generate audit trails. Covered in Chapter 10.
SQL Server Query Analyzer	A visual utility for making queries and SQL scripts. Used anytime you want to execute SQL statements, check queries, or perform index analysis. See Chapter 4.
SQL Server Service Manager	Manages and configures SQL services. Easier to use than the Services utility in the Control Panel. See Chapter 3.
Uninstall SQL Server 7.0	Runs InstallShield to uninstall SQL Server. (Don't use this when you want to add components. Run SQL Server Setup instead.)

Administration Wizards and the Taskpad

Administration wizards are designed to make database administration easier. Wizards guide you through common database administration tasks using a series of dialog boxes and free you from having to remember what to enter when. Over 20 wizards are provided in SQL Server; a partial list of wizards is shown in Figure 1-1. Most wizards are started in SQL Server Enterprise Manager.

Administration wizards can also be launched by selecting Taskpad entries in SQL Server Enterprise Manager (see Figure 1-2). The Taskpad is a new feature in SQL Server 7.0. Once you start working with the Taskpad, you'll discover it works much like a Web browser. You use the Taskpad to navigate through SQL Server

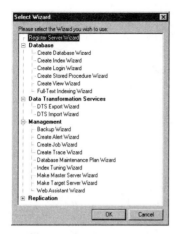

Figure 1-1.   *SQL Server Enterprise Manager provides many different wizards to make database administration easier.*

options by clicking on hypertext links. While some links access other Taskpad pages, others launch wizards or display database information pages. Buttons on the toolbar allow you to move backward or forward as well as refresh the display, if necessary.

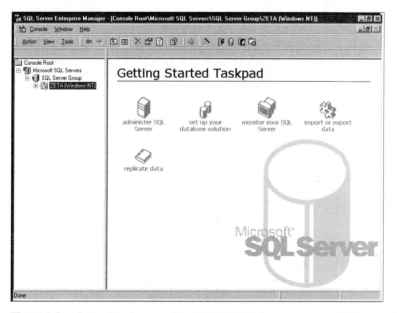

Figure 1-2.   *The Taskpad is one of the WYSIWYG enhancements for SQL Server 7.0.*

The Taskpad is usually enabled by default in full installations and disabled by default in desktop installations. To enable or disable the Taskpad, complete the following steps:

1. In SQL Server Enterprise Manager, select a database server entry. In Figure 1-2, the database server entry is labeled <COMPUTERNAME (OS)>, such as Zeta (Windows NT).

2. Choose Taskpad from the View menu.

Note You'll learn more about SQL Server Enterprise Manager in Chapter 3.

SQL Server also provides an additional wizard for migrating from previous versions. This wizard is called the Version Upgrade Wizard. Use this wizard to migrate databases from a SQL Server 6.5 database and import the data into an existing SQL Server 7.0 installation.

You run the Version Upgrade Wizard by selecting Start, choosing Programs, and then choosing the SQL Server Upgrade Wizard option on the Microsoft SQL Server-Switch submenu. During the installation you'll need to stop and restart both database servers; consequently, you'll probably want to perform this operation after regular business hours.

Command-Line Tools

The graphical administration tools provide just about everything you need to work with SQL Server. Still, there are times when you may want to work from the command line, especially if you want to automate installation, administration, or maintenance with scripts. Key command-line tools you'll use include BCP.EXE, ISQL.EXE, OSQL.EXE, TEXTCOPY.EXE, ODBCPING.EXE, REBUILDM.EXE, and REGREBLD.EXE. These command-line executables are usually stored in the mssql7\binn directory.

BCP

BCP is the bulk copy program. You can use BCP to import and export data. BCP's major advantage is speed. It's much faster than standard database import/export procedures. Unfortunately, its command-line syntax makes it much harder to use. The syntax for BCP is shown in Listing 1-1.

Listing 1-1. BCP Syntax and Usage

```
bcp {dbtable | query} {in | out | queryout | format} datafile
    [-m maxerrors]   [-f formatfile]   [-e errfile]
    [-F firstrow]   [-L lastrow]   [-b batchsize]
    [-n native type]  [-c character type] [-w wide character type]
    [-N keep non-text native] [-6 6x file format] [-q quoted id]
    [-C code page specifier] [-t field terminator] [-r row terminator]
    [-i inputfile]   [-o outfile]   [-a packetsize]
    [-S server name]  [-U username]  [-P password]
```
(continued)

Listing 1-1. *(continued)*

```
[-T trusted connection] [-v version]  [-R regional enable]
[-k keep null values] [-E keep identity values]
[-h "load hints"]
```

ISQL

ISQL is a SQL query tool that you can run from the command line. ISQL communicates with SQL Server through the DB Library and is used primarily because it runs within scripts. You'll find that ISQL has very little overhead, making it a good choice when system resources are a concern. Listing 1-2 shows the syntax for ISQL.

Listing 1-2. ISQL Syntax and Usage

```
isql   [-U login id]  [-P password]
   [-S server]   [-H hostname]   [-E trusted connection]
   [-d use database name] [-l login timeout] [-t query timeout]
   [-h headers]   [-s colseparator]   [-w columnwidth]
   [-a packetsize]  [-e echo input]   [-x max text size]
   [-L list servers]  [-c cmdend]
   [-q "cmdline query"] [-Q "cmdline query" and exit]
   [-n remove numbering] [-m errorlevel]
   [-r msgs to stderr]
   [-i inputfile]  [-o outputfile]
   [-p print statistics] [-b On error batch abort]
   [-O use Old ISQL behavior disables the following]
      <EOF> batch processing
      Auto console width scaling
      Wide messages
      default errorlevel is -1 vs 1
   [-? show syntax summary (this screen)]
```

When you start ISQL, you can issue Transact-SQL statements to run queries, execute stored procedures, and more. Because you are working at the command line, these commands aren't automatically executed and you need to use additional commands to tell ISQL when to execute statements, when to ignore statements, and so on. These additional statements must be entered on separate lines and are summarized in Table 1-2.

Table 1-2. Commands for Use with ISQL and OSQL

Command	Description
GO	Executes all statements entered up to the previous GO or RESET
RESET	Clears statements you have entered so they aren't executed
ED	Calls the editor
!! *command*	Executes the specified Windows NT shell command or script
QUIT	Exits ISQL
EXIT	Exits ISQL
CTRL+C	Ends a query without exiting from ISQL

OSQL

An alternative to ISQL is OSQL. You'll use OSQL to execute queries using ODBC connections instead of DB Library. The syntax for OSQL is shown in Listing 1-3. With OSQL, you can also use the commands shown previously in Table 1-2.

Listing 1-3. OSQL Syntax and Usage

```
osql    [-U login id]  [-P password]
   [-S server]    [-H hostname]   [-E trusted connection]
   [-d use database name] [-l login timeout] [-t query timeout]
   [-h headers]    [-s colseparator]   [-w columnwidth]
   [-a packetsize]  [-e echo input]   [-I Enable Quoted Identifiers]
   [-L list servers]  [-c cmdend]
   [-q "cmdline query"] [-Q "cmdline query" and exit]
   [-n remove numbering] [-m errorlevel]
   [-r msgs to stderr] [-V severitylevel]
   [-i inputfile]  [-o outputfile]
   [-p print statistics] [-b On error batch abort]
   [-O use Old ISQL behavior disables the following]
      <EOF> batch processing
      Auto console width scaling
      Wide messages
      default errorlevel is -1 vs 1
   [-? show syntax summary]
```

TEXTCOPY

TEXTCOPY is a command-line utility for importing and exporting text or images files with SQL Server. When you import with TEXTCOPY, data from a specified file is copied into SQL Server, replacing an existing text or image value. When you export with TEXTCOPY, a text or image value is copied from SQL Server into a specified file. The syntax and switches for TEXTCOPY are shown in Listing 1-4 and Table 1-3, respectively.

Listing 1-4. TEXTCOPY Syntax and Usage

```
TEXTCOPY [/S [sqlserver]] [/U [login]] [/P [password]]
   [/D [database]] [/T table] [/C column] [/W"where clause"]
   [/F file] [{/I | /O}] [/K chunksize] [/Z] [/?]
```

Table 1-3. TEXTCOPY Switches Defined

Switch	Definition
/?	Displays syntax and usage help.
/C column	Specifies the table column.
/D database	Sets the database to use. If database is not specified, the default database for the user login is used.
/F file	Sets the input/output file name.
/I	Input; specifies that you are copy into SQL Server from a file.

(continued)

Table 1-3. *(continued)*

Switches	Definitions
/K chunksize	Sets the size of the data transfer buffer in bytes. While the minimum value is 1024 bytes, the default value is 4096 bytes.
/O	Output; specifies that you are copying from SQL Server to a file.
/P password	Sets the login password. If password is not set, NULL is used.
/S sqlserver	Designates the SQL Server to connect to. If *sqlserver* is not specified, the local SQL Server is used.
/T table	Specifies the database table.
/U login	Sets the login to connect with. If login is not set, TEXTCOPY attempts to use a trusted connection.
/W "*where* clause"	Used to set the necessary *where* clause that must specify a single row in the designated table.
/Z	Displays debug information while running.

ODBCPING

If you need to verify an ODBC connection between a client and server, you can use ODBCPING. ODBCPING is a command-line utility with the following syntax:

```
odbcping [-S Server | -D DSN] [-U Login Id] [-P Password]
```

REBUILDM

REBUILDM is a utility for rebuilding the master database. Rebuilding the master database removes all database objects and data. Because of this, you'll need to re-create database objects and reload data by restoring backups of system and user databases. You only need to rebuild the master database in these situations:

- To repair a corrupted master database

- To change the character set, sort order, or Unicode collation

To start the Rebuild Master utility, type **rebuildm** on the command line. Then follow the prompts.

REGREBLD

REGREBLD is a utility for backing up and restoring SQL Server registry entries. You can use this tool to recover SQL Server registry settings if they ever get corrupted. You should always run Registry Rebuild from the mssql7\binn directory.

Tip The SQL Server installation program runs REGREBLD at the end of the installation process. This creates an initial Registry backup set for SQL Server.

Configuring and Tuning Microsoft SQL Server 7.0

Microsoft SQL Server 7.0 is designed to balance the workload dynamically and to self-tune configuration settings. For example, SQL Server can dynamically increase or decrease memory usage based on overall system memory requirements. SQL Server also manages memory efficiently, especially when it comes to queries and user connections—and memory is just one of dozens of areas where the configuration is automatically adjusted.

While self-tuning works in most cases, there are times when you'll need to configure SQL Server settings manually. For example, if you're running a large database with special constraints and the database isn't performing the way you expect it to, you may need to customize the configuration. You may also need to modify configuration settings for SQL Server accounts, authentication, and auditing. Key tools you'll use to modify configuration settings are

- **SQL Server Setup**   Allows you to add components, such as free-text search.
- **Enterprise Manager Server Properties dialog box**   Provides an easy-to-use interface that updates the database and registry settings for you.
- **Stored Procedures**   Lets you view and manage configuration settings through stored procedures, such as *sp_configure* and *xp_regwrite*. Note that you can only change some options of *sp_configure* when Show Advanced Options is set to 1, as in the following example:

```
exec sp_configure 'show advanced options', 1
```

- **SQLSERVR.EXE**   Starts SQL Server from the command line and can be used to set configuration parameters at startup.

In this chapter I use a task-oriented approach to explore how these tools are used to configure SQL Server.

Reconfiguring SQL Server Setup

Previous versions of SQL Server allowed you to run the setup program with special flags. These special flags could be used to change character sets, restore registry settings, and more. You don't need to run SQL Server 7.0 setup with special flags.

These operations have been replaced by Rebuild Master, Registry Rebuild, and a more intuitive setup wizard.

Changing Character Sets, Sort Order, or Unicode Collation

When you install SQL Server, the default character set, sort order, and Unicode collation are set. You can't change these settings on an existing SQL Server installation without rebuilding the master database. Further, after you do this, all user databases are detached and unreadable. To recover, you must re-create all your user databases. You can't restore the user databases from backup—the restore maintains the information that was set when the backup was created and may instead want to move the databases to another server via the Data Transformation Services (DTS), which are covered in Chapter 7.

But if you still want to proceed, you can change the default character set, sort order, and Unicode collation by completing the following steps:

1. Stop the MSSQLServer service if it's running. Select Start, choose Settings, choose Control Panel, and then double-click Services. This displays the Services utility.

2. In the Services utility, select the MSSQLServer service, as shown in Figure 2-1. Then click Stop.

3. If you are running other services that depend on the MSSQLServer service, such as SQLServerAgent, you will need to stop these as well. Choose Yes when prompted.

4. Run Rebuild Master from the command line using the following command:

   `rebuildm`

5. In Rebuild Master, click the Browse button, and then select the path to the Data directory from which the master database was originally installed (see Figure 2-2). Normally, the source directory is the SQL Server CD-ROM. For Intel x86 systems, set the path to the x86/Data directory. For Alpha systems, set the path to the alpha/Data directory.

Figure 2-1. *Stop the MSSQLServer service using the Services utility. Another way to do this is to use the SQL Server Service Manager.*

Figure 2-2. *Use Rebuild Master to change character set, sort order, and Unicode collation. But be careful because changing these settings detaches user databases and you must rebuild them from scratch.*

6. Click Settings, and then use the options of the Character Set/Sort Order/ Unicode Collation dialog box to configure the new server settings. Click OK when you're finished.

7. In Rebuild Master, click Rebuild. Rebuild Master copies the master database source files to the server and then begins remapping and reconfiguring the server.

Restoring the SQL Server Registry

Many of SQL Server's settings are stored in the registry. These settings can be backed up and restored using the Registry Rebuild utility REGREBLD.EXE. If there's a backup, you can even restore SQL Server after reinstalling the operating system.

Note   These settings are only for SQL Server. The backup and restore process doesn't back up registry settings for other applications and services. The registry backups have the .rbk extension and are stored in the MSSQL7\Binn directory.

SQL Server Registry Full Restore

To do a full restore of SQL Server registry entries, enter the utility name without parameters, such as

```
regrebld
```

The Registry Rebuild utility then tells you what is happening to the server step-by-step, such as

```
Restoring backed up registry settings ...
Registry setting successfully restored.
```

```
Verifying status of MSSQLServer service ...
Status has been verified.
Verifying status of SQLServerAgent service ...
Status has been verified.
Creating shortcuts ...
```

SQL Server Registry Restore from Backup

To restore the registry from backup, enter the command with the -Restore option, such as

```
regrebld -restore
```

By default, Registry Rebuild retrieves backups from the same directory as its executable. You can change this behavior by specifying a directory path after the -Restore option.

Backing Up SQL Server Registry Entries

To back up SQL Server registry entries, enter the command with the -Backup option, such as

```
regrebld -backup
```

You can also specify a destination directory for the registry backup, such as

```
regrebld -backup d:\sql\reg\backup
```

 Tip The backup procedure fails if the backup file already exists. Delete the existing file or store the backup in a different directory by specifying a directory path after the -Backup option.

Adding Components

SQL Server keeps track of those components you've installed and those you haven't. If you ever want to add components, just rerun the SQL Server Installation program from the distribution CD-ROM. The installation program detects currently installed components and then allows you to select additional components. Components you might want to add through the installation program include

- **Server components** Upgrade tools, replication support, and full-text search capabilities
- **Management tools** SQL Server Enterprise Manager, SQL Server Query Analyzer, SQL Server Profiler, DTC Client Support, and Replication Conflict Viewer
- **Books online** Help documentation, installed to the system's disk drive or accessed from a CD-ROM, or both
- **Development tools** Headers and libraries, Backup/Restore API, and Debugger Interface

Note As the installation dialog box says, selecting components already installed doesn't reinstall them and canceling components already installed doesn't remove them.

The SQL Server CD-ROM provides other tools that aren't part of the standard installation. These tools are accessed on the initial installation screen and include

- **SQL Server 7.0 OLAP services**   Used with online analytical applications and data warehousing

- **English Query**   Used with applications that allow plain-English queries of the SQL database

Configuring SQL Server with the Properties Dialog Box

Enterprise Manager provides the easiest way to configure SQL Server. In Enterprise Manager you access the properties dialog box of a registered server and then use the tabs and options provided to configure SQL Server. Behind the scenes, SQL Server executes commands that modify server settings. If the changes affect the master database or other databases, the stored procedure *sp_configure* is used to make changes in the sysconfigures system table. If the changes affect the Microsoft Windows Registry, the stored procedure *xp_regwrite* is used to update the Registry. SQL Server also uses stored procedures to read configuration settings. For example, the stored procedure *xp_regread* is used to read most registry settings.

Once you register a server in Enterprise Manager, you can connect to it and manage its configuration with the SQL Server Properties dialog box. To access this dialog box, complete the following steps:

1. Select Start, choose Programs, choose Microsoft SQL Server 7.0, and then choose Enterprise Manager.

2. Access the server group containing the server you want to work with, then right-click the server name in the Enterprise Manager tree view and choose Properties from the shortcut menu. This opens the dialog box shown in Figure 2-3.

3. You can now configure common SQL Server settings. For more advanced settings, you'll need to use a stored procedure, such as *sp_configure*.

As you can see on the following page, the SQL Server Properties dialog box has seven tabs. Each of them is discussed in the sections that follow. To obtain a summary of current settings in SQL Server Query Analyzer, run the following command:

```
exec sp_configure
```

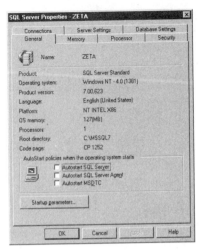

Figure 2-3. *The SQL Server Properties dialog box allows you to configure SQL Server without having to use stored procedures like* sp_configure. *Pointing and clicking is easy, so it's definitely recommended.*

Determining System and Server Information

General system and server information is available on the General tab of the SQL Server Properties dialog box (see Figure 2-3). The information provided by the General tab helps you determine the following:

- SQL Server edition: Standard, Small Business Server, or Enterprise
- Operating system version
- SQL Server version
- Default language
- Platform and chip architecture
- Amount of RAM installed on the system
- Number of CPUs
- SQL Server root directory location
- Code page for the current character set

Using the extended stored procedure *xp_msver*, you can obtain similar information by executing the following command:

```
exec xp_msver 'ProductName', 'ProductVersion', 'Language',
'Platform', 'WindowsVersion', 'PhysicalMemory', 'ProcessorCount'
```

> **Tip** You can use the SQL Query Analyzer to execute the command shown. Basic techniques for using this utility are covered later in this chapter in the section titled "Configuring SQL Server with Stored Procedures."

Configuring Startup

SQL Server provides many different ways to configure server startup. One of them is through the General tab of the SQL Server Properties dialog box. Use the check boxes in the Autostart Policies When The Operating System Starts area. These check boxes determine whether the related services start automatically when the operating system starts. You can use these check boxes as follows:

- **Configuring SQL Server startup**   To automatically start SQL Server (MSSQLServer service) when the system boots, select the Autostart SQL Server check box. Otherwise, clear the check box.

- **Configuring SQL Server Agent startup**   To automatically start SQL Server Agent (SQLServerAgent service) when the system boots, select the Autostart SQL Server Agent check box. Otherwise, clear the check box.

- **Configuring MSDTC startup**   To automatically start MS DTC (MSDTC service) when the system boots, select the Autostart MSDTC check box. Otherwise, clear the check box.

Enterprise Manager uses the stored procedure *xp_regwrite* to modify the service startup settings. These settings affect the startup value for the registry keys:

```
HKEY_LOCAL_MACHINE
    \SYSTEM
        \CurrentControlSet
            \Services
                \MSSQLServer
                \MSDTC
                \SQLServerAgent
```

Caution   Don't write directly to the Registry unless absolutely necessary. Use the Properties dialog box instead—that's what it's for.

Setting Startup Parameters

Startup parameters control how SQL Server starts and what options are set when it does. The easiest way to configure startup options is through the General tab of the SQL Server Properties dialog box. Click Startup Parameters to display the dialog box shown in Figure 2-4. You can now add and remove startup parameters.

Tip   Startup parameters can be passed to the command-line utility SQLSERVR.EXE as well. This utility starts SQL Server without using a service.

Adding Startup Parameters

You can add startup options by completing the following steps:

1. Enter a parameter in the Parameter field.

Figure 2-4. *Configure startup parameters for SQL Server by adding or removing options. Don't delete the default options (-d, -e, and -l) or you may have problems.*

2. Choose Add.

3. Click OK to apply the changes.

Removing Startup Parameters

You can remove startup parameters by completing the following steps:

1. Select the parameter, and then choose Remove.

2. Click OK to apply the changes.

Common Startup Parameters

Table 2-1 shows startup options and how they're used. The first three parameters (-d, -e, and -l) are the defaults for SQL Server. The remaining parameters allow you to configure additional settings.

Table 2-1. Startup Parameters for SQL Server

Parameter	Description	Example
-d\<path>	Sets the full path for the master database.	-dC:\MSSQL7\data\master.mdf
-e\<path>	Sets the full path for the error log.	-eD:\LOGS\ERRORLOG
-l\<path>	Sets the full path for the master database transaction log.	-lD:\LOGS\mastlog.ldf
-c	Prevents SQL Server from running as a service. This makes startup faster when you're running SQL Server from the command line.	
-f	Starts SQL Server with minimal configuration. Enables the *sp_configure* Allow Updates option, which is disabled by default.	

(continued)

Table 2-1. *(continued)*

Parameter	Description	Example
-m	Starts SQL Server in single-user mode. Only a single user can connect and the CHECKPOINT process isn't started.	
-n	Tells SQL Server not to log errors in the application event log.	
-p<level>	Sets the precision level for numeric and decimal data types. Default is 28 digits but the range is 1–38. Maximum precision (38) is assumed if you use the switch without setting a level.	-p38
-s<altreg>	Sets an alternative Registry key for SQL Server. This is used during startup instead of the default key.	-sHKEY_LOCAL_MACHINE\SYSTEM\CurrentControlSet\Services\MSSQLServerMod
-T<tnum>	Sets a trace flag. Trace flags set nonstandard behavior and are often used in debugging or diagnosing performance issues.	-T237
-t<tnum>	Sets an internal trace flag for SQL Server. Used only by SQL Server support engineers.	-t8837
-x	Disables statistics tracking for CPU time and cache-hit ratio. Allows maximum performance.	

Setting the Startup Service Account

SQL Server inherits rights and permissions from the startup service account. These permissions are used whenever SQL Server performs tasks on the local system or across the network. As discussed in the section of Chapter 1 titled "Services Accounts," you can use two types of accounts: local system accounts and domain accounts. If SQL Server only performs local operations, use the local system account. Otherwise, use a properly configured domain account.

Using the Local System Account

Specify the local system account for SQL Server startup by completing the following steps:

1. Access the Security tab of the SQL Server Properties dialog box.

2. Use the local system account by choosing the System Account option button in the Startup Service Account area.

3. Click Apply. Now the server can only access local resources.

Using a Domain Account

Specify a domain account for SQL Server startup by completing the following steps:

1. Set appropriate privileges for the SQL Server account and make sure the server can log on as a service.
2. From the SQL Server Properties dialog box, go to the Security tab)
3. Choose the This Account option button. Then type the designated account name and password. If necessary, specify the domain as part of the account name, such as cordata/wrstane, where cordata is the domain name and wrstane is the account name.
4. Click Apply.

These settings affect the ObjectName value for the registry key:

```
HKEY_LOCAL_MACHINE
    \SYSTEM
        \CurrentControlSet
            \Services
                \MSSQLServer
```

Authentication and Auditing

Authentication and auditing options are configured with the Security tab of the SQL Server Properties dialog box. This tab is shown in Figure 2-5.

Setting Authentication Mode

As discussed in the section of Chapter 1 titled "Authentication Enhancements," SQL Server can use combined domain and SQL Server authentication or domain

Figure 2-5. *Configure authentication and auditing with the Security tab's options.*

authentication only. To use combined authentication, select the SQL Server And Windows NT option button. Now users in Windows domains can access the server using a domain account, and other users can be logged on using a SQL Server logon ID.

To use domain authentication only, select the Windows NT Only option button. Now only users with a domain account can access the server. These settings affect the LoginMode value for the registry key:

```
HKEY_LOCAL_MACHINE
  \SOFTWARE
    \Microsoft
      \MSSQLServer
        \MSSQLServer
```

Tip   With combined authentication, SQL Server first checks to see if a new logon is a SQL Server logon. If the logon exists, SQL Server then uses the password provided to authenticate the user. If the logon doesn't exist, it uses domain authentication. Note also that domain authentication isn't available on SQL Server Desktop running on Microsoft Windows 95 or Windows 98.

Setting Auditing Level

Auditing allows you to track user access to SQL Server. You can use auditing with both authentication modes as well as with trusted and untrusted connections. When auditing is enabled, user logons are recorded in the Windows application log, the SQL Server error log, or both, depending on how you configure logging for SQL Server. The available auditing options are

- **None**   Disables auditing (the default setting)
- **Success**   Audits successful logon attempts
- **Failure**   Audits failed logon attempts
- **All**   Audits both successful and failed logon attempts

These settings affect the AuditLevel value for the registry key:

```
HKEY_LOCAL_MACHINE
  \SOFTWARE
    \Microsoft
      \MSSQLServer
        \MSSQLServer
```

Tuning Memory Usage

SQL Server is designed to manage memory needs dynamically and it does an excellent job in most cases. Using dynamic memory allocation, SQL Server can add memory to handle incoming queries, free up memory for another application you're starting, or reserve memory for possible needs. The default memory settings are the following:

- Dynamically configure SQL Server memory
- Minimum memory allocation of 0 megabytes (MB)
- Maximum memory allocation is set to the total amount of RAM on the system
- No memory is reserved specifically for SQL Server
- Minimum memory for query execution of 1024 kilobytes (KB)

You can change these settings if you like, but you need to be very careful about allocating too much or too little memory to SQL Server. Too little memory and SQL Server has to throttle back and may not handle tasks in a timely manner. Too much memory and SQL Server may take essential resources away from other applications like the operating system, which may result in excessive paging and a drain on overall system performance.

 Tip Statistics that can help you better allocate memory are the number of page faults per second and the cache-hit ratio. Page faults per second helps track paging to and from virtual memory. Cache-hit ratio helps track whether data being retrieved is in memory. You'll learn more about this in Chapter 10, "Monitoring and Profiling Microsoft SQL Server 7.0."

The following sections examine key areas of memory management. The primary way to configure memory usage is to use the Memory tab of the SQL Server Properties dialog box, shown in Figure 2-6. I'll also show you a better way to configure Windows memory usage for SQL Server.

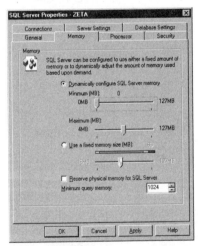

Figure 2-6. *Memory usage can be dynamically or manually configured, but keep in mind that you shouldn't change these settings unless you're experiencing performance problems.*

Working with Dynamically Configured Memory

With dynamically configured memory, SQL Server configures memory usage automatically, based on workload and available resources. Total memory usage varies between the minimum and maximum values you set. To use dynamically configured memory, complete the following steps:

1. Select the Dynamically Configure SQL Server Memory option button in the Memory tab.

2. If desired, set minimum and maximum memory usage values with the Minimum and Maximum sliders, respectively. It's recommended that you set the Maximum value at or near total RAM for stand-alone servers.

3. Click Apply.

You can use the stored procedure *sp_configure* to change the minimum and maximum settings. Use the following Transact-SQL commands:

```
exec sp_configure 'min server memory', <number of megabytes>
exec sp_configure 'max server memory', <number of megabytes>
```

Best Practice   With dynamically configured memory, you usually don't need to set minimum and maximum memory usage values. On a dedicated system running only SQL Server, however, you may achieve smoother operation by setting minimum memory to 4 MB + (24 KB * NumUsers) where NumUsers is the average number of users simultaneously connected to the server. You may also want to reserve physical memory for SQL Server. SQL Server uses about 3.5 MB for its code and internal structures. Additional memory is used as follows: 96 bytes for locks, 2880 bytes for open databases, and 276 bytes for open objects, which include all tables, views, stored procedures, extended stored procedures, triggers, rules, constraints, and defaults. To simplify tracking additional memory, I just add 500 KB. This gives a total of 4 MB.

Using Fixed Memory

If you want to override the dynamic memory management features, you can do this by setting a fixed memory size for SQL Server. Here are the steps you can use:

1. From the SQL Server Properties dialog box, go to the Memory tab, and select Use A Fixed Memory Size.

2. Allocate memory using the Fixed Memory slider.

3. Click Apply.

Caution   Setting fixed memory incorrectly can cause serious performance problems on SQL Server. Use fixed memory only in circumstances when you need to ensure that an exact amount of memory is available for SQL Server.

Reserving Physical Memory

You can also reserve memory specifically for SQL Server. When you reserve physical memory for SQL Server, the operating system doesn't swap out SQL Server memory pages even if that memory could be allocated to other processes when SQL Server is idle. On a dedicated system, reserving memory can improve SQL Server performance by cutting down on paging and cache hits.

To reserve physical memory for SQL Server, complete the following steps:

1. From the SQL Server Properties dialog box, go to the Memory tab and select Reserve Physical Memory For SQL Server.

2. Click Apply.

You can also use the stored procedure *sp_configure* to reserve physical memory. The Transact-SQL command you would use is

```
exec sp_configure 'set working set size', 1
```

Allocating Memory for Queries

By default, SQL Server allocates a minimum of 1024 KB of memory for query execution. This memory allocation is guaranteed per user and can be set anywhere from 512 KB to 2 gigabytes (GB). Increasing the minimum query size can improve the performance of queries that perform processor-intensive operations, such as sorting or hashing. If you set the value too high, however, you can degrade the overall system performance. Because of this, adjust the minimum query size only when you're having trouble executing queries quickly.

 Best Practice The default setting of 1024 KB RAM works in most cases. However, you may want to consider changing this value if the server operates in an extremely busy environment, with lots of simultaneous queries running in separate user connections, or in a relatively slow environment, with few (but large or complex) queries. In this case, four factors should determine your decision to adjust the minimum query size: the total amount of free memory (when the system is idle and SQL Server is running), the average number of simultaneous queries running in separate user connections, the average query size, and the query response time you hope to achieve. There's often a trade-off to be made with these values. You can't always get an instant response, but you can optimize performance based on available resources.

Use the following equation to get a starting point for the optimization: FreeMemory / (AvgQuerySize + AvgNumSimulQueries). For example, if the system has 200 MB of free memory, the average query size is 2 MB, and the average number of simultaneous queries is five, the optimal value for query size is 200 MB / (2+5) or 20 MB. Generally, this value represents the maximum you should assign given the current environment, and you'll want to adjust this value downward.

To allocate memory for queries, complete the following steps:

1. From the SQL Server Properties dialog box, go to the Memory tab and set a value for the Minimum Query Memory box. This value is set in kilobytes.
2. Click Apply.

You can also use the stored procedure *sp_configure* to set the minimum query size. The related command is

```
exec sp_configure 'min memory per query', <number of kilobytes>
```

Configuring Processors and Parallel Processing

Systems that use multiprocessors can take advantage of SQL Server's enhancements for parallel and symmetric multiprocessing. You can control how and when processors are used by SQL Server as well as when queries are processed in parallel. Standard and Small Business Server editions of SQL Server support up to four processors. Enterprise editions support up to 32 processors.

Optimizing CPU Usage

Processor settings are automatically configured and optimized when you install SQL Server. Don't change these settings without careful forethought. That said, you can manually configure processor usage by completing the following steps:

1. Select Start, choose Programs, choose Microsoft SQL Server 7.0, and then choose Enterprise Manager.
2. Right-click the server name in the Enterprise Manager tree view and choose Properties from the shortcut menu.
3. From the SQL Server Properties dialog box, go to the Processor tab, as shown in Figure 2-7.
4. Use the Processor list to determine which processors are used by SQL Server. Select the check box for processors you want to use and clear the check box for processors you don't want to use. The first CPU on the system is identified as CPU 0, the second as CPU 1, and so on.

Best Practice   If the system has more processors than SQL Server supports, SQL Server doesn't use all of them. For example, on an eight-way SMP system, SQL Server Standard can only use four processors. This leaves four processors for other applications and system-level tasks. While you may be tempted to assign SQL Server to the higher numbered processors (5, 6, 7, and 8), this isn't a good idea. Windows assigns deferred process calls associated with network interface cards (NICs) to the highest numbered processors. Here, if the system had 2 NICs, these calls would be directed to CPU 8 and CPU 7. Definitely, consult with the equipment manufacturer before changing these values.

5. Click Apply.
6. These settings take effect when the server is stopped and restarted.

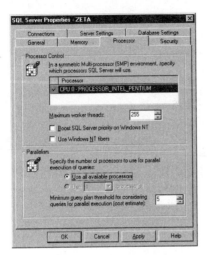

Figure 2-7. *Use the Processor tab to control which processors are used by SQL Server and when parallel processing is used. Read the notes before making changes.*

You can also use the stored procedure *sp_configure* to set the affinity mask. The related command is

```
exec sp_configure 'affinity mask', <integer value>
```

SQL Server interprets the integer value as a bit mask representing the processors you want to use. In this bit mask, CPU 0 is represented with bit 0, CPU 1 with bit 1, and so on. A bit value of 1 tells SQL Server to use the CPU. A bit value of 0 tells SQL Server not to use the CPU. For example, if you wanted to turn on support for processors 1, 2, and 5, you would have a binary value of

```
000100110
```

The corresponding integer value is 76:

```
64+8+4 = 76
```

Setting Parallel Processing
A lot of calculations go into determining when parallel processing is and isn't used. Generally, SQL Server processes queries in parallel

- When the number of CPUs is greater than the number of active connections.
- When the estimated cost for the serial execution of a query is higher than the query plan threshold. (The estimated cost refers to the elapsed time in seconds required to execute the query serially.)

That said, certain types of statements can't be processed in parallel unless they contain clauses. For example, UPDATE, INSERT, and DELETE aren't normally processed in parallel even if the related query meets the criteria. However, if the UPDATE or DELETE statements contain a *where* clause or an INSERT statement contains a SELECT clause, the *where* and SELECT can be executed in parallel. Changes are then serially applied to the database.

You can configure parallel processing by completing the following steps:

1. From the SQL Server Properties dialog box, go to the Processor tab.

2. To use all available processors for parallel processing (the maximum supported by SQL Server), select the Use All Available Processors option button.

3. To use a set amount of processors for parallel processing (up to the maximum supported by SQL Server), select the Use N Processors option button and then select the number of processors to use. A value of 1 tells SQL Server not to use parallel processing.

4. Set a cost estimate in the Minimum Query Plan Threshold field. You can use any value from 0 to 32,767. On a single CPU the cost threshold is ignored.

5. Click Apply. These changes take effect immediately. You don't need to restart the server.

The stored procedure *sp_configure* can be used to configure parallel processing. The Transact-SQL commands are

```
exec sp_configure 'max degree of parallelism', <integer value>
exec sp_configure 'cost threshold for parallelism', <integer value>
```

Note Transact-SQL is an enhanced version of the standard structured query language (SQL) that is used by SQL Server. You may also see Transact-SQL referenced as T-SQL.

Configuring Threading, Priority, and Fibers

Threads are a very important part of a multitasking operating system and enable SQL Server to do many things at once. Threads aren't processes, however. They're concurrent execution paths that allow applications to use the CPU more effectively. SQL Server tries to match threads to user connections. When the number of threads available is more than the number of user connections, there is at least a one-to-one ratio of threads to user connections, which allows each user connection to be handled uniquely. When the number of threads available is less than the number of user connections, SQL Server must pool threads; as a result, the same thread may serve multiple user connections, which can reduce performance and response time if additional resources are available and aren't being used.

Normally, the operating system handles threads in kernel mode but handles applications and user-related tasks in user mode. Switching between modes, such as when the kernel needs to handle a new thread, requires CPU cycles and resources. To allow the application to handle threading directly, you can use fibers. Switching fibers doesn't require changing modes and therefore can sometimes improve performance. Another way to improve performance is to increase the priority of SQL Server threads. Normally, threads have a priority of 1 to 31, and higher priority threads get more CPU time than lower priority threads. Higher priority threads can also preempt lower priority threads, forcing threads to wait until higher priority threads finish executing. By increasing thread priority, you can give the threads a higher preference for CPU time and ensure that other threads don't preempt them.

You configure worker threads, fibers, and thread priority using the SQL Server Properties dialog box. Go to the Processor tab and then use these options:

- **Maximum Worker Threads** Sets the maximum number of threads. By default, the field is set to 255. However, you can use any value from 10 to 1024 (except on the desktop version). On a busy server with lots of user connections, you may want to increase this value. On a slow server with few connections, you may want to decrease this value. Computers with multiple processors can concurrently execute one thread per CPU.

- **Boost SQL Server Priority On Windows NT** Increases the priority of SQL Server threads. Without boosting, SQL Server threads have a priority of 7 (normal priority). With boosting, SQL Server threads have a priority of 13 (high priority). On a dedicated system running only SQL Server, this option can improve performance. However, if the server runs other applications, the performance of those applications may be degraded.

- **Use Windows NT Fibers** Configures SQL Server to use fibers, which it can handle directly. SQL Server still needs threads to carry out tasks. SQL Server allocates one thread per CPU and then allocates one fiber per concurrent user connection, up to the Maximum Worker Threads value. You must restart the server for this option to take effect.

 Tip Fibers work best when the server has multiple CPUs and a relatively low user to CPU ratio. For example, on an Enterprise installation with 32 CPUs and 250 users, you may see a noticeable performance boost with fibers. But when you have eight CPUs and 5,000 users, you may see performance *decrease* with fibers.

You can use *sp_configure* to set fibers, maximum worker threads, and priority boost. The commands are

```
exec sp_configure 'lightweight pooling', <0 or 1>
exec sp_configure 'max worker threads', <integer value>
exec sp_configure 'priority boost', <0 or 1>
```

Configuring User and Remote Connections

Requests for data are handled through user connections to client systems. The client opens a connection with SQL Server, makes a request, and waits for a response from SQL Server. When the client is finished with its request, it closes the connection. Other servers and applications can also connect to SQL Server

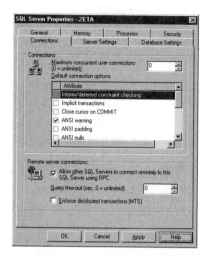

Figure 2-8. *The default connection settings seen in the Connections tab are usually sufficient. Note the original settings before you make any changes.*

remotely. To configure client connections and remote server connections, you can use the Connections tab in the SQL Server Properties dialog box.

As you see in Figure 2-8, there are many settings associated with client and server connections. The sections that follow examine these settings.

Setting Maximum User Connections

In the Connections tab, the Maximum Concurrent User Connections field allows you to configure the maximum number of user connections that SQL Server allows at any one time. By default, SQL Server manages the maximum number of user connections dynamically, and this is why the initial value is zero (0). SQL Server allows you to set this value to anywhere from 0 to 32,767. However, the actual number of user connections allowed really depends on hardware, application, and other server limitations. You can determine the number of user connections allowed on your system by executing the following command in SQL Server Query Analyzer:

```
select @@max_connections
```

To set the maximum number of user connections, complete the following steps:

1. From the SQL Server Properties dialog box, go to the Connections tab.

2. Type a new value in the Maximum Concurrent User Connections field and then click Apply.

3. Stop and restart the server for the changes to take effect.

You can also set the maximum user connections by using the following command:

```
exec sp_configure 'user connections', <integer value>
```

Best Practice You shouldn't need to change the maximum connections value. If you do, be careful. When the maximum number of connections is reached, users receive an error message and aren't able to connect until a connection becomes available. The only time you'll need to set this option is in an environment where you have a large number of users and need to limit the number of active connections to ensure that requests for connected users are handled in a timely manner. A better alternative is to add sufficient memory to the system or configure a cluster to balance the workload, or both. For large numbers of users, you should also ensure that SQL applications connect and then disconnect promptly when finished to free resources.

Default Connection Options

In the Connections tab you'll find a list box labeled Default Connection Options. You'll use the list box options to set default query-processing options for user connections. Select an option by selecting its related check box. Cancel an option by clearing its related check box. Any changes you make affect new logons only. Current logons aren't affected. Further, users can override the defaults by using SET statements, if necessary.

Table 2-2 provides a summary of the connection options as well as the default state for ODBC (open database connectivity) and OLE DB (object linking and embedding database, which may be different from the SQL Server default). You'll also find a list of commands you can use with *sp_configure*, the corresponding value for the configuration bit mask, and the SET commands used to override the default settings in a user session.

Table 2-2. Configuring Connection Options

Connection Option	Description	Default State	Bit Mask Value	SET Command
Interim/ deferred constraint checking	When on, disables deferred checking of foreign key constraints. This applies stricter referential integrity checking.	Off	1	DISABLE_DEF_ CNST_CHK
Implicit transactions	When on, uses transactions implicitly whenever statements are executed.	Off	2	IMPLICIT_ TRANSACTIONS

(continued)

Table 2-2. *(continued)*

Connection Option	Description	Default State	Bit Mask Value	SET Command
Close cursor on COMMIT	When on, automatically closes a cursor at the end of a transaction.	Off	4	CURSOR_CLOSE_ON_COMMIT
ANSI warning	When on, SQL Server displays null, overflow, and divide-by-zero errors. Otherwise, no error or null may be returned.	On	8	ANSI_WARNINGS
ANSI padding	When on, data in fixed-length fields are padded with trailing spaces to fill out the width of the column.	On	16	ANSI_PADDING
ANSI nulls	Controls how NULL is used with equality operators. When on, comparing anything with NULL gives an unknown result.	On	32	ANSI_NULLS
Arithmetic abort	When on, causes a query to terminate when an overflow or divide-by-zero error occurs.	On	64	ARITHABORT
Arithmetic ignore	Returns NULL when an overflow or divide-by-zero error occurs during a query.	On	128	ARITHIGNORE

(continued)

Table 2-2. *(continued)*

Connection Option	Description	Default State	Bit Mask Value	SET Command
Quoted identifier	When on, SQL Server interprets double quotation marks as indicating an identifier rather than as delimiting a string.	On	256	QUOTED_ IDENTIFIER
No count	When on, turns off the display of the number of rows returned in a query.	Off	512	NOCOUNT
ANSI null defined ON	When on, new columns are defined to allow nulls (if you don't explicitly allow or disallow nulls).	Off	1024	ANSI_NULL_ DFLT_ON
ANSI null defined OFF	When on, new columns are defined not to allow nulls (if you don't explicitly allow or disallow nulls).	Off	2048	ANSI_NULL_ DFLT_OFF

For *sp_configure*, the default options are set with the *user options* parameter

```
exec sp_configure 'user options', <integer bit mask value>
```

Here, the bit mask value is the sum of the numeric values for all the options you want to use. Each option has a corresponding SET command as well. When you make a connection, you can use the SET command to override the default setting for the session. For example, if you wanted to turn on ANSI padding, ANSI nulls, and ANSI warning, you'd use the bit mask value 56, such as

```
exec sp_configure 'user options', 56
```

In a user session, you could later turn these options on or off using

```
set ansi_padding on
set ansi_nulls off
```

Configuring Remote Server Connections

Connections from other servers are handled differently than user connections. You can determine whether servers can connect using remote procedure call

(RPC), how long it takes for remote queries to time out, and whether distributed transactions are used. To configure remote connections, complete these steps:

1. From the Server Properties dialog box, go to the Connections tab.

2. To allow servers to connect by means of RPC, select Allow Other Servers To Connect Via RPC. Remote servers can then log on to the server to execute stored procedures remotely. You must stop and restart the server if you change this option.

Caution RPC connections are allowed by default. If you change this be-havior, remote servers can't log on to SQL Server. This secures SQL Server from remote server access.

3. By default, queries executed by remote servers don't time out. To change this behavior, type a time-out value in the Query Time-Out field. Time-out val-ues are set in seconds, and the acceptable range of values is from 0 to 2,147,483,647.

4. Stored procedures and queries executed on the server can be handled as distributed transactions by using MS DTC. If you want to execute procedures in this way, select the Enforce Distributed Transactions check box. You must stop and restart the server if you change this option.

5. Click Apply.

These options can also be set with *sp_configure,* and the related Transact-SQL statements are

```
exec sp_configure 'remote access', <0 or 1>
exec sp_configure 'remote query timeout', <number of seconds>
exec sp_configure 'remote proc trans', <0 or 1>
```

Note A value of 0 is off and a value of 1 is on.

Server Settings

You use the Server Settings tab of the SQL Server Properties dialog box to con-figure general server settings. As shown in Figure 2-9, you can set the default language, general server behavior, and more.

Setting Default Language for SQL Server

The default language determines default display formats for dates as well as the names of months and days. All output is in U.S. English unless you're running a localized version of SQL Server. Localized versions of SQL Server are available for French, German, Japanese, and Spanish. On a localized server, there are two sets of system messages, one in U.S. English and one in the local language. If the default language is set to the local language, SQL Server messages are dis-played in the local language. Otherwise, they're displayed in U.S. English.

Figure 2-9. *General configuration options for the server are set in the Server Settings tab.*

In the Server Settings tab of the SQL Server Properties dialog box, you use the Default Language For User drop-down list box to set the default language and then choose Apply. Afterward, you must stop and restart the server for the changes to take effect. With *sp_configure*, the related Transact-SQL statement is

```
exec sp_configure 'default language', <language id number>
```

The language ID number for U.S. English is always 0.

Allowing and Disallowing System Updates

By default, users can only update the systems table with system-stored procedures, even if they have proper permissions. This is a valuable feature because it prevents users from executing statements that may corrupt the database or prevent SQL Server from starting. Still, you may want to change this behavior and allow direct updates to system tables. Once you allow modifications, anyone with proper permissions can update systems tables by executing statements or stored procedures. This is very risky. Rather than take chances, you may want to follow this procedure:

1. From the SQL Server Properties dialog box, go to the Server Settings tab.

2. Enable system table modifications by selecting Allow Modifications To Be Made Directly To The System Catalogs.

3. Click Apply, and then stop SQL Server.

4. Start SQL Server in single-user mode at the command line using

```
sqlservr -m
```

5. Make the necessary changes to the system tables.

6. From the SQL Server Properties dialog box, got to the Server Settings tab.
7. Disable system table modifications by clearing Allow Modifications To Be Made Directly To The System Catalogs.
8. Stop and restart the server.

With *sp_configure*, the related Transact-SQL statement is

```
exec sp_configure 'allow updates', <0 or 1>
```

Note If you use *sp_configure* to allow updates, you must use the *reconfigure with override* statement as well. Then stop and restart the server.

Allowing and Disallowing Nested Triggers

By default, SQL Server allows you to nest up to 32 levels of triggers. Nested triggers are useful for executing a series of tasks within a single transaction. For example, an action can initiate a trigger that starts another trigger, which can in turn start another trigger, and so on. Because the trigger is handled within a transaction, a failure at any level causes the entire transaction to roll back, which reverses all changes to the database. As a fail-safe measure, triggers are terminated when the maximum nesting level is exceeded. This protects against an infinite loop.

To allow or disallow nested triggers, complete the following steps:

1. From the SQL Server Properties dialog box, go to the Server Settings tab.
2. Set or clear Allow Triggers To Be Fired Which Fire Other Triggers (Nested Triggers).
3. Choose Apply.

With *sp_configure*, the related Transact-SQL statement is

```
exec sp_configure 'nested triggers', <0 or 1>
```

Controlling Query Execution

The Query Governor disallows execution of any query that has a running time that exceeds a specified query cost. The query cost is the estimated time, in seconds, required to execute a query, and it's estimated prior to execution based on the query engine's analysis of execution time. By default, the Query Governor is turned off, meaning there is no maximum cost. To set the Query Governor, complete the following steps:

1. From the SQL Server Properties dialog box, go to the Server Settings tab.
2. Select Use Query Governor To Prevent Queries Exceeding Specified Cost.
3. In the Query Governor field, type a maximum query cost limit. The valid range is from 0 to 2,147,483,647. A value of 0 disables the Query Governor. Any other value sets a maximum query cost limit.
4. Choose Apply.

With *sp_configure*, the related Transact-SQL statement is

```
exec sp_configure 'query governor cost limit', <limit>
```

You can also set a per connection query cost limit in Transact-SQL using

```
set query_governor_cost_limit <limit>
```

 Tip Before you set the Query Governor, you should use Query Analyzer to estimate the cost of current queries you're running on the server. This will give you a good idea of a value to use for the maximum query cost. You can also use Query Analyzer to optimize queries.

Setting the Default SQL Mail Profile

E-mail facilities can be used with SQL Server in two key ways. You can

• Configure stored procedures that are triggered by e-mail through SQL Mail.

• Send notifications to designated operators through SQLAgentMail.

These SQL Server features can use separate mail profiles, or they can use the same mail profile. The profile(s) must be configured on the server and associated valid e-mail account(s). Afterward, you need to

1. Tell SQL Server about the SQL Mail profile by accessing the SQL Mail Configuration dialog box and then entering the profile name in the Profile Name field. Once you configure mail properly, you can access the SQL Server Properties dialog box and enter a mail logon name for SQL Mail in the Mail Login Name field of the Server Settings dialog box.

2. Tell SQL Server Agent about the SQLAgentMail profile by accessing the SQL Server Agent Properties dialog box and then entering the profile name in the Mail Profile field of the General tab.

 Note You'll find detailed information on SQL Mail and SQL Server Agent in Chapter 3 and Chapter 12, respectively.

Configuring Year 2000 Support

SQL Server allows you to insert or modify dates without specifying the century part of the date. However, to be Year 2000 compliant, SQL Server interprets two-digit dates as being within a certain time span. By default, this time span is from 1950 to 2049. With this setting, all two-digit dates from 50 to 99 are treated as having 19 in front of them and all two-digit dates from 00 to 49 are treated as having 20 in front of them. Thus, SQL Server would interpret a two-digit year of 99 as 1999 and a two-digit year of 02 as 2002.

To maintain backward compatibility, Microsoft recommends that you leave the setting at the default value. You can, however, change this value by completing the following steps:

1. From the SQL Server Properties dialog box, go to the Server Settings tab.
2. In the When A Two-Digit Year Is Entered, Interpret It As A Year Between list box, select a value that is the ending year of the time span you want to work with. The valid range for the ending year is 1753 to 9999.
3. Choose Apply.

Note The time span affects all databases on the current server. Note also some older OLE clients only support a date range of 1931 to 2030. To be compatible with these clients, you may want to type **2030** as the ending year for the time span.

With *sp_configure*, the related Transact-SQL statement is

```
exec sp_configure 'two digit year cutoff', <ending year>
```

Database Settings

You use the Database Settings tab of the SQL Server Properties dialog box to configure server-wide database settings. As shown in Figure 2-10, you can use the tab to set index fill, backup and restore options, and checkpoint execution.

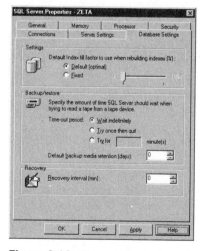

Figure 2-10. *You set general configuration options for the databases in the Database Settings tab.*

Setting the Index Fill

The default index fill determines how much space SQL Server should reserve when it creates a new index using existing data. A tradeoff is involved when setting the fill factor. Setting the fill factor too high slows down SQL Server when adding data to a table. However, setting a fill factor too low can affect read performance by an amount inversely proportional to the fill factor. For example, a fill factor of 25 percent can degrade read performance by a factor of 4 (or 4 times normal) but makes large updates faster initially. Ideally, you'll balance the need to quickly make updates against the need for good read performance and select a fill factor that makes sense for your situation.

 Best Practice The fill factor is used only when an index is created and is not maintained afterward. This allows you to add, delete, or update data in a table without worrying about maintaining a specific fill factor. Because of this, the empty space in the data pages can fill if you make extensive additions or modifications to the data. To redistribute the data, re-create the index and specify a fill factor when you do so. Indexes are discussed more in Chapter 11.

By default, the index fill is set to 0 but the valid range is from 0 to 100. The setting of 0 is an optimized setting for SQL Server. Any other value is an actual fill percentage.

SQL Server handles the optimized setting in much the same way as a fill percentage of 100. Here, SQL Server creates clustered indexes with full data pages and nonclustered indexes with full leaf pages. But unlike an index fill of 100, the optimized setting of 0 leaves room for growth in the upper level of the index tree. On the other hand, with an index fill of 100, there's no room for growth, which is why this value should only be used with read-only tables where you'll never add data.

If you need to, you can override the default when you create indexes. But you have to remember to do this. You can also set a fixed index fill as the default by completing the following steps:

1. From the SQL Server Properties dialog box, go to the Database Settings tab.
2. Select the Fixed option button.
3. Use the Fixed slider to set a fill percentage. A low fill factor allows more room for insertions without requiring page splits, but the index takes up more space. A high fill factor allows less room for insertions that don't require page splits, but the index uses less space.
4. Choose Apply.

With *sp_configure*, the related Transact-SQL statement is

```
exec sp_configure 'fill factor', <integer percentage>
```

Backup and Restore Time-Out

SQL Server backups are often made on tape devices. When you work with tape devices and the DB-Library, you may want to control whether or not you want to enforce a read/write time-out. The default is to have DB-Library "wait indefinitely" for a response from SQL Server, which is sometimes less than ideal. With an indefinite time-out, you won't necessarily get errors that let you know that you're having backup problems. To change this behavior, you may want to set a specific time-out, such as "try once and then quit" or "try for a certain number of minutes and then quit." You set the time-out period by completing the following steps:

1. From the SQL Server Properties dialog box, go to the Database Settings tab.
2. To set an indefinite time-out, select the Wait Indefinitely option button.
3. To try once and then quit, select the Try Once And Then Quit option button.
4. To try for a specified amount of time, select the Try For N Minutes option button and then enter the time-out period in the field provided.
5. Click Apply.

The time-out preference changes are made to the Tapeloadwaittime value for the registry key

```
HKEY_LOCAL_MACHINE
  \SOFTWARE
    \Microsoft
      \MSSQLServer
        \MSSQLServer
```

Backup and Restore Retention

As you'll learn in Chapter 6, SQL Server has many features to help you back up and restore data. When you write data to tapes using DB-Library, you can specify the number of days to maintain old files. This value is called the retention period, and you set it by completing the following steps:

1. From the SQL Server Properties dialog box, go to the Database Settings tab.
2. Enter the number of days you'd like to maintain old files in the Default Backup Media Retention (Days) field. The minimum value is 0, which specifies that old files are always overwritten. The valid range is from 0 to 365.
3. Click Apply.

With *sp_configure*, the related Transact-SQL statement is

```
exec sp_configure 'media retention', <number of days>
```

Flushing Cache with Checkpoints

Database checkpoints flush all cached data pages to the disk and are done on a per-database basis. In SQL Server you control how often checkpoints occur using the recovery interval. By default, the recovery interval is set to 0, which allows

SQL Server to dynamically control when checkpoints occur. This usually means that checkpoints occur about once a minute on active databases. Unless you're experiencing performance problems that are related to checkpoints, you shouldn't change this option.

You set the checkpoint interval manually by completing the following steps:

1. From the SQL Server Properties dialog box, go to the Database Settings tab.
2. Enter the checkpoint time in minutes in the Recovery Interval field. The valid range is from 0 to 32,767. This is a server-wide setting.
3. Click Apply.

With *sp_configure*, the related Transact-SQL statement is

```
exec sp_configure 'recovery interval', <number of minutes>
```

Configuring SQL Server with Stored Procedures

You can configure many areas of SQL Server through the SQL Server Properties dialog box. As you've learned in this chapter, you can also configure SQL Server with stored procedures, such as *sp_configure*. You execute stored procedures and other queries in Query Analyzer. Query Analyzer is a client tool that sends commands to the SQL Server query engine, which in turn parses, compiles, and executes the commands.

The following sections explain how you can configure SQL Server using Query Analyzer and stored procedures. You'll find more detailed coverage of Query Analyzer in other chapters.

Starting Query Analyzer

You can start Query Analyzer using any of these techniques:

- Select Start, choose Programs, choose Microsoft SQL Server 7.0, and then choose Query Analyzer.
- Run ISQLW.EXE at the command line.
- From the Enterprise Manager, select the Tools menu, and then select the SQL Server Query Analyzer option.

When you start Query Analyzer from the menu or the command line, you have to specify connection information using the dialog box shown in Figure 2-11. The fields of this dialog box are used as follows:

- **SQL Server** Use this option to select the database server to which you want to connect. If the server isn't available on the drop-down list box, you can type in a server name or use the ellipsis button to display a dialog box showing active SQL Servers on the network.

Figure 2-11. *Use the Connect To SQL Server dialog box to select the server you want to use and then specify connection information. If you start Query Analyzer in Enterprise Manager you can often bypass this dialog box.*

- **Start SQL Server If Stopped** Starts the MSSQLServer service and the database if it's stopped.

- **Use Windows NT Authentication** Uses your current domain account and password to establish the database connection. This only works if Windows NT authentication is enabled and you have appropriate privileges.

- **Use SQL Server Authentication** Allows you to specify a SQL Server logon ID and password.

If you're working with an active database in Enterprise Manager and have already authenticated the connection, Query Analyzer automatically connects to the currently selected database server and uses this authentication information to log on. If there is no active database connection or if the logon fails, you'll see the dialog box shown previously in Figure 2-11.

Tip Query Analyzer normally connects you to the master database on the active server. You can use the DB drop-down list box on the Query Analyzer toolbar to change to any of the available databases on the server.

Changing Settings with *sp_configure*

The Query Analyzer window is normally divided into two panes (see Figure 2-12). The top pane is for entering queries. The bottom pane is for displaying results. If you don't see the bottom pane, don't worry. It's automatically displayed when you type a query. You can also set the pane to display by default. Select the Show Results Pane option on the Window menu.

As you know, you can use *sp_configure* to view and change SQL Server configuration settings. Two types of configuration settings are available: those that are dynamic and those that aren't. In this instance, a dynamic setting is one that you

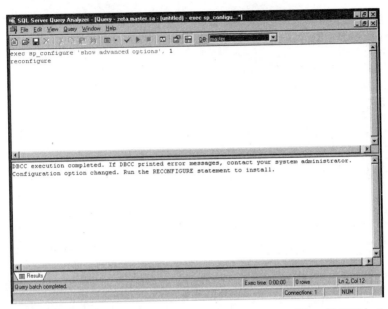

Figure 2-12. *Query Analyzer is a dressed up version of the old ISQL/w in SQL Server 6.5. It even uses the same executable name, ISQLW.EXE. Still, it's friendlier and easier to use.*

can change without having to stop and restart SQL Server. To execute *sp_configure* or other types of queries, type a command in the top pane and then click the toolbar's Execute Query button (it's the green arrow). You can also execute commands using these key sequences:

- F5
- Ctrl+E
- Alt+X

Whenever you use *sp_configure* to modify settings, the changes don't actually take place until you also execute the RECONFIGURE command, as shown in Figure 2-12. Some highly risky settings can only be changed with the RECON-FIGURE WITH OVERRIDE command. Additionally, *sp_configure* settings are divided into two categories: standard and advanced. Standard commands can be executed at any time, but advanced commands can only be executed when Show Advanced Options is set to 1. With this setting in effect, you can modify both standard and advanced settings by following this procedure:

1. In Query Analyzer, type

```
exec sp_configure 'show advanced options', 1
reconfigure
```

Note   You could later disable advanced options by setting this value to 0.

2. Execute the commands by pressing Ctrl+E.

3. Clear the query windows by clicking on the toolbar's Clear Query Window button.

4. Now type one *sp_configure* command for each option you want to change.

5. Type **RECONFIGURE** (or **RECONFIGURE WITH OVERRIDE**).

6. Execute the commands by pressing Ctrl+E.

7. Stop and start the server if you changed any nondynamic settings. (See Tables 2-3 and 2-4 for details.)

Configuration Parameters

Table 2-3 provides a summary of the standard configuration parameters. You'll find parameters listed in alphabetical order with the minimum, maximum, and default values shown. The dynamic parameter column tells you whether the setting is dynamic. If you see a "No" in this column, you'll need to stop and restart the server to enforce changes.

Table 2-3. Quick Reference Summary for Standard Configuration Parameters

Parameter Name	Description	Minimum Value	Maximum Value	Default Value	Dynamic Yes/No
allow updates	Allow updates to systems tables.	0	1	0	Yes
default language	Sets language formatting for dates. With localized versions, can change to local language or U.S. English.	0	9999	Varies; 0 is U.S. English.	Yes
language in cache	Determines number of languages that can be held in language cache.	3	100	3	No
max text repl size	Sets maximum number of bytes to be written to a replicated column.	0	2147483647	65536	Yes

(continued)

Table 2-3. *(continued)*

Parameter Name	Description	Minimum Value	Maximum Value	Default Value	Dynamic Yes/No
nested triggers	Determines whether nested triggers are allowed.	0	1	1	Yes
remote access	Controls access from remote servers. 0 denies access.	0	1	1	No
remote login timeout	Sets remote logon time-out in seconds. 0 sets no time-out.	0	2147483647	5	Yes
remote proc trans	Use DTC for distributed transactions.	0	1	0	Yes
remote query timeout	Sets time-out in seconds for queries from remote servers. 0 sets no time-out.	0	2147483647	0	Yes
show advanced options	Set to 1 to turn on advanced options.	0	1	1	Yes
user options	Sets global defaults for user connections using a bit mask.	0	4095	0	Yes

Table 2-4 provides a summary of the advanced configuration parameters. To view or change these parameters, the parameter Show Advanced Options must be set to 1. Note also that some advanced options can't be changed (they can only be viewed).

Table 2-4. Quick Reference Summary for Advanced Configuration Parameters

Parameter Name	Description	Minimum Value	Maximum Value	Default Value	Dynamic Yes/No
affinity mask	Associates threads with processors.	0	2147483647	0	No

(continued)

Table 2-4. *(continued)*

Parameter Name	Description	Minimum Value	Maximum Value	Default Value	Dynamic Yes/No
cost threshold for parallelism	Helps determine when queries are processed in parallel.	0	32767	5	Yes
cursor threshold	-1 to generate synchronous key sets for cursors. 0 sets asynchronous. Other values perform row comparison.	-1	2147483647	-1	Yes
default sortorder ID	Shows default sort order (must rebuild master).	0	255	52	No
extended memory size	Sets extended memory support with EMA (Enterprise only).	0	2147483647	0	No
fill factor	Sets index fill factor percentage. 0 lets SQL Server configure.	0	100	0	No
index create memory	Sets KB of memory used when creating index to sort data.	704	1600000	0	Yes
language neutral full-text	1 sets language neutral option for Unicode data.	0	1	0	No
lightweight pooling	1 switches to fibers.	0	1	0	Yes
locks	Sets the number of available locks.	5000	2147483647	0	No

(continued)

Table 2-4. *(continued)*

Parameter Name	Description	Minimum Value	Maximum Value	Default Value	Dynamic Yes/No
max async IO	Sets the maximum number of asynchronous I/O requests to issue.	1	255	32	No
max degree of parallelism	With SMP, sets number of threads to execute a parallel plan.	0	32	0	Yes
max server memory	Sets maximum memory in MB used by SQL Server.	4	2147483647	Varies	Yes
max worker threads	Sets the maximum number of threads.	10	1024	255	Yes
media retention	Sets number of days to retain backup media.	0	365	0	No
min memory per query	Sets minimum memory in KB to reserve for queries.	512	2147483647	1024	Yes
min server memory	Sets minimum memory (MB) used by SQL Server.	0	2147483647	0	Yes
network packet size	Sets the byte size of network packets.	512	65535	4096	Yes
open objects	Sets maximum number of open objects. 0 for SQL control.	0	2147483647	0	No
priority boost	Set to 1 to boost thread priority.	0	1	0	No

(continued)

Table 2-4. *(continued)*

Parameter Name	Description	Minimum Value	Maximum Value	Default Value	Dynamic Yes/No
query governor cost limit	Sets cost limit for queries. 0 turns off limit.	0	2147483647	0	No
query wait	Sets time-out value for queries.	-1	2147483647	-1	Yes
recovery interval	Sets time interval in minutes for checkpoints. 0 for SQL control.	0	32767	0	Yes
resource time-out	Sets number of seconds to wait for a resource to be released.	5	2147483647	10	Yes
scan for startup procs	Set to 1 to scan for stored procedure to execute on startup.	0	1	0	No
set working set size	1 sets no swapping for memory.	0	1	0	No
spin counter	Sets maximum number of attempts at accessing a resource.	1	2147483647	10000	Yes
time slice	Sets the time in milliseconds that a process can take before yielding to other processes.	50	1000	100	No
two digit year cutoff	Sets date range for two-digit dates.	1753	9999	2049	Yes

(continued)

Table 2-4. *(continued)*

Parameter Name	Description	Minimum Value	Maximum Value	Default Value	Dynamic Yes/No
Unicode comparison style	View Unicode sorting option (must rebuild master to change.)	0	2147483647	Varies	No
Unicode locale ID	View Unicode local ID (must rebuild master to change.)	0	2147483647	Varies	No
user connections	Controls maximum number of user connections. Set to 0 for unlimited.	0	32767	0	No

Recovering from a Bad Configuration

SQL Server 7.0 has many safeguards that help you avoid configuration settings that keep SQL Server from starting. Still, you may occasionally find that a configuration change prevents SQL Server from starting. In this case, you can recover the server by completing the following steps:

1. Log on to the affected server locally or remotely through Telnet.

2. Make sure that the MSSQLServer service for the server is stopped. If it isn't, stop the service using the following command:

   ```
   net stop MSSQLSERVER
   ```

3. Start SQL Server from the command line with the following option:

   ```
   sqlservr -f
   ```

4. The -f option starts SQL Server in single-user mode with a minimum configuration. This ensures that the bad configuration isn't loaded.

5. Wait for the server to start up. SQL Server should write a few pages of output to the screen. Leave the server running.

6. In another command prompt window or Telnet session, start ISQL with the username of a SQL account with administrator privileges and password,

   ```
   isql -U username -P password
   ```

7. If you've accessed ISQL properly, you should see the prompt change to 1>

8. Reverse the changes made to the configuration by entering commands much like you would in Query Analyzer. The key difference is that you execute the commands with *go*, as in the following example:

```
sp_configure 'max server memory', 128
go
reconfigure
go
```

9. When finished, exit ISQL by typing **exit**.

10. At the window running SQL Server from the command line, press Ctrl+C. Then, when prompted, type **Y** for Yes. This stops SQL Server.

11. Restart SQL Server as you normally would. If you've made the appropriate changes, the server should start normally. Otherwise, repeat this procedure.

Part II

Microsoft SQL
Server 7.0 Administration

In this part, you'll find the essential tasks for administering Microsoft SQL Server 7.0. Chapter 3 details management techniques for server groups and servers. You'll also learn how to control services and server processes. The core administration tasks for creating and managing databases are covered in Chapter 4, with a logical follow on to SQL Server security in Chapter 5. To manage server security, you'll create user logons, configure logon permissions, and assign roles.

Chapter 3

Managing the Enterprise

Microsoft SQL Server 7.0 Enterprise Manager is the primary tool you'll use to manage database servers. Other tools you may want to use to manage local and remote servers are Microsoft SQL Server Service Manager, Microsoft Performance Monitor, and Microsoft Event Viewer. You'll use Service Manager to manage SQL-related services, like MSSQLServer and SQLServerAgent. You'll use Performance Monitor to track SQL Server activity and performance. You'll use Event Viewer to examine events generated by SQL Server, which can provide helpful details on problems. Enterprise Manager and Service Manager are covered in this chapter. For detailed information on Performance Monitor and Event Viewer, see Chapter 10.

Starting, Stopping, and Pausing SQL Server

SQL Server has two modes of operation. It can run as a command-line application (SQLSERVR.EXE) or as a service. You'll use the command-line application when you need to troubleshoot problems or modify configuration settings in single-user mode. Other than that, the normal technique is to run SQL Server as a service.

Managing SQL Server Service with Service Manager

SQL Server Service Manager is the primary tool you'll use to manage SQL Server services. Most DBAs prefer SQL Server Service Manager to the alternatives because you can manage both local and remote servers. You can also configure these services to start automatically. Start SQL Server Service Manager by double-clicking the SQL Server shortcut on the taskbar or by clicking Start, then Programs, then Microsoft SQL Server 7.0, and then Service Manager. This opens the dialog box shown in Figure 3-1.

You can manage the SQL Server service with Service Manager by completing the following steps:

1. Use the Server drop-down list box to select an available server, or type the server name.

2. On the Services drop-down list box, select MSSQLServer.

Figure 3-1. *SQL Server Service Manager makes it easy to manage services on local and remote systems.*

3. The status of the currently selected service is shown on the status bar. In Figure 3-1, for example, MSSQLServer is running on the selected server.

4. Use the available options to work with the service as follows:

- Select Start/Continue to start the service.
- Select Pause to temporarily stop the service.
- Select Stop to stop the service.
- Select Auto-start Service When OS Starts in order to have SQL Server automatically start when the system boots.

 Note On Microsoft Windows 95/98 you can only manage local resources with Service Manager. The reason for this is that these "services" are actually running as executables on Windows 95/98.

Managing SQL Server
Service from the Command Line

When you run SQL as a service, you can start, stop, and pause SQL Server as you would any other service. On a local system, you could use the Services utility in the Control Panel to start, stop, or pause the service. On a remote system, you could connect to the system using Telnet and then issue one of the following NET commands:

- **NET START MSSQLSERVER** Starts SQL Server as a service
- **NET STOP MSSQLSERVER** Stops SQL Server when running as a service
- **NET PAUSE MSSQLSERVER** Pauses SQL Server when running as a service
- **NET CONTINUE MSSQLSERVER** Resumes SQL Server when running as a service

Managing the SQL Server Command-Line Executable

The SQL Server command-line executable provides an alternative to the SQL Server service. When SQL Server is installed on a local system, you start SQL Server by typing **sqlservr** at the command line. On a remote system, you connect to the system using Telnet and then issue the startup command. Either way, SQL Server reads the default startup parameters from the registry and starts execution. You can also enter startup parameters and switches that override the default settings. The available parameters were summarized in Table 2-1 in Chapter 2. You can still connect Enterprise Manager to the server (though when you do, it may incorrectly report that it's starting the MSSQLServer service).

To stop SQL Server, complete the following steps:

1. Press Ctrl+C to break into the execution stream.

2. When prompted, press N to stop SQL Server.

Using SQL Server Enterprise Manager

With its graphical point-and-click interface, Enterprise Manager makes server, database, and resource management a snap. Using Enterprise Manager, you can manage both local and remote servers by establishing a connection to SQL Server and then administering the resources. If you've disabled remote server connections to a particular server, however, you can only work with the server locally (by logging in to the system at the keyboard and then running the local management tools) or through a Telnet session.

Getting Started with Enterprise Manager

To run Enterprise Manager, choose Start, then Programs, then Microsoft SQL Server 7.0, and then Enterprise Manager. As shown in Figure 3-2, Enterprise Manager presents information in a directory tree structure. The left pane is called the Console Root, and it can be used to work your way down through successive levels of server hierarchy, including

- **Microsoft SQL Servers**   The top level of the SQL Server hierarchy
- **SQL Server groups**   Groupings of related SQL Servers as defined by you
- **SQL Servers**   Entries for individual SQL Servers and their related resource folders

The right pane shows resources you can work with, such as databases or logons. If you have the Taskpad enabled, the right pane also shows tasks you can perform. (To enable or disable the Taskpad, select a SQL Server in the Console Root and then choose the Taskpad option on the View menu.)

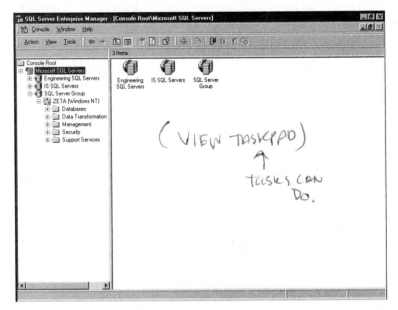

Figure 3-2. *Enterprise Manager is a Microsoft Management Console (MMC) snap-in. You can add other snap-ins to it or add Enterprise Manager to an MMC you already use. Choose Add/Remove Snap-In from the Console menu and then follow the prompts.*

Managing SQL Server Groups

You use SQL Server groups to organize sets of SQL Servers. You define these server groups and can organize them by function, department, or any other criteria. Creating a server group is easy. You can even create subgroups within a group if you want to. If you make a mistake, you can delete groups as well.

Creating a Server Group

Create a server group or a subgroup by completing the following steps:

1. In Enterprise Manager's Console Root (the left pane), right-click Microsoft SQL Servers or any group-level entry.

2. On the shortcut menu, click New SQL Server Group. This displays the dialog box shown in Figure 3-3.

3. In the Server Groups dialog box, type a name for the new group in the Name field.

4. Top level groups follow the Microsoft SQL Servers entry in the console hierarchy. Create a top level group by selecting the Top Level Group option button.

Figure 3-3. *Use the Server Groups dialog box to create new server groups or subgroups.*

5. Subgroups are organized under their primary group, such as Engineering SQL Servers. Create a subgroup by clicking the Sub-Group Of option button and then choosing the primary group from the list provided.

6. Click OK.

Deleting a Server Group

Delete a group or subgroup by completing the following steps:

1. In Enterprise Manager's Console Root, click the plus sign (+) next to the group or subgroup you want to delete. If the group has servers registered in it, move them to a different group, as described later in this chapter under "Moving a Server to a New Group."

2. Select the group or subgroup entry.

3. Press Delete.

Adding SQL Servers to a Group

When you register a SQL Server for use with Enterprise Manager, you can choose which group you want the server to be in. You can even create a new group specifically for this server. Server registration is covered in the following section.

Managing Servers

Servers and databases are the primary resources you manage in Enterprise Manager. Click a server group in the Console Root and the right pane shows you which servers are available for this group. If the server you want to work with isn't shown, you'll need to register it. After that, you can connect to the server to work with it and disconnect when you're finished. You can start the registration process using any of the following techniques:

- From the Action menu, select New SQL Server Registration.

- Right-click any server or group-level entry in Enterprise Manager's Console Root and then choose New SQL Server Registration.

- Select the Wizards option on the Tools menu and then double-click the Registry Server Wizard entry.

If you've opted not to use the Registry Server Wizard, you'll go straight to the manual registration process. Otherwise, you'll use a wizard to register the server.

 Tip You can't use SQL Server 7.0 Enterprise Manager to administer SQL Server 6.5. However, you can register a 6.5 server in Enterprise Manager for SQL Server 7.0. Then, when you access the server in Enterprise Manager for SQL Server 7.0, the Enterprise Manager for SQL Server 6.5 is displayed automatically, provided the SQL Server 6.5 administration tools are installed.

Registering a Server with a Wizard

The Register SQL Server Wizard makes server registration a point-and-click process. You can register multiple servers at the same time, create new groups for these servers, and more. Just complete the following steps:

1. After you start the registration process, you'll see the Register SQL Server Wizard dialog box shown in Figure 3-4. As shown, the first dialog box window provides an introduction, so click Next to continue.

Figure 3-4. *The Register SQL Server Wizard makes it easy to register multiple servers. But if you don't like using wizards, select From Now On I Want To Perform This Task Without Using A Wizard.*

2. Use the Available Servers list to select the SQL Servers you want to register and then click Add to add the server to the Added Servers list. These servers should all have the same authentication account or logon account or both. Click Next to continue.

Tip Sometimes it takes a while for servers to broadcast their names over the network. If the server you want to use isn't listed, just type the name directly in the Available Servers field and then click Add.

3. Select the authentication mode you want to use, either Windows NT authentication or SQL Server authentication. With Windows NT authentication, you use the current domain logon for authentication. With SQL Server authentication, you use a separate SQL Server logon ID and password. Click Next to continue.

4. If you're using SQL Server authentication, the next screen asks you to specify how to log on to SQL Server. For automatic login, choose Login Automatically Using My SQL Server Account Information and then type a SQL Server logon ID and password. For manual login with each connection, choose Prompt For The SQL Server Account Information When Connecting. Click Next to continue.

5. Select an existing server group or create a new server group for the server or servers you're registering. Click Next to continue.

6. The wizard lists the server or servers you're registering. Click Finish to complete the process and begin registration.

7. The Register SQL Server Message dialog box appears and tells you the status of each server. If a server failed to register, click Properties and edit the registration properties for the server. To stop registration of a server that isn't responsive, click Stop. To complete the process, click Close.

Registering a Server Manually

If you don't want to use the wizard, you can manually register each server that you want to work with individually. To do this, complete the following steps:

1. In Enterprise Manager's Console Root, right-click any server or group-level entry and then choose New SQL Server Registration. If the Wizard dialog box comes up, click From Now On I Want To Perform This Task Without Using A Wizard and then click Next. This displays the Registered SQL Server Properties dialog box shown in Figure 3-5.

2. In the Server field, type the name of the server you want to register. If you're unsure of the server name, use the build button (...) to display a dialog box showing active SQL Servers on the network.

3. Select the authentication mode you want to use, either Windows NT authentication or SQL Server authentication. With Windows NT authentication, you use the current domain logon for authentication. With SQL Server authentication, you use a separate SQL Server logon ID and password.

Figure 3-5. *Manual registration puts everything you need in one convenient location, but you can't simultaneously register multiple servers.*

4. If you're using SQL Server authentication, type a SQL Server logon ID and password. Or select Always Prompt For Login Name And Password.

5. Using the Server Group drop-down list box, select an existing server group for the server or click the build button (...) to create a new group.

6. To display server state in the console, select Display SQL Server State In Console. Otherwise, clear this check box and you won't see the start, stop, or pause symbols in the server icon.

> **Tip** The server state is continually refreshed using remote procedure calls (RPCs). To cut down on network traffic, you may want to disable this feature. In addition, the server state may not be displayed when you're running Enterprise Manager on Windows 95 and Windows 98. Windows 95 and Windows 98 don't have the necessary Windows NT networking facilities.

7. To display system databases and system objects, select Show System Databases And System Objects. If you clear this option, system databases and objects are hidden, and you can only display them by editing the registration properties. The system databases are master, msdb, model, and tempdb.

> **Tip** In Enterprise Manager, you can edit the registration properties by right-clicking on the server name and selecting Edit SQL Server Registration Properties.

8. To automatically start the MSSQLServer service when connecting, select Automatically Start SQL Server When Connecting.

Tip   Clearing this option may prevent the accidental starting of SQL Server by other administrators when you're working on the server system (and it is recommended). After all, you don't want someone to accidentally start the server when you're shutting it down or performing some other type of maintenance.

9. Click OK to start the registration process. If Enterprise Manager is unable to connect to the server, you'll see an error dialog box. Choose Yes to register the server regardless of the error. Choose No to modify the registration properties and try again.

Editing Registration Properties

You can change the registration properties at any time by right-clicking on the SQL Server entry in Enterprise Manager's Console Root and then selecting Edit SQL Server Registration Properties. Afterward, use the Registered SQL Server Properties dialog box as described in the "Registering a Server Manually" section of this chapter. The only property you can't change is the server name.

Moving a Server to a New Group

To move the server to a new group, complete the following steps:

1. Right-click the SQL Server entry in Enterprise Manager's Console Root and then select Edit SQL Server Registration Properties from the shortcut menu.

2. In the Edit SQL Server Registration Properties dialog box, use the Server Group drop-down list box to select a new group.

3. Click OK.

Deleting a Server Registration

If you change a server name or remove a server, you may want to delete the server registration in Enterprise Manager so that Enterprise Manager no longer tries to connect to a server that can't be accessed. Right-click the server entry in the Console Root and then select Delete SQL Server Registration. You could also select the server entry in the Console Root and press Delete.

Connecting to a Server

Once you've registered a server, connecting to it is easy. Right-click the server entry in Enterprise Manager's Console Root and then select Connect on the shortcut menu. Or double-click the server entry to establish a connection and display the server's properties dialog box.

Note   Enterprise Manager connects to other SQL Servers through RPC. If you've disabled remote access to a server, however, you won't be able to connect to that server in Enterprise Manager.

Disconnecting from a Server

When you're finished working with a server, you may want to disconnect from it. This cuts down on the back-and-forth RPC calls to the server. To disconnect, right-click the server's entry in Enterprise Manager and then choose Disconnect from the shortcut menu.

Starting, Stopping, and Configuring SQLServerAgent

SQLServerAgent runs as a service and is used to schedule jobs, alerts, and other automated tasks. Once you schedule automated tasks, you'll usually want SQLServerAgent to start automatically when the system starts. This ensures that these tasks are performed as expected. Using SQL Server Service Manager, you can control the related service (SQLServerAgent) just as you do the MSSQLServer service. For details, see the section of this chapter titled "Managing SQL Server Service with Service Manager."

To configure SQLServerAgent, you'll use Enterprise Manager. Although Chapter 12 covers the agent configuration in detail, the basic steps are as follows:

1. Start Enterprise Manager and then in the left pane (Console Root) click the plus sign (+) next to the server on which you want to manage SQL Server Agent.

2. Click the Management folder.

3. Right-click the SQLServerAgent icon and then select Properties from the shortcut menu. You can now configure SQLServerAgent.

4. The SQL Server Agent shortcut menu also lets you start and stop the SQL Server Agent service. Click Start to start the service or click Stop to stop the service.

Starting, Stopping, and Configuring the Microsoft Distributed Transaction Coordinator

Microsoft Distributed Transaction Coordinator (MS DTC) is a transaction manager that allows client applications to work with multiple sources of data in one transaction. When a distributed transaction spans two or more servers, the servers coordinate the management of the transaction using MS DTC. When a distributed transaction spans multiple databases on a single server, SQL Server manages the transaction internally.

SQL Server applications can call MS DTC directly to start an explicit distributed transaction. Distributed transactions can also be started implicitly by

- Calling stored procedures on remote servers running SQL Server
- Updating data on multiple OLE DB data sources
- Enlisting remote servers in a transaction

If you work with transactions under any of the previously listed scenarios, you'll want DTC to be running on the server and you'll probably also want DTC to start automatically when the server starts. As with SQL Server itself, DTC runs as a service. This service is named MSDTC. As you learned in the section of this chapter titled "Managing SQL Server Service with Service Manager," you can control the MSDTC service with Service Manager.

You can also start and stop DTC in Enterprise Manager by completing the following steps:

1. Start Enterprise Manager and then in the left pane (Console Root) click the plus sign (+) next to the server on which you want to manage DTC.

2. Click the Support Services folder.

3. Right-click Distributed Transaction Coordinator and then click Start to start the service or click Stop to stop the service.

Installing and Configuring Full-Text Search

Full-text search allows extensive word searches of textual data and is an additional component you can add to the SQL Server installation. (For details, see the section of Chapter 2 titled "Adding Components.") Once you install the full-text search component, you can manage full-text searches as described in the following sections.

Using Full-Text Searches

As far as administration goes, full-text searches depend on two factors: 1) that you install the necessary components and 2) that you start the related service, which is called the Microsoft Search service. When you start the search service, SQL Server creates full-text indexes of textual data contained in databases. The service manages the indexes and provides the primary mechanism for examining the data it contains.

Note   In Enterprise Manager's Support Services folder, the Microsoft Search service is referred to as Full-Text Search. Don't let the terminology confuse you. These services are one and the same, and the correct name is Microsoft Search service.

The concept of a full-text index may be a bit different than you may be used to. In SQL Server, a full-text index stores information about keywords and their location within a specific column. These text indexes are created for each table in the database, and groups of indexes are contained in catalogs, which are stored separately from the databases to which they belong.

Further, full-text indexes are defined on base tables and not on views, system tables, or temporary tables. Indexes are populated with key values that have information about the significant words in a table, such as the column they're in and their location in the column. In Transact-SQL you can test rows against a full-text search condition using *contains* and *freetext*. You can also return the set of rows that match a full-text search condition using the functions *containstable* and *freetexttable*.

Starting, Stopping, and Configuring the Microsoft Search Service

Microsoft Search is a service that performs the necessary management and search tasks for full-text indexes and their related catalogs. Again, these indexes and catalogs are created automatically when you start and stop the search service. Using SQL Server Service Manager, you can control the search service (SQL Server Agent) just as you do the MSSQLServer service. For details, see the section of this chapter titled "Managing SQL Server Service with Service Manager." If SQL Server uses full-text searches, you'll want to make sure that Microsoft Search starts automatically when the system boots.

Managing Catalogs and Full-Text Searches

Catalogs are stored separately from the databases themselves and although you don't have control over the where's and how's, you still should know where the related information is stored. To examine current catalog information, complete the following steps:

1. Start Enterprise Manager and then in the left pane (Console Root) click the plus sign (+) next to the server using full-text search.

2. Click the Support Services folder.

3. Right-click the Full-Text Search icon and then select Properties from the shortcut menu. This opens the Full-Text Search Service Properties dialog box shown in Figure 3-6.

Figure 3-6. *The Full-Text Search Service Properties dialog box shows where important catalog files and logs are located.*

4. The Full-Text Search Service Properties dialog box has two tabs, General and Performance. The General tab provides the following information:
   - The default location of catalog files
   - The location of temporary files used with full-text searching
   - The location of error logs

5. The Performance tab gives you the following options to optimize full-text searching:

   System Resource Usage   Sets the relative amount of system resources used for full-text indexing. The range of values is from Background (priority 1) to Dedicated (priority 5). The default priority is 3 for Normal. If you set a priority lower than 3, other applications that are running have higher priority for system resources. If you set a priority higher than 3, Microsoft Search will have higher priority than most other applications running on the server.

   Connect Time-Out   Sets the number of seconds to wait for a server connection before indexing a table and the number of seconds to wait for data to be returned from SQL Server. The default is 20 seconds.

6. Click Apply to apply the changes.

Real World   The System Resource Usage setting can really affect performance of the server, and you should rarely set the priority higher than 3. The exceptions would be if you make extensive use of full-text searching or if you use full-text searching almost exclusively.

Cleaning Up Old Catalogs

Although the full-text search components do a good job of maintaining indexes and cleaning up after themselves, you'll want to keep an eye on the number and size of catalog files. You'll also want to regularly clean up old catalogs. You do this by completing the following steps:

1. Start Enterprise Manager and then in the left pane (Console Root) click the plus sign (+) next to the server using full-text search.

2. Click the Support Services folder.

3. Right-click the Full-Text Search icon and then select Cleanup Catalogs from the shortcut menu.

4. When prompted, choose Yes to start cleanup. Cleanup may take a few minutes, depending on the size of the catalogs.

Managing SQL Mail and SQLServerAgent Mail

SQL Mail and SQLServerAgent Mail are core facilities of SQL Server. You use SQL Mail to trigger stored procedures and return result sets by e-mail. You use SQLServerAgent Mail to send e-mail and pager notifications. Both facilities rely on a MAPI-complaint e-mail service. SQL Mail runs via the MSSQLServer service. SQLServerAgent Mail, on the other hand, runs through the SQL Server Agent service. The sections that follow explain how you configure and test the mail client needed by SQL Mail and SQLServerAgent Mail, then examines configuring SQL Mail and SQLServerAgent Mail.

Setting Up SQL Server as a Mail Client

SQL Mail and SQLServerAgent Mail can make use of your existing e-mail infrastructure to send and receive messages as long as your e-mail server is MAPI compliant and you configure SQL Server as a valid mail client. The easiest mail service to configure a client for is Microsoft Exchange. If you're running Microsoft Exchange, you must

1. Set up an Exchange mailbox for SQL Mail and SQLServerAgent Mail. Or, if you prefer, set up separate mailboxes for these facilities.

Tip By default, the SQL Mail service runs in the same security context as MSSQLServer service. Because of this, the Exchange mailbox must be configured for a domain account that can run the MSSQLServer service. SQLServerAgent Mail runs through the SQL Server Agent service and, likewise, the Exchange mailbox must be configured for a domain account that can run the SQL Server Agent service.

2. Install compatible mail client software on the server, such as Microsoft Outlook. The key components of the client used by SQL Mail and SQLServerAgent Mail are the MAPI extensions. Watch out, because you can modify these extensions accidentally when you install service packs, e-mail applications, or other applications that use e-mail.

3. Set up a mail profile for each account using the Mail and Fax utility on the Control Panel. You should configure the profiles to point to the Mail Exchange Server and the Exchange mailbox.

Tip Be sure to use a profile name that's easy to identify as the SQL Mail or SQLServerAgent Mail profile, or both. This will make it easier for others to work with the profiles and will help prevent accidental deletion.

Testing the Mail Installation

Once you configure SQL Mail as a mail client(s), you should test the installation using the following procedure:

1. Log on to the system running SQL Server using a domain account set up for SQL Server.
2. Start the mail client using the new mail profile.
3. Test the configuration by sending a message addressed to the mailbox for SQL Mail.
4. If the message doesn't show up in the mail client's inbox, you may have improperly configured SQL Mail. Take a close look at each step of the configuration and then repeat this test.
5. Repeat this process to test SQLServerAgent Mail.

Configuring SQL Mail

After you determine that SQL Server can send and receive mail with the mail client, you're ready to complete the configuration. You need to tell SQL Server about the profile. You do this by completing the following steps:

1. Start Enterprise Manager and then in the left pane (Console Root) click the plus sign (+) next to the server using SQL Mail.
2. Click the Support Services folder.
3. Right-click the SQL Mail icon and then select Properties from the shortcut menu. This opens the dialog box shown in Figure 3-7.

Figure 3-7. *In the SQL Mail Configuration dialog box, type the profile name in the field provided and then click Test.*

4. Type the profile name in the field provided or use the drop-down list box to select any of the available profiles on the server. If you want to test the configuration, click Test.

5. SQL Mail should be configured to start automatically when the server starts. This ensures that mail can be sent and received when the server is running. To enable automatic startup, select Autostart SQL Mail When SQL Server Starts.

6. Click OK.

Configuring SQLServerAgent Mail

Next, you need to tell SQL Server about the profile for SQLServerAgent Mail. You do this by completing the following steps:

1. In Enterprise Manager, access the Management folder on the server using SQLServerAgent.

2. Right-click on the SQL Server Agent icon in the left pane and then, from the shortcut menu, select Properties.

3. Type the profile name in the Mail Profile field or use the drop-down list box to select any of the available profiles on the server. If you want to test the configuration, click Test.

4. Click OK.

Managing Server Activity

As a database administrator, it's your job to make sure that SQL Server runs smoothly. One of the ways you do this is by actively monitoring the server. By monitoring server activity, you can

- Keep track of user connections and locks
- View processes and commands that active users are running
- Check the status of locks on processes and objects
- See blocked or blocking transactions
- Ensure that processes complete successfully and detect errors if they don't

When problems arise, you can send a message to a user who is running a process or even terminate a process, if necessary.

 Note For more detailed coverage of monitoring SQL Server, see Chapter 10. In that chapter, you'll learn how to use Performance Monitor and SQL Server Profiler to keep track of SQL Server activity, performance, and errors.

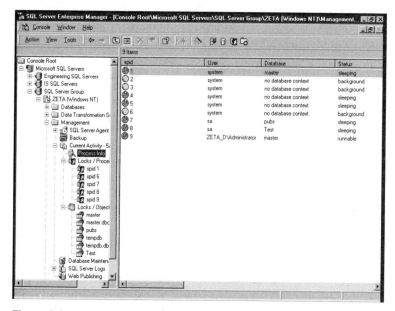

Figure 3-8. *Process Info provides a detailed look at processes and the user connections running them.*

Examining Process Information

Process information provides detailed information about the status of processes, current user connections, and other server activity. You can view process information by completing the following steps:

1. Start Enterprise Manager and then in the left pane (Console Root) click the plus sign (+) next to the server you want to examine.

2. Click the Management folder and then select Current Activity. The Current Activity entry shows a date and time when the activity snapshot was taken.

3. Choose the Process Info entry in the Console Root or double-click Process Info in the right pane. You should see a summary of process activity similar to that shown in Figure 3-8.

4. Process information isn't updated automatically and occasionally you'll have to refresh it. To do this, right-click Current Activity and select Refresh on the shortcut menu.

Initially, processes are sorted by process ID, but they can be ordered by any of the available information categories summarized in Table 3-1. Click a category header to sort processes based on that category. Click a category header a second time to do a reserve sort on the category.

Table 3-1. Process Information Used in Database Administration

Category	Description
SPID	Server process ID of the current user process.
User	User running the process by SQL Server ID or domain account, depending on the authentication technique used.
Database	The database being used. Some server processes are started before the master database is brought online, and these have no database context.
Status	The status of the process, which is usually runnable, sleeping, or background. A runnable process is active. A sleeping process is waiting for input or a lock. A background process is running in the background and periodically performing tasks.
Open Transactions	The number of open transactions.
Command	The command being executed or the last command executed.
Application	The application connecting to the server and running the process, such as SQL Server Query Analyzer.
Wait Time	The elapsed wait time in milliseconds.
Wait Type	Specifies whether the process is waiting or not waiting.
Wait Resource	The resource the process is waiting for (if any).
CPU	The amount of processor time being used by the process.
Physical I/O	The physical input/output used by the process.
Memory Usage	The amount of memory the process is using in KB.
Login Time	When the connection was established.
Last Batch Time	The time when the last command was executed using the connection.
Host	The host from which the connection originated.
Network Library	The network library used to establish the connection.
Network Address	The network address for the connection.
Blocked By	The number of connections blocking this process.
Blocking	The number of connections waiting for this process to finish.

Locks by Process ID and Object

Locks can be tracked by process ID and object. Either technique provides the same information; it's just presented in a different way. You can view locks by process ID or object by completing the following steps:

1. Start Enterprise Manager and then in the left pane (Console Root) click the plus sign (+) next to the server you want to examine.

2. Click the Management folder and then select Current Activity. The Current Activity entry shows a date and time when the activity snapshot was taken.

3. With processes, you can view a summary of all objects the process is locking. Click Locks/Process ID and then select the process you want to examine, such as SPID 1.

4. With objects, you can see a list of all processes with locks on the object. Click Locks/Object and then select the database object you want to examine, such as master.

5. Lock statistics aren't updated automatically, and you'll occasionally have to refresh the view. To do this, right-click Current Activity and select Refresh on the shortcut menu.

Although locks by process ID and locks by object are presented in a slightly different manner, the information contained in the listing is almost identical. With process ID, you see a list of objects the process has a lock on. With objects, you see a list of processes that have locks on the object. Beyond this, you'll also see information on the type, status, and mode of the lock as well as the lock owner, the resource being locked, and the index being locked (if applicable)—all of which are summarized in Table 3-2.

Table 3-2. Lock-Related Information Used in Database Administration

Category	Type	Description
Lock Type	RID	Row identifier. Used to lock a single row within a table.
	KEY	A row lock within an index. Used to protect key ranges.
	PAG	A lock on a data or index page.
	EXT	A lock on a contiguous group of eight data or index pages.
	TAB	A lock on an entire table, including all data and indexes.
	DB	A lock on a database.
Lock Mode	S	Shared; used for read-only operations, such as a SELECT statement.
	U	Update; used when reading/locking an updateable resource. Prevents some deadlock situations.
	X	Exclusive; allows only one session to update the data. Used with data modification operations, such as INSERT, DELETE, and UPDATE.
	Intent	Used to establish a lock hierarchy.
	Sch-S	Schema stability; used when checking the schema of a table.
	Sch-M	Schema modification; used when modifying the schema of a table.
	BU	Bulk update; used when bulk-copying data.

(continued)

Table 3-2. *(continued)*

Category	Type	Description
Status	GRANT	The lock was obtained.
	WAIT	The lock is blocked by another process.
	CNVT	The lock is being converted; that is, it's held in one mode but waiting to acquire a stronger lock mode.
Owner	curs	The lock owner is a cursor.
	sess	The lock owner is a user session.
	xact	The lock owner is a transaction.
Index	Index Name	The index associated with the designated resource. With clustered indexes, you'll see a table name instead.
Resource	RID	A row identifier for a locked row within a table; listed by <file id>:<page>:<row id>/ where row id is a row within the specified page.
	KEY	A key shown as a hexadecimal number and used internally by SQL Server.
	PAG	A page number; listed by <file id>:<page>, where file id is the file id in the sysfiles table and page is the logical page number within that file.
	EXT	The first page number in the extent being locked; listed by <file id>:<page>.
	TAB	Table identifier.
	DB	Database identifier.

Troubleshooting Deadlocks and Blocking Connections

Two common problems you may see are deadlocks or blocking connections. Deadlocks and blocking connections can occur in just about any database environment, especially when lots of users are making connections to databases.

- Deadlocks occur when two users have locks on separate objects and each wants a lock on the other's object. Each user waits for the other to release the lock, and this doesn't happen.

- Blocking connections occur when one connection holds a lock and a second connection wants a conflicting lock type. This forces the second connection to either wait or block the first.

Both deadlocks and blocking connections can degrade server performance.

Although deadlock and blocking situations can be detected and corrected by SQL Server, you can help speed up this process by identifying potential problems and taking action, if necessary. Process information can tell you when deadlocks or blocking occur. You'll want to examine these columns: Wait Time, Wait Type, Wait Resource, Blocking, and Blocked By. When you have a deadlock or blocking situation, you'll want to take a closer look at the locks on the objects that are causing problems. This manner is described earlier in the "Locks by Process ID and Object" section of this chapter. You may also want to stop the offending processes. Follow the steps described in the section below entitled "Killing Server Processes."

Tracking Command Execution in SQL Server

Sometimes you'll want to track the commands that users are executing; you can do this by using the Current Activity resource viewer. The steps you take are the following:

1. Start Enterprise Manager and then in the left pane (Console Root) click the plus sign (+) next to the server you want to examine.

2. Click the Management folder and then select Current Activity. The Current Activity entry shows a date and time when the activity snapshot was taken.

Tip If the snapshot is old, you can refresh the snapshot by right-clicking Current Activity and selecting Refresh on the shortcut menu.

3. Select Process Info. The entries in the User column can help you track user sessions and the processes they are using.

4. Double-click a process to display the dialog box shown in Figure 3-9. This dialog box shows the last command executed by the user.

5. To track commands being executed by the user, click Refresh.

6. To kill the process, click Kill Process. Then, when prompted, choose Yes.

7. To send a message to the user running the process, click Send Message.

Figure 3-9. *The Process Details dialog box displays the last command or batch executed in the session. Note that the title line also shows the user logon ID, process ID, and originating host.*

Figure 3-10. *Use the Send Message dialog box to send a message using the Messenger service. If you want to send a message to a different host, choose the Using Hostname option button and then type the new hostname.*

Sending Messages to Users Based on Connections

While you're examining processes and server activity, you may want to send messages to users based on connections. To do this, complete the following steps:

1. Start Enterprise Manager and then in the left pane (Console Root) click the plus sign (+) next to the server you want to examine.

2. Click the Management folder and then select Current Activity. The Current Activity entry shows a date and time when the activity snapshot was taken.

3. Select Process Info and then right-click a process being used by a user you want to send a message to.

4. On the shortcut menu, select Send Message. This opens the dialog box shown in Figure 3-10.

5. In the Message area, type the text of the message.

6. Select a destination using the option buttons provided. You can send a message to the user or to the user's computer.

7. Click Send to send the message.

 Note When you send mail to users, you use the Windows Alerter and Messenger services and not SQL Mail. These services must be running on SQL Server and on the user's system. A good resource about Windows NT services and service management is *Microsoft Windows NT Server 4.0 Administrator's Pocket Consultant*.

Killing Server Processes

Processes that are using up CPU time or blocking may need to be stopped. To do this, complete the following steps:

1. Start Enterprise Manager and then in the left pane (Console Root) click the plus sign (+) next to the server you want to examine.

2. Click the Management folder and then select Current Activity. The Current Activity entry shows a date and time when the activity snapshot was taken.

3. Select Process Info and then right-click the process you want to stop.

Note When you start SQL Server the process IDs 1 to 6 are started by the system. These processes shouldn't be killed. If you are concerned about these processes, you should stop and restart the MSSQLServer service rather than trying to kill these processes.

4. On the shortcut menu, select Kill Process. Then, when prompted, click Yes.

Chapter 4

Core Database Administration

Core database administration tasks revolve around creating, manipulating, and supporting databases. In Microsoft SQL Server 7.0, a database is a collection of data and the objects that represent and interact with that data. Tables, views, stored procedures, triggers, and constraints are typical database objects.

A single SQL Server can have up to 32,767 databases, and each database can have over 2 billion objects. These are theoretical limits, of course, but they demonstrate that SQL Server can handle just about any chore. To perform most administration tasks, you'll need to log in to the database using an account that has the sysadmin role, such as the local sysadmin account (sa). Detailed information on roles and SQL Server security is in Chapter 5.

Database Files and Logs

Each SQL Server database is associated with a transaction log. A transaction log is a history of modifications to the database, and SQL Server uses it to ensure database integrity. All changes to the database are first written to the transaction log and then applied to the database. If the database update is successful, the transaction is completed and recorded as successful. If the database update fails, SQL Server uses the transaction log to restore the database to its original state (which is called rolling back the transaction). This two-phase commit process makes it possible for SQL Server to automatically restore a database in case of power failure, server outage, or other problems that occur when you enter a transaction.

SQL Server databases and transaction logs are contained in separate database files. This means that each database always has at least two files associated with it— a data file and a log file. Databases also can have secondary data files. These database files store the following information:

- **Primary data files** Every database has one primary data file. These files store data and maintain records of other files used in a database. These files end with the .mdf extension.

- **Secondary data files** These files store additional data for a database. These files end with the .ndf extension.

- **Transaction log files** Every database has at least one transaction log file. This file contains information necessary to restore the database. Log files end with the .ldf extension.

> **Note** SQL Server also uses backup devices. Backup devices are logical drives that map to files, named piped or physical devices, such as tape drives.

Database files are set when the database is created or modified. By allowing for multiple database files, SQL Server can create databases that span multiple disk drives and can grow in size as needed. Although the size of a SQL Server database is often measured in gigabytes (GB), databases can range in size from 1 megabyte (MB) to a theoretical limit of 1 terabyte (TB).

As you set out to work with databases, keep in mind that SQL Server is designed to automatically expand databases as necessary. This means that master, tempdb, msdb, and other critical databases won't run out of space under normal conditions—provided, of course, that there's file space on the configured drives and that you don't set a maximum database size manually. System databases are the most important ones on the server. You should never directly update tables in system databases. Instead, you should use the appropriate management tools or stored procedures to modify the databases, if necessary. The only exception is the model database, which you can update with settings for new databases.

Database Administration Basics

Most of your database administration work is done through Enterprise Manager. You'll use Enterprise Manager to perform many common database administration tasks, including

- Viewing database information
- Checking default and system databases
- Examining database objects

Each of these tasks is examined in the sections that follow.

Viewing Database Information in Enterprise Manager

SQL Server organizes information using a top-down hierarchy that goes from server groups to servers to databases to objects. Following this, you must work your way down to the database level in order to view the databases installed on a particular server. If you have registered with a server and have connected to it previously, you can view its databases by completing the following steps:

1. Start Enterprise Manager and then in the left pane (Console Root) click the plus sign (+) next to the server group you want to work with. If the MSSQL-Server service is stopped, you'll need to restart it before accessing the server.

2. Click the plus sign (+) next to the server you want to work with and then select the Databases folder.

Note If you haven't authenticated the server connection, you may need to provide a SQL logon account and password. You may also need to reestablish a connection with the server. In either case, enter any necessary information and then click OK/Yes to continue.

3. You should see a list of the databases available on the server. Now select a database in the left pane or double-click its icon in the right pane.

4. With the Taskpad enabled (by selecting Taskpad from the View menu, if necessary), the right pane should provide access to three different views:

   * **General** Displays database owner, creation date, total size, and other important database information; also provides quick access links to start key administration tasks, such as backup database and restore database.

   * **Tables & Indexes** Displays the available tables and indexes in the databases. The tables are listed alphabetically along with their associated indexes and clustered indexes. You'll find the total table size and the number of rows in a particular table as well.

   * **Space Allocated** Displays a summary of the disk space allocated for database files. The summary is broken down by data files and transaction files as well as by used and free space.

Real World If only the general information is provided for a database, you may not have the appropriate permissions to access additional information, or you may need to reinitialize your database connection. Do this by exiting Enterprise Manager and restarting it.

5. To view database information, click any of the view links in the right pane, either General, Tables & Indexes, or Space Allocated. Figure 4-1 shows the General view.

Figure 4-1. *The General view provides a summary of the selected database and also gives quick access to start key administration tasks.*

Viewing Database Information Using SQL

You can also use Transact-SQL to examine database information. Transact-SQL is an enhanced version of the standard structured query language that is used by SQL Server. Start Query Analyzer and then use the following command:

```
sp_helpdb <dbname>
```

where dbname is the name of the database you want to examine.

When you view database information in this way, you get an overview of the database as well as a listing of current data and log files. A summary of this information is shown in Table 4-1.

Table 4-1. Database Properties Viewable Using SQL

Column Name	Description
created	The date the database was created.
db_size	The total size of the database including all data and log files.
dbid	The unique identifier for the database on the current server.
filegroup	The filegroup associated with the file. Filegroups allow you to group sets of database files together.
fileid	The unique identifier for the file in the current database.

(continued)

Table 4-1. *(continued)*

Column Name	Description
filename	The full filename and path.
growth	The number of megabytes or percent the file grows by.
maxsize	The maximum file size. Unlimited means there is no limit.
name	The name of the database or file (without a file extension).
owner	The database owner.
size	The current size of a file.
status	The database status.
usage	The way the file is used, such as data only or log only.

Checking System and Sample Databases

A new SQL Server installation includes the system and sample databases listed in Table 4-2. System databases are critical to the proper operation of SQL Server, and a key part of administration is backing up and maintaining these databases. Sample databases, on the other hand, are only meant to provide examples and don't need regular maintenance. The sample databases take up only 6 MB of disk space, and rather than deleting them, you may want to keep them around for testing and for use in demonstrations.

Table 4-2. Summary of System and Sample Databases

Database Name	Database Type	Description
master	System	Maintains information on all databases installed on the server. This database is modified anytime you create databases, manage accounts, or change configuration settings. Back up the master regularly.
model	System	Provides a template for all new databases. If you want new databases to have certain properties or permissions, put these changes in the model database and then all new databases will inherit the changes.
tempdb	System	Provides a temporary workspace for processing queries and handling other tasks. This database is re-created each time SQL Server is started and is based on the model database.
pubs	Sample	Provides a sample database and is often used to demonstrate SQL/Transact-SQL commands.
Northwind	Sample	Provides a sample database with application programming interface (API) examples.

(continued)

Table 4-2. *(continued)*

Database Name	Database Type	Description
msdb	System	Used by the SQL Server Agent service when performing handling alerts, notifications, and scheduled tasks. All the information in this database is accessible using Enterprise Manager options.

Examining Database Objects

The key elements of a SQL Server database are referred to as objects. The objects you can associate with a database include tables, views, stored procedures, extended stored procedures, users, roles, rules, defaults, user-defined data types, and full-text catalogs. To examine this information, complete the following steps:

1. Start Enterprise Manager and then in the left pane (Console Root) click the plus sign (+) next to the server group you want to work with.

2. Click the plus sign (+) next to the server you want to work with again and then, if necessary, authenticate yourself or establish a connection, or both.

3. Click the Databases folder.

4. Click the plus sign (+) next to the database you want to work with a third time and you should see a list of available objects.

5. In the left pane, click the object you want to view.

 More Info Each of these objects is covered in detail in the appropriate chapter. For example, you'll find more information on tables in Chapter 11.

Creating Databases

SQL Server uses the model database as the basis of new databases. If you want new databases to have the same setup, you should modify the model database and then create the necessary new databases. Otherwise, you'll need to manually modify the settings of each new database. The easiest way to create a new database is to use Enterprise Manager. You can also create databases using Transact-SQL.

Creating Databases in Enterprise Manager

In Enterprise Manager you set database properties with buttons and input fields and let SQL Server do all the behind-the-scenes SQL work. You create a database using the default options by completing these steps:

1. Start Enterprise Manager and then in the left pane (Console Root) click the plus sign (+) next to the server group you want to work with.

2. Click the plus sign (+) next to the server you want to work with again and then, if necessary, authenticate yourself or establish a connection, or both.

3. Right-click the Databases folder and then select New Database from the short-cut menu. This opens the Database Properties dialog box shown in Figure 4-2.

4. Select the General tab and type a name for the database. Although database names can be up to 128 characters, you'll be better able to track the data-base if it has a short but descriptive filename.

Note   The names of database objects are referred to as identifiers. Identifiers can contain from 1 to 128 characters (except for local tem-porary tables, which can have from 1 to 116 characters) and must fol-low the specific naming conventions for the identifier class to which they belong. Generally, if the identifier name uses spaces or begins with a number, you must use brackets ([]) or double quotes (" ") to delimit the name when referencing it in Transact-SQL commands.

5. Click OK and SQL Server creates the database.

To customize the creation process, follow steps 1 through 4 (but not 5) in the previous example and then continue with these steps:

1. In the File Name field, type a name for the primary data file associated with this database. By default, SQL Server bases the data filename on the database name. For example, if you type Sample as the database name, the data file is named Sample_Data.

Figure 4-2. *Use the Database Properties dialog box to create new databases and to update the settings of existing databases. If you want to create databases with a wizard instead, select the Wizards option on the Tools menu. In the Wizards dialog box select Database, and then double-click Create Database Wizard.*

2. In the Location field, type the full path to the data file. The primary data file must end with the .mdf extension. By default, SQL Server uses the default data location you selected when you installed the server. Click Location to find a new path or enter a new path directly.

3. In the Initial Size field, type an initial size for the database in megabytes. Use a size that makes sense for the amount of data that the database will store. By default, new databases have the same size as the model database. The size range for databases is from 1 MB to 1 TB.

Tip Setting the initial database size to a reasonable value cuts down on the overhead that may be associated with growing the database. Whether you grow the database manually or SQL Server grows it automatically, the database is locked until the growth is complete. This can cause delays in processing queries and handling transactions.

Note Keep in mind that you cannot shrink a database to be smaller than its size when created. However, you can shrink individual data and log files to be smaller than their initial creation size by using the DBCC SHRINKFILE statement. With DBCC SHRINKFILE, you must shrink each file individually, rather than trying to shrink the entire database.

4. The File Group field shows which filegroup the data file belongs to. By default, all files are placed in the primary group. While the primary data file must be in the primary group, other data files can be placed in different filegroups. Filegroups provide additional options for determining where data is stored and how it's used, as well as how data is backed up and restored.

Tip Filegroups are designed primarily for large databases and advanced administration. If your database might grow to 1 GB or larger, consider using filegroups. Otherwise, you really don't need to use filegroups. That said, the primary reason to use filegroups is to improve database response time. You do this by allowing database files to be created across multiple disks or accessed by multiple disk controllers, or both.

5. Secondary data files provide an additional location for data. If you want to configure secondary data files, start on a new line and then repeat steps 1 through 4. Secondary data files must end with the .ndf extension.

6. After configuring data files, you need to configure file properties for the database. By default, data files are set to grow automatically by 10 percent each time the data files need to be expanded, and there's no limit on the maximum file size.

7. Click the Transaction Log tab shown in Figure 4-3. You can now configure one or more transaction log files in much the same way that you configured the data files. Type file name, location, initial size, and filegroup information. Be sure to name the log files with the .ldf extension.

Figure 4-3. *Use the Transaction Log tab to configure the size, location, and features of the transaction log.*

Real World The Autogrow feature is a good one, and I heartily recommend using it so databases don't run out of space. That said, however, the default option for file growth can lead to problems. With a 10 percent growth rate, a 500 MB database grows by a whopping 50 MB each time a data file needs to be expanded, and a server with multiple databases may run out of space as a result of the growth factor. I prefer to set the growth in megabytes, with 1 MB as a minimum growth size. When you grow in megabytes, you know exactly how much the database will grow each time. You may also want to configure an alert to notify you when the database grows to a certain size. Configuring alerts is covered in Chapter 12.

Note Sizing the transaction log can be tricky. You don't want to rob the system of needed space for data, but at the same time you want to make sure that the transaction logs aren't continually getting resized (as I noted previously, the file gets locked when it's being expanded). I recommend 2–3 MB as a minimum for most databases and 25 percent of total data file size on a moderately active database. Note also that placing transaction logs on separate drives from data files can usually improve database performance.

8. Set file properties for the transaction logs. Here, the default options usually work fine and you don't need to change anything.

9. Click OK to complete the creation process. Afterward, you should set options and permissions for the database. Setting options is covered later in the section entitled "Setting Database Options." Setting permissions is covered in Chapter 5, "Microsoft SQL Server 7.0 Security."

Creating Databases Using SQL

Another way to create a database is to use the CREATE DATABASE command. This command has options that are similar to those in the Database Properties tab, and the best way to learn how the command works is to first create databases in Enterprise Manager and then try CREATE DATABASE.

The syntax and usage for CREATE DATABASE is shown in Listing 4-1.

Listing 4-1. CREATE DATABASE Syntax and Usage

Syntax

```
CREATE DATABASE database_name
[ ON [PRIMARY]
  [ <filespec> [,...n] ]
  [, <filegroup> [,...n] ]
]
[ LOG ON { <filespec> [,...n]} ]
[ FOR LOAD | FOR ATTACH ]
<filespec> ::=
( [ NAME = logical_file_name, ]
  FILENAME = 'os_file_name'
  [, SIZE = size]
  [, MAXSIZE = { max_size | UNLIMITED } ]
  [, FILEGROWTH = growth_increment] ) [,...n]
<filegroup> ::=
FILEGROUP filegroup_name <filespec> [,...n]
```

Usage

```
CREATE DATABASE Sample
ON
PRIMARY ( NAME = Sample1,
  FILENAME = 'c:\mssql7\data\sampledat1.mdf',
  SIZE = 100MB,
  MAXSIZE = UNLIMITED,
  FILEGROWTH = 10%),
  ( NAME = Sample2,
  FILENAME = 'c:\mssql7\data\sampledat2.ndf',
  SIZE = 100MB,
  MAXSIZE = UNLIMITED,
  FILEGROWTH = 10%)
LOG ON
  ( NAME = SampleLog1,
  FILENAME = 'c:\mssql7\data\samplelog1.ldf',
  SIZE = 3MB,
  MAXSIZE = UNLIMITED,
  FILEGROWTH = 5MB)
```

Setting Database Options

New databases inherit options from the model database. After you create a database, you can modify these settings at any time by using Enterprise Manager or Transact-SQL.

Setting Database Options in Enterprise Manager

To set database options in Enterprise Manager, complete the following steps:

1. Start Enterprise Manager and then in the left pane (Console Root) click the plus sign (+) next to the server group you want to work with.

2. Click the plus sign (+) next to the server you want to work with again and then click the plus sign (+) next to the Databases folder.

3. Right-click the database you want to work with and then, from the shortcut menu, choose Properties. This opens the Properties dialog box shown in Figure 4-4. For details see the following section, "Database Options for Enterprise Manager and Transact-SQL."

4. In the Properties dialog box, click the Options tab. You can now configure options for the database by selecting or clearing the appropriate check boxes.

5. Click OK when you're finished. Your changes take effect immediately, and you don't need to restart the server.

Figure 4-4. *After creating a database, you should set its options in the Properties dialog box.*

Database Options for Enterprise Manager and Transact-SQL

You use database options to configure individual databases. In most SQL Server editions, all database options are set to FALSE by default, except for Auto Create Statistics and Auto Update Statistics, which are set to TRUE by default in the model database. If you change these options in the model database, your default options will be different. In the following list, database Properties dialog box options are listed with initial caps or by the related SQL command in lowercase, or both.

- **ANSI NULL Default (ANSI null default)**   When TRUE, changes the database default to NULL when no value is specified. You can override this setting by explicitly stating NULL or NOT NULL when you create user-defined data types or column definitions.

- **ANSI Nulls (ANSI nulls)**   When TRUE, any comparison to a null value evaluates to NULL. Otherwise, comparisons of non-Unicode values evaluate to TRUE only when both values are NULL.

- **ANSI Warnings (ANSI warnings)**   When TRUE, SQL Server displays warnings when it otherwise may not. For example, if TRUE, divide-by-zero errors are displayed. Otherwise, they aren't.

- **Auto Close (autoclose)**   When TRUE, the database is closed and resources are freed up when the last user connection ends and all database processes are completed. The database reopens automatically when a user tries to use the database again. In the SQL Server Desktop edition, this option is set to TRUE by default. All other editions set this option to FALSE by default. When FALSE, the database remains open even if no users are currently using it.

   Tip   With the Desktop edition, Autoclose is a useful feature that allows databases to be treated like any other file. When the database is closed, you're free to move, copy, or change it.

- **Auto Create Statistics (auto create statistics)**   When TRUE, statistics are automatically created by SQL Server for columns used in a *where* clause. These statistics are used to better determine how to evaluate a query, which in turn can improve query performance.

- **Auto Shrink (autoshrink)**   When TRUE, data and log files can be reduced in size and compacted automatically. The idea is that when records are deleted or purged, you can let SQL Server automatically reduce the size of data or log files, or both. However, log files are only reduced in size when you back up the transaction log or set the Truncate Log On Checkpoint option to TRUE. In the SQL Server Desktop edition, this option is set to TRUE by default. All other editions set this option to FALSE by default. Note also that you can't set this option on a read-only database.

Note Several caveats apply to Autoshrink. The Autoshrink option is only applied when more than 25 percent of a file contains unused space. This in turn causes SQL Server to reduce the file size so that only 25 percent of file space is free or to set the file size to its original size setting, whichever is greater. The process that shrinks the database is the server process ID 6; it checks the database size at 30-minute intervals. As with Autogrow, the database is locked when SQL Server shrinks files, which can reduce query response time. Because of this, I don't recommend using this option and prefer to periodically run the DBCC SHRINK-DATABASE command or to schedule this task on a recurring basis, as outlined later in the section entitled "Compacting and Shrinking a Database Manually."

- **Auto Update Statistics (auto update statistics)** When TRUE, existing statistics are automatically updated if data in the related tables changes. Otherwise, existing statistics aren't automatically updated and can only be updated manually.

- **concat null yields null** When TRUE, concatenating a string containing NULL with other strings results in NULL. Otherwise, the null value is treated as an empty string.

- **cursor close on commit** When TRUE, open cursors are closed automatically when a transaction is committed. This behavior is in compliance with SQL-92 but isn't set to TRUE by default. As a result, cursors remain open across transaction boundaries and close only when the related connection is closed or when the cursor is explicitly closed.

Note SQL-92 is the most widely used version of the SQL standard and is sometimes referred to as ANSI SQL.

- **DBO Use Only (dbo use only)** When TRUE, only the database owner can access the database. Use this option when you're modifying a database and temporarily want to block access to it.

- **default to local cursor** When TRUE, cursors are created with local scope unless otherwise specified, and as a result, the cursor name is valid only within this scope. When FALSE, cursors not explicitly set to LOCAL are created with a global scope and can be referenced in any stored procedure, batch, or trigger that the connection executes.

- **merge publish** When TRUE, the database can be used for merge replication publications. If you use the Replication Wizard to configure replication, this setting is changed for you automatically.

- **offline** When TRUE, the database is offline and can be mounted or dismounted as necessary. You'll often want to use this option with removable media, such as CDs.

- **published** When TRUE, permits the tables of a database to be published for replication. This option is also set by the Replication Wizard.

- **Read Only (read only)** When TRUE, data can be read but not modified. Use this option to prevent users from changing data and modifying database configuration settings. When this option is set, several caveats apply: automatic recovery is skipped at system startup, locking does not take place, and the database will not shrink.

- **Recursive Triggers (recursive triggers)** When TRUE, a trigger can execute recursively. Triggers can be executed directly or indirectly. With a direct trigger, a trigger in Table A1 modifies Table A1, which in turn causes the trigger to fire again. With an indirect trigger, a trigger in Table A1 could modify data in Table A2, which in turn has a trigger that modifies data in Table A1, and this causes the original trigger to fire again.

- **Select Into/Bulk Copy (select into/bulkcopy)** When TRUE, certain SQL commands aren't logged in the transaction log. These commands include using SELECT INTO with a permanent table, running fast bulk copy, using UPDATETEXT or WRITETEXT without logging, and using a table load. If you set this option to TRUE and execute any command that bypasses the transaction log, you can't recover the database from transaction logs and BACKUP LOG commands are prohibited. Instead, use BACKUP DATABASE to backup the entire database and then later you can back up from the log (provided you don't run anymore commands that bypass the transaction log).

- **Single User (single user)** When TRUE, only one user at a time can connect to the database. Before you can set this option, all users must log out of the database. If necessary, kill the user processes as detailed in Chapter 3.

- **subscribed** When TRUE, the database can be subscribed to a replicated (or published) database.

- **torn page detection** When TRUE, SQL Server automatically detects incomplete I/O operations known as torn pages. If a torn page is detected during a user connection, an I/O error is raised and the user connection is terminated. If a torn page is detected during recovery, the database is marked suspect. In either case, you may want to restore the database from backup and apply any backup transaction logs.

> **Tip** You can use battery-backed disk caches to ensure that data is successfully written to disk or not written at all. But don't set torn page detection to TRUE.

- **Truncate Log on Checkpoint (trunc. log on chkpt.)** When TRUE, the transaction log can be automatically truncated. Basically, this allows the log to be cleared out once transactions have been committed. After the transaction log has been cleared out, you can only perform BACKUP/RESTORE at the database level (and not with the transaction log). In the SQL Server Desktop edition, this option is set to TRUE by default. All other editions set this option to FALSE by default.

Tip Checkpoints occur at various times. A checkpoint is issued for each database when the MSSQLServer service shuts down normally. Checkpoints do not occur when the SHUTDOWN WITH NOWAIT statement is used. A checkpoint is executed in a single database when a database is changed with *sp_dboption*. SQL Server also automatically issues a checkpoint on a database as necessary to ensure that the designated recovery interval can be achieved and when the log becomes 70% full.

Note The transaction log must be large enough to store all active trans- actions. Otherwise, you can't roll back transactions. In a deployment environment, you should only use this option when you can rely solely on database backups and do not supplement with transaction log backups. Note also that the tempdb database is always truncated on CHECKPOINT, regardless of the setting of this option.

- **Use Quoted Identifiers (quoted identifier)** When TRUE, identifiers must be delimited by double quotation marks ("...") and literals must be delimited by single quotation marks ('...'). All strings that are delimited by double quotation marks are interpreted as object identifiers and don't have to follow the Transact-SQL rules for identifiers.

Viewing, Changing, and Overriding Database Options

Although Enterprise Manager makes it easy to set database options, you'll often want to view or change options using SQL commands. To do this, you can use the *sp_dboption* stored procedure or individual SET commands or both. Key tasks you'll want to perform with these commands are

Displaying an options list To display a list of available options, type the following command:

```
EXEC sp_dboption
```

Viewing database option settings To view the current option settings for a database, type

```
EXEC sp_dboption <dbname>
```

where dbname is the name of the database you want to examine, such as

```
EXEC sp_dboption 'Subs'
```

Changing database options To set or change a database option, type

```
EXEC sp_dboption <dbname>, <option>, {TRUE | FALSE}
```

where dbname is the name of the database you want to examine and option is the name of the option to set, such as

```
EXEC sp_dboption 'Subs', 'trunc. log on chkpt.', TRUE
```

Overriding database options Use SET options for individual sessions or database drivers to override default settings. You can also check options using properties of the *Databaseproperty* function. See the "Default Connection Options" section of Chapter 2 for more information.

Managing Database and Log Size

With SQL Server 7.0, you can manage database and log size either automatically or manually. You can configure either technique in Enterprise Manager or through Transact-SQL. This section looks primarily at configuration through Enterprise Manager.

Configuring SQL Server to Automatically Manage File Size

To configure automatic management of database and log size in Enterprise Manager, complete the following steps:

1. Start Enterprise Manager and then work your way down to the Databases folder using the entries in the left pane.

2. Right-click the database you want to work with, and then select Properties from the shortcut menu.

3. Click the General tab. Under File Properties, select the Automatically Grow File check box, and then set the file growth in megabytes or as a percentage of file size.

4. Click the Transaction Log tab. Under File Properties, select the Automatically Grow File check box, and then set the file growth in megabytes or as a percentage of file size.

5. Optionally, click the Options tab and select the Autoshrink check box. Autoshrink compacts and shrinks the database periodically.

6. Click OK when you're finished. Your changes take effect immediately; you don't need to restart the server.

 Note See the section of this chapter entitled "Creating Databases in Enterprise Manager" for detailed tips and advice on sizing databases and transaction logs.

Expanding Databases and Logs Manually

Sometimes you'll want to increase the size of a database or log file. You can do this by completing the following steps:

1. Start Enterprise Manager and then work your way down to the Databases folder using the entries in the left pane.

2. Right-click the database you want to work with and then, from the shortcut menu, select Properties.

3. To expand a database, click the General tab and then enter a larger file size in the Space Allocated field for a primary or secondary data file.

Tip   You could also create and size a new secondary file for the database. The advantage to using a new file rather than an existing file is that SQL Server doesn't need to lock what may be an active database file in order to expand the database.

4. To expand a log, click the Transaction Log tab and then enter a larger file size in the Space Allocated field for a primary or secondary log file. (You could also create and size a new transaction log file.)

Tip   With data and log files, the new file size must be larger than the current size. If it isn't, you'll get an error. The reason for this is that shrinking the database is handled in a different way. See the next section entitled "Compacting and Shrinking a Database Manually" for details.

5. Click Apply to make the changes. SQL Server locks the database while expanding it, which blocks access.

More Info   You can also expand files using Transact-SQL. The command you use is ALTER DATABASE. See the "Altering a Database" section later in this chapter for more information.

Compacting and Shrinking a Database Manually

Compacting and shrinking a database is a bit different from expanding it, and you'll often want finer control over the process than you get with the Autoshrink option. Fortunately, you can manually manage this process, and you can also schedule this process on a recurring basis.

To manually compact or shrink database files (both data and log files) in Enterprise Manager, complete the following steps:

1. Start Enterprise Manager and then work your way down to the Databases folder using the entries in the left pane.

2. Right-click the database you want to work with and, from the shortcut menu, select All Tasks. From the All Tasks menu, choose the Shrink Database option.

3. You should see the Shrink Database dialog box shown in Figure 4-5. The Database Disk Space Information area shows the total amount of space allocated to all database files and the amount of space used. Use this information to help you decide whether you really want to shrink the database.

Figure 4-5. *Shrinking a database is easy with Enterprise Manager's Shrink Database dialog box. Just make your selections and click OK, or schedule the task on a recurring basis.*

4. To compact the database, select Re-Organize Database + Move Data Pages To The Beginning Of The Files. By reorganizing data pages, you move data pages to the beginning of the data files.

5. To shrink the database, select Shrink Database Files + Truncate Trailing Free Space From The End Of Files. By shrinking data and log files, you remove unneeded space from the end of the file, leaving only approximately 25 percent of free space for expansion.

 Note Log files aren't reduced in size immediately. Instead, the size is reduced when the transaction log is backed up or the log is truncated, whichever occurs first. Also, you normally can't shrink a database smaller than the model database (which is the database template).

6. Click Apply to begin or continue to Step 7 for scheduling. SQL Server locks the database while shrinking it, which blocks access.

7. The property settings you make in this dialog box are saved and unique to the current database. If you want to use these properties to shrink the database on a recurring basis, select Periodically Check To See If The Database Disk Space Can Be Shrunk and then click Schedule. You can now schedule this task as explained in Chapter 12, "Database Automation and Maintenance."

Another way to shrink a database is to use Transact-SQL. Two commands are provided:

```
DBCC SHRINKDATABASE
    ( database_name [, target_percent]
    [, {NOTRUNCATE | TRUNCATEONLY}]
    )
```

```
DBCC SHRINKFILE
  ( {file_name | file_id }
    { [, target_size]
    | [, {EMPTYFILE | NOTRUNCATE | TRUNCATEONLY}]
    }
  )
```

You use DBCC SHRINKDATABASE to shrink all data files in the database and DBCC SHRINKFILE to shrink a specific data file. In either case, these commands reduce file size to approximately 25 percent free space by default, or file size can be set to a specific free space percentage. By default, the command also compacts the database. You can override this option with TRUNCATEONLY or specify that you only want to compact the database with NOTRUNCATE.

The following command compacts and then shrinks the Customer database to 50 percent free space:

```
DBCC SHRINKDATABASE
  ( Customer, 50% )
```

Note The DBCC SHRINKFILE command is the only technique you can use to shrink individual data and log files smaller than their initial creation size. With DBCC SHRINKFILE, you must shrink each file individually, rather than trying to shrink the entire database. Additionally, the truncation options for DBCC SHRINKDATABASE and DBCC SHRINKFILE only apply to data files and are ignored for log files. Transaction logs aren't truncated with these commands.

Manipulating Databases

Other core administration tasks that you'll often need to perform include renaming, dropping, detaching, copying, and moving databases. These tasks are examined in the sections that follow.

Renaming a Database

User databases can be renamed using the SP_RENAMEDB command. To do this, complete the following steps:

1. Ask all users to disconnect from the database and end any open Enterprise Manager connections to the database. If necessary, kill the user processes as detailed in Chapter 3.

2. Start Query Analyzer and then put the database in single-user mode. The following example puts a database called Customer in single-user mode:

```
use master
exec sp_dboption Customer, 'single user', true
```

Tip You execute commands in Query Analyzer by clicking Execute Query or by pressing F5. With ISQL or OSQL, you can execute commands by entering the *go* statement.

3. Rename the database using the SP_RENAMEDB command. In the following example, the Customer database is renamed cust:

```
exec sp_renamedb 'Customer', 'cust'
```

4. After you run the SQL commands, set the renamed database back to multiuser mode. The following example sets the cust database to multiuser mode:

```
exec sp_dboption cust, 'single user', false
```

5. Be sure that all commands, applications, and processes that use the old database name are pointed to the new database name. If you don't, you'll have problems.

Dropping and Deleting a Database

In SQL Server 7.0, dropping and deleting a database are the same thing. When you drop a database, you remove the database and its associated files from the server. Once a database is dropped, it's permanently deleted and can't be restored without using a backup. To delete references to a database without removing the database files, use SP_DETACH_DB, as described in the following section of this chapter, "Attaching and Detaching Databases."

You can drop a database by completing the following steps:

1. Close all user connections to the database.

2. Start Enterprise Manager and then work your way down to the Databases folder using the entries in the left pane.

3. Right-click the database you want to drop and then select Delete.

4. When prompted, choose Yes to delete the database.

 Note You can't drop a database that's being used by SQL Server or by other users. For example, if you're restoring the database or the database is published for replication, you can't delete it. You also can't delete the database if there are any active user sessions.

5. Optionally, back up the master database as detailed in Chapter 6, "Database Backup and Recovery." Backing up the master database ensures that the most current system information is stored and that information for the old database won't be accidentally restored with the master database.

You can also delete a database with the DROP DATABASE command. The syntax and usage for this command is shown in Listing 4-2.

Listing 4-2. DROP DATABASE Syntax and Usage

Syntax

```
DROP DATABASE database_name [,...n]
```

Usage

```
DROP DATABASE 'Customer', 'Agencies', 'Resources'
```

Attaching and Detaching Databases

The SP_DEATTACH_DB and SP_ATTACH_DB commands are designed primarily for use in moving database files or disabling databases without deleting their files. When you detach a database, you remove references to the server in the master database but don't delete the related database files. Detached databases aren't displayed in Enterprise Manager and aren't accessible to users. If you want to use the database again, you can reattach it with the SP_ATTACH_DB or SP_ATTACH_SINGLE_FILE_DB commands. Attaching a database creates a new database that references data stored in existing data and log files.

Detaching a database When you detach a database, you can specify whether you want to update the statistics before you do. Updating statistics makes the database easier to use with read-only media; otherwise, it really isn't needed. To update statistics, set the skipchecks flag to TRUE. Detach a database using SP_DETACH_DB, as shown in Listing 4-3.

Listing 4-3. SP_DETACH_DB Syntax and Usage

Syntax

```
exec sp_detach_db [@dbname =] 'dbname'
[, [@skipchecks =] 'skipchecks']
```

Usage

```
exec sp_detach_db 'sample', 'true'
```

Tip You can't detach system databases, and you can only detach user databases when they aren't in use. Furthermore, before detaching a user database, you may want to close all current connections, put the database in single-user mode, and then run the detach operation.

Attaching a database with multiple files When you reattach a database with SP_ATTACH_DB, you can specify up to 16 files to associate with the database. This filename list must include the primary file, which contains pointers to the original locations of all other database files, and all files that have changed location. Attach the database using SP_ATTACH_DB, as shown in Listing 4-4.

Listing 4-4. SP_ATTACH_DB Syntax and Usage

Syntax

```
exec sp_attach_db [@dbname =] 'dbname',
[@filename1 =] 'filename_n' [,...16]
```

Usage

```
exe sp_attach_db 'Sample',
   'c:\mssql7\data\sample_data.mdf',
   'c:\mssql7\data\sample_log.ldf'
```

Attaching a database with only a data file   Old transaction logs may not be needed in a new database. Because of this, you may only want to restore a data file and let SQL Server create a new log file for you. To do this, use the SP_ATTACH_SINGLE_FILE_DB command, as shown in Listing 4-5.

Listing 4-5. SP_ATTACH_SINGLE_FILE_DB Syntax and Usage

Syntax

```
exec sp_attach_single_file_db [@dbname =] 'dbname',
[@physname =] 'physical_name'
```

Usage

```
exec sp_attach_single_file_db 'Customer',
   'c:\mssql7\data\customer_data.mdf'
```

Copying Databases with Attach

One of the key reasons for using SP_ATTACH_DB is to create a copy of an existing database. When you do this, you copy the database's existing files to a new location and then attach them with SP_ATTACH_DB. The steps you take are the following:

1. Start Query Analyzer and then run the SP_HELPDB command for the database you want to copy, such as

   ```
   exec sp_helpdb Customer
   ```

2. Note the absolute file path location of all data and log files for the database.

3. Start Microsoft Windows Explorer and then access the folders containing the database's data and log files. Use Copy to copy each file in turn and then use Paste to insert the files at the desired location. Be sure to rename the files, if necessary.

4. In Query Analyzer, use SP_ATTACH_DB to create a new database using the files you just copied, such as

   ```
   exec sp_attach_db 'Customer2',
     'c:\mssql7\data\cust2_data.mdf',
     'c:\mssql7\data\cust2_log.ldf'
   ```

5. In Enterprise Manager, configure the new database, as necessary.

Moving Databases with Detach and Attach

You can use the SP_DETACH_DB and SP_ATTACH_DB commands to move database files to new locations. For example, if you create a database and put all the files in one location, you may want to put the data files and transaction logs on separate drives later. You would do this by detaching the database, moving database files as necessary, and then reattaching the database so that it points to the new file locations.

Moving a database is much like copying a database. You move a database by completing the following steps:

1. Close all active connections to the database you want to move and then put the database in single-user mode by typing

```
exec sp_dboption Customer, 'single user', true
```

2. Start Query Analyzer and then run the SP_HELPDB command for the database you want to copy, such as

```
exec sp_helpdb Customer
```

3. Note the absolute file path location of all data and log files for the database.

4. Use SP_DETACH_DB to detach the database by typing

```
exec sp_detach_db 'sample', 'true'
```

5. Start Windows Explorer and then access the folders containing the database's data and log files. Use Cut to cut files you want to move and then use Paste to insert these files at the desired location.

6. In Query Analyzer, use SP_ATTACH_DB to reattach the database. Be sure to reference the new location for files, such as

```
exec sp_attach_db 'Customer',
  'c:\cust\data\cust_data.mdf',
  'c:\cust\data\cust_data2.ndf',
  'd:\cust\logs\cust2_log.ldf'
```

Moving a Database to Another Server

You can also move databases to a new server. You detach the database, move the related data and log files to the new server, and then reattach them. You can follow the same procedure described in the previous section, "Moving Databases with Detach and Attach."

Tip   The source and destination servers must have the same code page, sort order, Unicode collation, and Unicode locale settings. If they don't, you have to use import/export as described in Chapter 7.

Altering a Database

Enterprise Manager gives you an easy way to modify the configuration of a database. Another way to modify a database is to use the ALTER DATABASE command. You can use ALTER DATABASE to

- Add new data and log files to a database. All files must be placed in the same filegroup.
- Modify properties of data and log files, such as by increasing file size, changing the maximum size, or setting file growth rules.
- Add a new filegroup to a database.
- Modify the properties of an existing filegroup, such as by determining whether the filegroup is read-only or read-write and which filegroup is the default.
- Remove files and filegroups from a database. These elements can only be removed when they don't contain data.

The ALTER DATABASE command is designed to make one database change at a time and has the syntax shown in Listing 4-6. The examples in the listing show how you could use ALTER DATABASE to perform key administration tasks. You can use Query Analyzer or ISQL/OSQL. Execute commands with either the Execute Command button or the *go* statement, respectively.

Listing 4-6. ALTER DATABASE Syntax and Usage

Syntax

```
ALTER DATABASE database
{ ADD FILE <filespec> [,...n] [TO FILEGROUP filegroup_name]
  | ADD LOG FILE <filespec> [,...n]
  | REMOVE FILE logical_file_name
  | ADD FILEGROUP filegroup_name
  | REMOVE FILEGROUP filegroup_name
  | MODIFY FILE <filespec>
  | MODIFY FILEGROUP filegroup_name filegroup_property
}
<filespec> ::=
(NAME = logical_file_name
  [, FILENAME = 'os_file_name' ]
  [, SIZE = size]
  [, MAXSIZE = { max_size | UNLIMITED } ]
  [, FILEGROWTH = growth_increment
```

Usage: Adding a File to a Database

```
ALTER DATABASE Customer
ADD FILE
```

(continued)

Listing 4-6. *(continued)*

```
( NAME = Customerdata2,
  FILENAME = 'c:\mssql7\data\customerdat2.ndf',
  SIZE = 10MB,

MAXSIZE = 500MB,
  FILEGROWTH = 5MB )
```

Usage: Adding a Filegroup

```
ALTER DATABASE Customer
ADD FILEGROUP Secondary
```

Usage: Adding Files and Placing Them in a Filegroup

```
ALTER DATABASE Customer
ADD FILE
( NAME = Customerdata3,
  FILENAME = 'c:\mssql7\data\customerdat3.ndf',
  SIZE = 10MB,
  MAXSIZE = UNLIMITED,
  FILEGROWTH = 5MB),
( NAME = Customerdata4,
  FILENAME = 'c:\mssql7\data\customerdat4.ndf',
  SIZE = 10MB,
  MAXSIZE = UNLIMITED,
  FILEGROWTH = 5MB)
TO FILEGROUP Secondary
```

Usage: Setting the Default Filegroup

```
ALTER DATABASE Customer
MODIFY FILEGROUP Secondary DEFAULT
```

Usage: Modifying a File

```
ALTER DATABASE Customer
MODIFY FILE
(NAME = Customerdata3,
  SIZE = 20MB)
```

Usage: Removing a File from a Database

```
USE Customer
DBCC SHRINKFILE (Customerdata3, EMPTYFILE)
ALTER DATABASE Customer
REMOVE FILE Customerdata3
```

Note The EMPTYFILE option of DBCC SHRINKFILE empties a file by moving its data to other files in the same filegroup. You can then use the REMOVE FILE option of ALTER DATABASE to delete the file.

Tips and Techniques

All great administrators have a few tricks up their sleeves to help manage databases more efficiently and to keep things running smoothly. Here are a few tricks you should keep in mind.

Moving and Resizing tempdb

The tempdb database contains temporary tables created by users or SQL Server, or both. Unlike in previous versions of SQL Server, you can't put tempdb in memory, and SQL Server doesn't store complete transactions for temporary tables either. With temporary tables, SQL Server stores only enough information to roll back a transaction and not enough to redo a transaction.

The tempdb database is created each time you start the MSSQLServer service, which ensures that the database starts clean. As with other databases, the default structure of tempdb is based on the model database. This means that each time you start SQL Server, a snapshot is taken of the current model database and applied to tempdb.

By default, tempdb has a size of 8 MB and is set to automatically grow the database by 10 percent when necessary. On a busy server, this 8 MB can fill up quickly, and as a result the server may need to frequently expand tempdb. Unfortunately, when tempdb is being expanded, SQL Server locks the database. This can slow down queries and make the server seem unresponsive. To improve the performance of tempdb, you can do a couple of things:

- Permanently expand tempdb to accommodate space needs during busy periods. To do this, follow the steps described in the section of this chapter entitled "Expanding Databases and Logs Manually." Even if the model database is smaller, tempdb will retain this new size.

- By default, tempdb is stored in the same location as other data. Unfortunately, you can't move a system database, but you can create a secondary data file for tempdb and put this file on its own drive.

Creating Secondary Data and Log Files

Secondary data and log files can improve the performance of busy databases and can help make large databases easier to manage. One occasion to create secondary files is when you want to distribute the load over several drives. For example, you could place the primary file on drive D, secondary files on drive E, and transaction logs on drive F. See the section of Chapter 1 titled "SQL Server 7.0 and Your Hardware" for more tips on drives and RAID arrays.

Another reason to create secondary files is to make it easier to restore a large database. For example, if you have a 10 GB database in a single file, you can only restore the database on a 10 GB drive, which you may not have at 3 A.M.

on a Tuesday if a drive fails. Instead, create several smaller files for the database, such as five 2 GB files, and then you can restore these files to several smaller drives, if necessary.

You can create secondary data or log files by completing the following steps:

1. Start Enterprise Manager and then work your way down to the Databases folder using the entries in the left pane.

2. Right-click the database you want to work with and, from the shortcut menu, select Properties.

3. To set a secondary data file, click the General tab and then, in the Database Files area, type a new filename, location, initial size, and filegroup.

4. To set a secondary log file, click the Transaction Log tab and then, in the Transaction Log Files area, type a new filename, location, initial size, and filegroup.

5. Click Apply to make the changes.

Preventing Transaction Log Errors

The transaction log is essential to the smooth running of SQL Server. If the log fills up or otherwise fails, SQL Server can't process most types of queries. To ensure that the transaction log runs smoothly, you may want to use these techniques:

- To reduce the load on the transaction log, use SQL commands that aren't logged. This invalidates the transaction logs, as explained in Chapter 6.

- To ensure that the log is cleaned out periodically, set the database option Truncate Log On Checkpoint. This invalidates the transaction logs, as explained in Chapter 6.

- To prevent the log from running out of space, don't set a maximum file size but do increase the frequency of the log backup and watch the amount of free drive space closely.

- To ensure that transactions can be recovered, increase the permanent size of the log and increase the frequency of the log backup.

Resolving a Filegroup Is Full Error

When a data file can't be written to, you'll see a Filegroup Is Full error. This error usually occurs when the data file has reached its maximum size or you've run out of file space. To reduce the chances of this error recurring, you can use the following techniques:

- Don't set a maximum file size.
- Watch the amount of free drive space closely.
- Schedule data files to be compacted periodically.
- Remove unused tables, indexes, or objects.

Creating a New Database Template

The model database is used as the basis of all new databases. If you modify the options and properties of the model, any new databases created on the server will inherit these options and properties.

Chapter 5

Microsoft SQL Server 7.0 Security

Microsoft SQL Server 7.0 is being used increasingly, both inside and outside organizations. Whether employees, contractors, or outside users access the databases, your job as an administrator is to efficiently manage that database access. You do this by creating user logins, configuring login permissions, and assigning roles. The permissions and roles you assign determine which actions users can perform, as well as what kinds of data they can access.

Your primary goals in managing security should be to

- Balance the user's need for access to data against your need for protection from unauthorized access to data

- Restrict database permissions so that users are less likely to execute harmful commands and procedures (whether maliciously or accidentally)

- Close off other security holes, such as those that may be caused by ordinary users being members of the Windows NT Administrators group

Note If you're working with the Desktop edition of SQL Server, the Microsoft Windows 95 or 98 system hosting SQL Server can only use SQL Server logins. Thus, Windows NT authentication, domain user's accounts, and domain group accounts aren't available.

SQL Server 7.0 Security

You control access to databases with the components of the SQL Server security model. These components include

- SQL Server authentication modes
- Server logins
- Permissions
- Roles

SQL Server 7.0 Authentication Modes

The SQL Server security model has two authentication modes:

- **Windows NT Authentication only** Works best when the database is accessed within the organization only
- **Mixed security** Works best when outside users may access the database or when you don't use Windows domains

You configure these security modes on the server level, and they apply to all databases on the server.

Windows NT Authentication

With Windows NT Authentication, you can use the user and group accounts available in the Windows domain for authentication. This lets domain users access databases without your having to provide a separate SQL Server login ID and password. The benefits of this are that domain users don't have to keep track of multiple passwords, and if they update their domain password, they don't have to change SQL Server passwords as well. However, users are still subject to all the rules of the Windows security model, and you can use this model to lock accounts, audit logins, and force users to change their passwords periodically.

When you use Windows NT Authentication, SQL Server authenticates users automatically based on their user account names or their group membership. If the user or the user's group has been granted access to a database, the user is automatically granted access to the database. By default, two local accounts are configured to use SQL Server. These accounts are the local Administrators group account and the local Administrator user account. (I include Administrator because it is a member of the Administrators group by default in Windows NT.) Local accounts are displayed as BUILTIN\<AccountName> or COMPUTERNAME\ <AccountName> in Enterprise Manager. For example, Administrators is displayed as BUILTIN\Administrators.

 Real World Domain accounts are the best way to manage users who access the database from within the organization. Also, if you assign users to domain groups and then configure access for these groups in SQL Server, you cut down on the amount of administration you have to do. For example, if you assign users in the marketing department to a marketing group and then configure this group in SQL Server, you have only one account to manage instead of 10, 20, 50, or more. When employees leave the organization or change departments, you don't have to delete user accounts. When new employees are hired, you don't have to create new accounts either—you just ensure that they are added to the correct group in Windows NT.

Mixed Security and SQL Server Logins

With mixed security, you use both Windows NT Authentication and SQL Server logins. SQL Server logins are primarily used by users outside the company, such as those who might access the database from the Internet. Applications that access SQL Server from the Internet can be configured to use specific accounts automatically or to prompt the user for a SQL Server login ID and password.

With mixed security, SQL Server first determines whether the user is connecting using a valid SQL Server login. If the user has a valid login and has the proper password, the user connection is accepted. If the user has a valid login but has an improper password, the user connection is refused. SQL Server only checks the Windows NT account information if the user doesn't have a valid login. Here, SQL Server determines whether the Windows NT account has permission to connect to the server. If the account has permission, the connection is accepted. Otherwise, the connection is refused.

All SQL Server databases have built-in SQL Server logins with special purposes. These logins are sa, guest, and dbo, and they are discussed next under "Server Logins."

Server Logins

You configure access to SQL Server using server logins or the roles to which those logins belong, or both. Just as there are two authentication modes, there are also two kinds of server logins. You create domain logins using domain accounts, which can be user accounts, local group accounts, or global group accounts. You create SQL Server logins by specifying a unique login ID and password. Several logins are configured by default, and these include

- The local Administrators group
- The local Administrator account
- The sa login
- The guest login (a special login configured but not automatically enabled)
- The dbo user (a special database user)

These logins are examined in the sections that follow.

Working with Administrators

Administrators is a local group on the database server. This group's members normally include the local Administrator user account and any other users set to administer the system locally. In SQL Server this group is granted the System Administrators (sysadmin) server role by default.

Note In Enterprise Manager, server roles are identified by full names, such as System Administrators, and regular names, such as sysadmin. When you reference server roles in procedures or Transact-SQL, you'll use the regular name, such as sysadmin. Unfortunately, SQL Server 7.0 doesn't have full names for database roles, which isn't consistent with the precedent set for server roles.

Working with Administrator

Administrator is a local user account on the server. This account provides administrator privileges on the local system, and you use it primarily when you install a system. If the host computer is part of a Windows NT domain, the Administrator account usually has domain-wide privileges as well. In SQL Server this account is granted the System Administrators server role by default.

Working with the sa Login

The sa login is the system administrator's account for SQL Server. With the new integrated and expanded security model, sa is no longer needed and is primarily provided for backward compatibility with previous SQL Server versions. As with other administrator logins, sa is granted the System Administrators server role by default. When you install SQL Server, the sa login isn't assigned a password. You should set a password for this account to prevent unauthorized access to the server.

 Best Practice Because the sa login is widely known to malicious users, you may want to delete or disable this account whenever possible. Instead make system administrators members of the System Administrators server role and have them log on using their own logins. Anyone with the System Administrators server role can then log in and administer the server. If you ever get locked out of the server, you can log on to the server locally using an account with local administrator privileges and then reset passwords or assign privileges, as necessary.

Working with the Guest Login

The guest login is a special login that you can add to a database to allow anyone with a valid SQL Server login to access the database. Users who access a database by way of the guest account assume the identity of the guest user and inherit all the privileges and permissions of the guest account. For example, if you configure the domain account GOTEAM to access SQL Server, GOTEAM can access any database with a guest login and when GOTEAM does, that person is granted all the permissions of the guest account.

By default, the guest login doesn't exist in newly created databases but can be added to or deleted from all databases except master and tempdb. Most users access master and tempdb as guests. Because of this, you can't remove the guest account from these databases. Don't worry, a guest has limited permissions and privileges in master and tempdb.

Before using the guest login, you should note the following:

- The guest login is a member of the public server role and inherits the permissions of this role.
- The guest account must be assigned to a database before anyone can access it as a guest.

- The guest login is only used when a user account has access to SQL Server, but it doesn't have access to the database through this user account.

Working with the dbo User

The database owner, or dbo, is a special type of database user and is granted special privileges. Generally speaking, the user who created a database is the database owner. The dbo is implicitly granted all permissions on the database and can grant these permissions to other users. Because members of the System Administrators server role are mapped automatically to the special user dbo, logins with the System Administrators role can perform any tasks that a dbo can.

Objects created in SQL Server databases also have owners. These owners are referred to as the database object owners. Objects created by a member of the System Administrators server role belong to the dbo user automatically. Objects created by users who aren't members of the System Administrators server role belong to the user creating the object and must be qualified with the name of that user when referenced by other users. For example, if GOTEAM is a member of the System Administrators server role and creates a table called Sales, Sales belongs to dbo and is qualified as dbo.Sales, or simply Sales. However, if GOTEAM isn't a member of the System Administrators server role and creates a table called Sales, Sales belongs to GOTEAM and must be qualified as GOTEAM.Sales.

Note   Technically, dbo isn't a "special login," but you may see it referred to as such. You can't log in to a server or database as dbo, but you may be the person who created the database or a set of objects in it.

Permissions

Permissions determine the actions that users can perform on SQL Server or in a database and are granted according to login ID, group memberships, and role memberships. Users must have appropriate permissions before they can perform any action that changes database definitions or accesses data. Three types of permissions are used in SQL Server:

- Object permissions
- Statement permissions
- Implicit permissions

Object Permissions

Object permissions control access to tables, views, columns, and stored procedures. You control access to these objects by granting, denying, or revoking the ability to execute particular statements or stored procedures. For example, you can grant a user the right to SELECT information from a table, but deny the right to INSERT, UPDATE, or DELETE information in the table. Table 5-1, on the following page, provides a summary of object permissions.

Table 5-1. Object Permissions

Object Type	Possible Actions
Column	SELECT and UPDATE
Row	N/A (assigned at the table level as they might affect multiple columns)
Stored procedure	EXECUTE
Table	SELECT, INSERT, UPDATE, DELETE, and REFERENCES
View	SELECT, INSERT, UPDATE, and DELETE

Statement Permissions

Statement permissions control administration actions, such as creating a database or adding objects to a database. Only members of the System Administrators role and database owners can assign statement permissions. By default, normal logins aren't granted statement permissions, and you must specifically grant these permissions to logins that aren't administrators. For example, if a user needs to be able to create views in a database, you would assign the CREATE VIEW permission to the user's login. Table 5-2 provides a summary of statement permissions that you can grant, deny, or revoke.

Table 5-2. Statement Permissions

Permission	Description
CREATE DATABASE	Determines whether the login can create databases. The user must be in the master database or a member of the System Administrators server role.
CREATE DEFAULT	Determines whether the user can create a default value for a table column.
CREATE PROCEDURE	Determines whether the user can create a stored procedure.
CREATE RULE	Determines whether the user can create a table column rule.
CREATE TABLE	Determines whether the user can create a table.
CREATE VIEW	Determines whether the user can create a view.
BACKUP DATABASE	Determines whether the user can back up the database.
BACKUP LOG	Determines whether the user can back up the transaction log.

Implied Permissions

Only members of predefined system roles or database/database object owners can perform implied permissions. Implied permissions for a role can't be changed or applied to other accounts (unless these accounts are made members of the role). For example, members of the System Administrators server role can perform any activity in SQL Server. They can extend databases and kill processes. You can't revoke or assign these rights to other accounts individually. Database and database object owners also have implied permissions. These permissions allow them to perform all activities with either the database or the object they own, or with both. For example, a user who owns a table can view, add, change, and delete data. That user can also alter the table definition and control the table's permissions.

Roles

Roles are a lot like Windows NT groups in that they allow you to easily assign permissions to a group of users, and they can have built-in permissions (implicit permissions) that can't be changed. Two types of roles are available:

- **Server roles** Applied at the server level
- **Database roles** Applied at the database level

Server Roles

You use server roles to grant server administration capabilities. If you make a login a member of a role, users who use this login can perform any tasks permitted by the role. For example, members of the System Administrators role have the highest level of permissions on SQL Server and can perform any type of task.

Server roles are set at the server level and are predefined. This means that these permissions affect the entire server and you can't change the permission set. The sections that follow provide a summary of each server role from the lowest level role (Database Creators) to the highest level role (System Administrators).

Database Creators (dbcreator)   The dbcreator role is designed for users who need to create and modify databases. Members of this role can add members to dbcreator and perform these tasks: ALTER DATABASE, CREATE DATABASE, and *sp_renamedb*.

Disk Administrators (diskadmin)   The diskadmin role is designed for users who need to manage disk files. Members of this role can add members to diskadmin and perform these tasks: DISK INIT, DISK MIRROR, DISK REFIT, DISK REINIT, DISK REMIRROR, *sp_addumpdevice*, *sp_diskdefault*, and *sp_dropdevice*.

Process Administrators (processadmin)   The processadmin role is designed for users who need to control SQL Server processes. Members of this role can add members to processadmin and kill processes.

Security Administrators (securityadmin)   The securityadmin role is designed for users who need to manage logins, create database permissions, and read error logs. Members of this role can add members to securityadmin; grant, deny, and revoke CREATE DATABASE; and read the error logs. They can also perform these tasks: *sp_addlinkedsrvlogin*, *sp_addlogin*, *sp_defaultdb*, *sp_defaultlanguage*, *sp_denylogin*, *sp_droplinkedsrvlogin*, *sp_droplogin*, *sp_grantlogin*, *sp_helplogins*, *sp_remoteoption*, and *sp_revokelogin*.

Server Administrators (serveradmin)   The serveradmin role is designed for users who need to set server-wide configuration options and shut down the server. Members of this role can add members to serveradmin and perform these other tasks: DBCC PINTABLE, RECONFIGURE, SHUTDOWN, *sp_configure*, and *sp_tableoption*.

- **Setup Administrators (setupadmin)** The setupadmin role is designed for users who need to manage linked servers and control startup procedures. Members of this role can add members to setupadmin; add, drop, and configure linked servers; and control startup procedures.

- **System Administrators (sysadmin)** The sysadmin role is designed for users who need complete control over SQL Server and installed databases. Members of this role can perform any activity in SQL Server.

Database Roles

When you want to assign permissions at the database level, you can use database roles. Database roles are set on a per-database basis, which means that each database has its own set of roles. SQL Server 7.0 supports three types of database roles:

- User-defined standard roles
- User-defined application roles
- Predefined (or fixed) database roles

Standard roles allow you to create roles with unique permissions and privileges. You can use standard roles to logically group users together and then assign a single permission to the role rather than having to assign permissions to each user separately. For example, you could create a role called Users that allows users to SELECT, INSERT, and UPDATE specific tables in the database but doesn't allow them to perform any other tasks.

Application roles allow you to create password-protected roles for specific applications. For example, a user could connect through a Web-based application called NetReady; this application would activate the role and the user would then gain the role's permissions and privileges. User or other roles can't be assigned to an application role. Instead, the application role is activated when the application connects to the database.

SQL Server also has predefined database roles. Predefined roles are built in and have permissions that can't be changed. You use predefined roles to assign database administration privileges, and you can assign a single login to multiple roles. These privileges are summarized in the sections that follow.

public The public database role is the default role for all database users. Users inherit the permissions and privileges of the public role, and this role represents their minimum permissions and privileges. Any roles to which you assign a user, beyond the public role, add permissions and privileges. If you want all database users to have specific permissions, assign the permissions to the public role.

db_accessadmin The db_accessadmin role is designed for users who need to add or remove logins in a database. Members of this role can perform these tasks on the selected database: *sp_addalias*, *sp_adduser*, *sp_dropalias*, *sp_dropuser*, *sp_grantdbaccess*, and *sp_revokedbaccess*.

db_backupoperator   The db_backupoperator role is designed for users who need to back up a database. Members of this role can perform these tasks on the selected database: BACKUP DATABASE, BACKUP LOG, CHECKPOINT, DBCC CHECKALLOC, DBCC CHECKCATALOG, DBCC CHECKDB, DBCC TEXTALL, DBCC TEXTALLOC, AND DBCC UPDATEUSAGE.

db_datareader   The db_datareader role is designed for users who need to view data in a database. Members of this role can select all data from any user table in the database.

db_datawriter   The db_datawriter role is designed for users who need to modify any data in any user table in the database. Members of this role can perform these tasks on any objects in the selected database: DELETE, INSERT, and UPDATE.

db_ddladmin   The db_ddladmin is designed for users who need to perform tasks related to SQL Server's data definition language (DDL). Members of this role can issue any DDL statement except for GRANT, REVOKE, or DENY. Members can also perform these tasks in the selected database: REFERENCES, *sp_changeobjectowner*, *sp_procoption*, *sp_recompile*, *sp_rename*, and *sp_tableoption*.

db_denydatareader   The db_denydatareader role is designed to restrict access to data in a database by login. Members of this role can deny or revoke SELECT permissions on any object in the database.

db_denydatawriter   The db_denydatawriter role is designed to restrict modifications permissions in a database by login. Members of this role can deny or revoke INSERT, UPDATE, and DELETE permissions on any object in the database.

db_securityadmin   The db_securityadmin role is designed for users who need to manage permissions, object ownership, and roles. Members of this role can perform any of the following tasks in the selected database: DENY, GRANT, REVOKE, *sp_addapprole*, *sp_addrole*, *sp_addrolemember*, *sp_approlepassword*, *sp_changeobjectowner*, *sp_dropapprole*, *sp_droprole*, and *sp_droprolemember*.

db_owner   The db_owner role is designed for users who need complete control over all aspects of the database. Members of this role can assign permissions, modify database settings, perform database maintenance, and perform any other administration task on the database.

Managing Server Logins

SQL Server can use Windows domain logins as well as SQL Server's own logins. If you've configured the server for mixed security, you can use both login types. Otherwise, you can only use Windows domain logins.

Viewing and Editing Existing Logins

To view or edit an existing login, follow these steps:

1. Start Enterprise Manager and then access the server you want to work with.

2. In the server's Security folder, select the Logins entry in the left pane. The right pane now displays the current logins, as shown in Figure 5-1. From this information you can learn the following:

   - **Name** The login name.
   - **Type** The login type, which is Standard for SQL Server logins, Windows NT User for domain user accounts, and Windows NT Group for domain group accounts.
   - **Server Access** The type of access permission the user has to the server. Permit means the user can access the server. Deny means the user can't access the server.
   - **Default Database** The default database for the user.
   - **User** The username that the login is known by in the database.
   - **Default Language** The default language for the user.

3. To view server role and database access permissions for a user, double-click the user's entry in the right pane. This opens the SQL Server Login Properties dialog box.

4. You can now edit the properties for this account using the fields of the General, Server Roles, and Database Access tabs.

To view a login with Transact-SQL, use *sp_helplogins*. The syntax and usage for this command is shown as Listing 5-1.

Figure 5-1. *Select the Logins entry to display current logins in the right pane.*

Listing 5-1. *sp_helplogins* **Syntax and Usage**

Syntax

```
sp_helplogins [[@LoginNamePattern =] 'login']
```

Usage

```
EXEC sp_helplogins 'goteam'
```

Creating Logins

You create new logins in Enterprise Manager by using either the Create Login Wizard or the Login Properties dialog box. Because the steps are almost identical with either method, I'll focus on the Login Properties dialog box and let you apply these techniques to the Create Login Wizard dialog boxes if you would rather use the wizard. To access the wizard, from the Tools menu, select Wizards. Then click the plus sign next to Database and double-click Create Login Wizard.

Tip   If you want to use Windows domain user or group accounts, you must create these accounts in the Windows domain and then create the related SQL Server logins. To create domain accounts, you can use User Manager For Domains or ask a domain administrator to set up the necessary accounts.

To create a SQL Server login, follow these steps:

1. Start Enterprise Manager and then access the server you want to work with.
2. In the server's Security folder, right-click the Logins entry and select New Login. This opens the SQL Server Login Properties dialog box, shown in Figure 5-2.

Figure 5-2. *To create new logins, you can use the SQL Server Login Properties dialog box or the Create Login Wizard.*

3. In the Name field, type the name of the account you want to use, such as Sales or WRSTANEK.

4. If you're creating a login for a domain account, select the Windows NT Authentication option button and then use the Domain combo box to select the domain you want to use. You can also type the domain name into the combo box. The domain name should now appear in the Name field.

5. If you want to create a new SQL Server login, select the SQL Server Authentication option button and then enter the SQL Server password for the login.

6. Specify the default database and default language for the login. Assigning a default database doesn't give the login permission to access the database. Instead, it merely specifies the database that's used when no database is specified in a command.

7. Click OK to create the login. If you're creating a SQL Server login, confirm the password by reentering it when prompted.

8. No roles or access permissions have been assigned. Refer to the sections later in this chapter entitled "Configuring Server Roles" and "Controlling Database Access and Administration" to learn how to configure these options.

You can also create logins with Transact-SQL. To create a login for a domain account, use *sp_grantlogin,* as shown in Listing 5-2.

Listing 5-2. *sp_grantlogin* **Syntax and Usage**

Syntax

```
sp_grantlogin [@loginame =] 'login'
```

Usage

```
EXEC sp_grantlogin 'GALAXY\Sales'
```

To create a new SQL Server login, use *sp_addlogin,* as shown in Listing 5-3.

Listing 5-3. *sp_addlogin* **Syntax and Usage**

Syntax

```
sp_addlogin [@loginame =] 'login'
    [,[@passwd =] 'password']
    [,[@defdb =] 'database']
    [,[@deflanguage =] 'language']
    [,[@sid =] 'sid']
    [,[@encryptopt =] 'encryption_option']
```

Usage

```
EXEC sp_addlogin 'webtr', 'webtester', 'Customer', 'us_english'
```

Note Although *sp_grantlogin* and *sp_addlogin* allow users to connect to SQL Server, the logins can't access databases. To configure database access, you need to run *sp_grantdbaccess* for each database the login needs access to. See the "Controlling Database Access and Adminis- tration" section for details.

Granting or Denying Server Access

When you create a new login or modify an existing login based on a Windows account, you can explicitly grant or deny access to the server for this login. Explicitly denying access to the server is useful when a particular Windows account should be temporarily restricted from accessing the server.

To grant or deny access for an existing login, complete the folowing steps:

1. Start Enterprise Manager and then access the server you want to work with.
2. In the server's Security folder, select the Logins entry in the left pane.
3. In the right pane, double-click the account you want to work with. This opens the SQL Server Login Properties dialog box shown previously in Figure 5-2.
4. To grant access to the server, select the Grant Access option button.
5. To deny access to the server, select the Deny Access option button.

Note Denying access to the server doesn't prevent users from logging in to SQL Server. Rather, it prevents them from using their Windows domain account to log in. Users can still log in if they have a valid SQL Server login ID and password.

6. Click OK.

You can also grant or deny logins with Transact-SQL. To grant a login for a domain account, use *sp_grantlogin*, as shown in Listing 5-4.

Listing 5-4. *sp_grantlogin* **Syntax and Usage**

Syntax

```
sp_grantlogin [@loginame =] 'login'
```

Usage

```
EXEC sp_grantlogin 'GALAXY\WRSTANEK'
```

To deny access to the server for the account, use *sp_denylogin*, as shown in Listing 5-5.

Listing 5-5. *sp_denylogin* **Syntax and Usage**

Syntax

```
sp_denylogin [@loginame =] 'login'
```

Usage

```
EXEC sp_denylogin ' GALAXY\WRSTANEK '
```

Removing Logins

When a user leaves the organization or a login is otherwise not needed, you should remove the login from SQL Server. To do this, complete the following steps:

1. Start Enterprise Manager and then access the server you want to work with.

2. In the server's Security folder, select the Logins entry in the left pane.

3. Right-click the login you want to remove and then select Delete from the shortcut menu.

4. When prompted, choose Yes to confirm that you want to delete the login.

The stored procedures that you use to delete SQL Server logins are *sp_revokelogin* and *sp_droplogin*. Use *sp_revokelogin* to delete Windows user and group accounts, as shown in Listing 5-6.

Listing 5-6. *sp_revokelogin* **Syntax and Usage**

Syntax

```
sp_revokelogin [@loginame =] 'login'
```

Usage

```
EXEC sp_revokelogin ' GALAXY\WRSTANEK '
```

Use *sp_droplogin* to remove a SQL Server login, as shown in Listing 5-7.

Listing 5-7. *sp_droplogin* **Syntax and Usage**

Syntax

```
sp_droplogin [@loginame =] 'login'
```

Usage

```
EXEC sp_droplogin 'TempUser'
```

Changing Passwords

Windows user and group accounts are managed in the Windows domain. Users can change their own passwords or can ask the Windows administrator to reset their password, if necessary. For SQL Server logins, passwords are changed through Enterprise Manager using the following steps:

1. Start Enterprise Manager and then access the server you want to work with.

2. In the server's Security folder, select the Logins entry in the left pane.

3. Double-click the login you want to change. This opens the SQL Server Login Properties dialog box.

4. Type the new password in the Password field and then click OK.

5. When prompted, reenter the password to confirm it and then click OK.

To change passwords with Transact-SQL, use *sp_password,* as shown in Listing 5-8.

Listing 5-8. *sp_password* Syntax and Usage

Syntax

```
sp_password [[@old =] 'old_password',] {[@new =] 'new_password'}
   [,[@loginame =] 'login']
```

Usage

```
EXEC sp_password 'changeme' 'h4rt5' 'GOTEAM'
```

Configuring Server Roles

Server roles set server-wide administrator privileges for SQL Server logins. Server roles can be managed by role or by individual logins.

Assigning Roles by Login

To assign or change server roles for a login, follow these steps:

1. Start Enterprise Manager and then access the server you want to work with.

2. In the server's Security folder, select the Logins entry in the left pane.

3. Double-click the login you want to configure. This opens the SQL Server Login Properties dialog box.

4. Select the Server Roles tab, as shown in Figure 5-3.

5. Grant server roles by selecting the check boxes next to the roles you want to use. Server roles are discussed in the section of this chapter entitled "Server Roles."

6. When you're finished configuring server roles, click OK.

Figure 5-3. *Grant server roles by selecting the check boxes next to the roles you want to use.*

You can also configure server roles with Transact-SQL. The *sp_addsrvrolemember* stored procedure adds a login to a server role and can be used as shown in Listing 5-9.

Listing 5-9. *sp_addsrvrolemember* **Syntax and Usage**

Syntax

```
sp_addsrvrolemember [@loginame =] 'login', [@rolename =] 'role'
```

Usage

```
EXEC sp_addsrvrolemember 'GALAXY\WRSTANEK' 'sysadmin'
```

The *sp_dropsrvrolemember* command removes a login from a role and can be used as shown in Listing 5-10.

Listing 5-10. *sp_dropsrvrolemember* **Syntax and Usage**

Syntax

```
sp_dropsrvrolemember [@loginame =] 'login', [@rolename =] 'role'
```

Usage

```
EXEC sp_dropsrvrolemember 'GALAXY\WRSTANEK' 'sysadmin'
```

Assigning Roles to Multiple Logins

The easiest way to assign roles to multiple logins is to use the Server Roles Properties dialog box. To access this dialog box and configure multiple logins, follow these steps:

1. Start Enterprise Manager and then access the server you want to work with.

Figure 5-4. *The Server Role Properties dialog box lets you configure multiple logins to use a particular server role.*

2. In the server's Security folder, select the Server Role entry in the left pane.

3. In the right pane, double-click the server role you want to configure. This opens the Server Role Properties dialog box shown in Figure 5-4.

4. To add logins, click Add and then in the Add Members dialog box, select the logins to add. Multiple logins can be selected by holding down Ctrl or Shift as you click login names.

5. To remove a login, select a login and then click Remove.

6. Click the Permissions tab to see the permissions associated with this server role.

7. When you're finished configuring server roles, click OK.

Controlling Database Access and Administration

You control database access and administration with database users and roles. Database users are the logins that have the right to access the database. Database access roles set administration privileges and other database permissions.

Assigning Access and Roles by Login

For individual logins, you can grant access to databases and assign roles as follows:

1. Start Enterprise Manager and then access the server you want to work with.

2. In the server's Security folder, select the Logins entry in the left pane.

Figure 5-5. *Use the Database Access tab to grant database access and then select roles the user should have on the currently selected database.*

3. Double-click the login you want to configure. This opens the SQL Server Login Properties dialog box.

4. Select the Database Access tab, as shown in Figure 5-5.

5. Select the check box for a database that the login should have access to. Then, in the Permit In Database Role list box, select the check boxes next to the database roles that this login should have on the currently selected database.

6. Repeat step 5 for other databases the login should have access to.

7. When you're finished configuring database roles, click OK.

Assigning Roles for Multiple Logins

At the database level, you can assign database roles to multiple logins. To do this, complete the following steps:

1. Start Enterprise Manager and then work your way down to the Databases folder using the entries in the left pane.

2. In the Databases folder, click the plus sign (+) next to the database you want to work with.

3. In the left pane, select Roles to display a list of database roles in the right pane.

4. Double-click the role you want to configure. This opens the Database Role Properties dialog box shown in Figure 5-6.

5. To add role members, click Add. Then, in the Add Role Members dialog box, select the logins you want to add. Multiple logins can be selected by holding down Ctrl or Shift as you click login names.

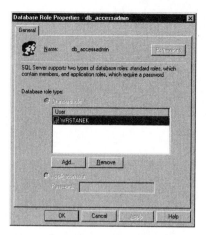

Figure 5-6. *The Database Role Properties dialog box lets you configure multiple logins to use a particular database role.*

6. To remove a role member, select a login and then choose Remove.

7. When you're finished configuring database roles, click OK.

Creating Standard Database Roles

Although predefined roles have a specific set of permissions that can't be changed, you can set permissions for roles you create for a particular database. For example, suppose that a database has three different types of users: normal users who need to view data, managers who need to be able to modify data, and developers who need to be able to modify database objects. If this is the case, you can create three roles to handle these user types. Then you only need to manage these roles and not the many different user accounts.

To create a standard database role, complete the following steps:

1. Start Enterprise Manager and then work your way down to the Databases folder using the entries in the left pane.

2. In the Databases folder, click the plus sign (+) next to the database you want to work with.

3. Right-click Roles and then select New Database Role from the shortcut menu. This opens the Database Role Properties dialog box shown in Figure 5-7.

4. Type a name for the role in the Name field.

Tip Use a name that's short but descriptive, such as Normal Users, Editors, or Testers and Developers.

Figure 5-7. *When creating a database role, the Name field can be edited but you can't configure permissions until after you create the role.*

5. Select the Standard Role option button.

6. To add role members, click Add. Then, in the Add Role Members dialog box, select the logins to add. You can select multiple logins by holding down Ctrl or Shift as you click login names.

7. Click OK.

8. The new role should be displayed in Enterprise Manager's right pane. Double-click its entry to reopen the Database Role Properties dialog box.

9. Click Permissions and then use the Permissions tab to configure database access permissions for this role. See "Managing Database Permissions" for more information.

Creating Application Database Roles

Application roles are designed to be used by applications that access the database and don't have logins associated with them. You can configure an application role by completing the following steps:

1. Start Enterprise Manager and then work your way down to the Databases folder using the entries in the left pane.

2. In the Databases folder, click the plus sign (+) next to the database you want to work with.

3. Right-click Roles and then select New Database Role from the shortcut menu. This opens the Database Role Properties dialog box shown previously in Figure 5-7.

4. Type a name for the role in the Name field.

5. Select the Application Role option button and then type a password for this role in the Password field. You won't be asked to confirm this password.

6. Click OK.

7. The new role should be displayed in Enterprise Manager's right pane. Double-click its entry to reopen the Database Role Properties dialog box.

8. Click Permissions and then use the Permissions tab to configure database access permissions for this role. See "Managing Database Permissions" for more information.

Revoking Access Rights and Roles by Login

To revoke access rights or remove a user from a role in a database, complete the following steps:

1. Start Enterprise Manager and then work your way down to the Security folder using the entries in the left pane.

2. In the Security folder, select the Logins entry in the left pane.

3. Double-click the login you want to configure. This opens the SQL Server Login Properties dialog box.

4. Select the Database Access tab.

5. Clear the check box for a database that the login should not have access to. Then, in the Permit In Database Role list box, clear the check boxes next to the database roles that this login should not have on the currently selected database.

6. Repeat step 5 for other databases the login should not have access to or rights on.

7. When you're finished, click OK.

Deleting User-Defined Roles

To delete a user-defined role, complete the following steps:

1. Start Enterprise Manager and then work your way down to the Databases folder using the entries in the left pane.

2. In the Databases folder, click the plus sign (+) next to the database you want to work with.

3. In the left pane, click Roles.

4. Select the role you want to delete and then press the Delete key.

5. When prompted, choose Yes to confirm that you want to delete the role.

Transact-SQL Commands for Managing Access and Roles

SQL Server provides different commands for managing database access and roles. These commands are summarized in Listing 5-11.

Listing 5-11. Commands for Managing Database Access and Roles

Database Access

```
sp_grantdbaccess [@loginame =] 'login'
  [,[@name_in_db =] 'name_in_db' [OUTPUT]]
sp_revokedbaccess [@name_in_db =] 'name'
```

Predefined Roles

```
sp_dbfixedrolepermission [[@rolename =] 'role']
```

Database Standard Roles

```
sp_addrole [@rolename =] 'role' [,[@ownername =] 'owner']
sp_droprole [@rolename =] 'role'
sp_helprole [[@rolename =] 'role']
```

Database Role Members

```
sp_addrolemember [@rolename =] 'role',
  [@membername =] 'security_account'
sp_droprolemember [@rolename =] 'role',
  [@membername =] 'security_account'
sp_helprolemember [[@rolename =] 'role']
```

Application Roles

```
sp_addapprole [@rolename =] 'role', [@password =] 'password'
sp_dropapprole [@rolename =] 'role'
sp_setapprole [@rolename =] 'role' ,
  [@password =] {Encrypt N 'password'} | 'password'
  [,[@encrypt =] 'encrypt_style']
```

Managing Database Permissions

Database permissions can be assigned by the database owner, members of sysadmin, and members of securityadmin. The available permissions include

- **Grant**   Gives permission to perform the related task. With roles, all members of the role inherit the permission.

- **Revoke**   Removes prior grant permission but doesn't explicitly prevent a user or role from performing a task. A user or role could still inherit grant permission from another role.

- **Deny** Explicitly denies permission to perform a task and prevents the user or role from inheriting the permission. Deny takes precedence over all other grant permissions.

Note Deny is a Transact-SQL command and isn't part of the ANSI SQL-92 standard.

You can assign grant, deny, and revoke permissions at the database level or the object level. You can also assign permissions using database roles. For more information, see "Controlling Database Access and Administration" in this chapter.

Assigning Database Permissions for Statements

At the database level, you can grant, revoke, or deny permission to execute data definition language statements, such as CREATE TABLE or BACKUP DATABASE. These statements were previously summarized in Table 5-2.

In Enterprise Manager, you grant, revoke, or deny database permissions for statements by completing the following steps:

1. Work your way down to the Databases folder using the entries in the left pane.
2. Right-click the database you want to work with and then, from the shortcut menu, select Properties.
3. Click the Permissions tab, as shown in Figure 5-8.

Figure 5-8. *The Permissions tab lets you assign statement permissions at the database level. The key icon indicates a role. The person icon indicates a user.*

4. To assign default permissions for all users, assign permissions to the public role. To assign permissions for individual users or roles, click the entries to the right of the User/Role name. A check mark grants permission. A red X denies permission. Clear a check mark to revoke permission.

5. Click Apply or OK to assign the permissions.

With Transact-SQL, you use the GRANT, REVOKE, and DENY commands to assign permissions. Listing 5-12 shows the syntax and usage of GRANT.

Listing 5-12. GRANT Syntax and Usage

Syntax

```
GRANT {ALL | statement[,...n]}
TO security_account[,...n]

GRANT
   {ALL [PRIVILEGES] | permission[,...n]}
   {
     [(column[,...n])] ON {table | view}
     | ON {table | view}[(column[,...n])]
     | ON {stored_procedure | extended_procedure}
   }
TO security_account[,...n]
[WITH GRANT OPTION]
[AS {group | role}]
```

Usage

```
GRANT CREATE DATABASE, CREATE TABLE
TO Users, [GALAXY\Sales]

GRANT SELECT
ON customer..customers
TO public

GRANT INSERT, UPDATE, DELETE
ON customer..customers
TO Devs, Testers
```

Listing 5-13 shows the syntax and usage of REVOKE.

Listing 5-13. REVOKE Syntax and Usage

Syntax

```
REVOKE {ALL | statement[,...n]}
FROM security_account[,...n]

REVOKE [GRANT OPTION FOR]
   {ALL [PRIVILEGES] | permission[,...n]}
```

```
{
    [(column[,...n])] ON {table | view}
    | ON {table | view}[(column[,...n])]
    | {stored_procedure | extended_procedure}
}
{TO | FROM}
    security_account[,...n]
[CASCADE]
[AS {group | role}]
```

Usage

```
REVOKE CREATE TABLE, CREATE DEFAULT
FROM Devs, Testers

REVOKE INSERT, UPDATE, DELETE
FROM Users, [GALAXY\Sales]
```

Listing 5-14 shows the syntax and usage of DENY.

Listing 5-14. DENY Syntax and Usage

Syntax

```
DENY{ALL | statement[,...n]}
TO security_account[,...n]

DENY
    {ALL [PRIVILEGES] | permission[,...n]}
    {
        [(column[,...n])] ON {table | view}
        | ON {table | view}[(column[,...n])]
        | ON {stored_procedure | extended_procedure}
    }
TO security_account[,...n]
[CASCADE]
```

Usage

```
DENY CREATE TABLE
TO Devs, Testers

DENY INSERT, UPDATE, DELETE
ON customer..customers
TO Users, [GALAXY\Sales]
```

Object Permissions by Login

Object permissions apply to tables, views, and stored procedures. Permissions you assign to these objects include SELECT, INSERT, UPDATE, and DELETE. A summary of permitted actions by object was listed previously in Table 5-1.

Figure 5-9. *Use the Permissions tab to assign object permissions. The glasses icon indicates a view. The table icon indicates a table. The icon with the wavy blue lines indicates a stored procedure.*

In Enterprise Manager, you grant, revoke, or deny object permissions by completing the following steps:

1. Work your way down to the Databases folder using the entries in the left pane.
2. Click on the plus sign (+) next to the database you want to work with and then select Users.
3. In the right pane, you should see a list of database users. Double-click the user you want to configure. This opens the Database User Properties dialog box.
4. Click Permissions to display the Permissions tab, as shown in Figure 5-9.
5. To assign object permissions, select the List All Objects option button. The entries to the right of the Object and Owner names are used to assign permissions. A check mark grants permission. A red X denies permission. Clear a check mark to revoke permission.
6. Click Apply or OK to assign the permissions.

Object Permissions for Multiple Logins

You can also assign permission by object and in this way assign object permissions for multiple logins. To do this, complete the following steps:

1. Start Enterprise Manager and work your way down to the Databases folder using the entries in the left pane.
2. Click on the plus sign (+) next to the database you want to work with and then select the type of objects you want to work with—Tables, Views, or Stored Procedures.

Figure 5-10. *Use the Object Properties dialog box to assign permissions by object rather than by login or role.*

3. In the right pane, double-click the table, view, or stored procedure you want to configure. This opens a properties dialog box.

4. In the properties dialog box, click Permissions. This opens the Object Properties dialog box shown in Figure 5-10.

5. To assign permissions for logins, select the List All Users option button. You use the entries to the right of the User / DB Roles / Public names column to assign permissions. A check mark grants permission. A red X denies permission. Clear a check mark to revoke permission.

Transact-SQL commands for assigning permissions were listed previously in the section of this chapter entitled "Assigning Database Permissions for Statements."

Part III

Microsoft
SQL Server 7.0
Data Administration

This part of the book covers Microsoft SQL Server 7.0 data administration. Chapter 6 starts by detailing how to create a backup and recovery plan. The chapter then dives into common tasks for creating and restoring backups. In Chapter 7, you'll find tasks for importing and exporting data. Chapter 8 focuses on integrating SQL Server databases with other SQL Server databases and with other data sources. You'll find detailed discussions on distributed queries, distributed transactions, Distributed Transaction Coordinator, and linking remote servers. Chapter 9 explores data replication. You'll learn all about the latest replication techniques, including merge replication and immediately updating subscribers.

Database Backup and Recovery

Information is the fuel that drives the enterprise, and often the most critical information is stored in databases. Databases are where you'll find an organization's customer account information, partner directories, product knowledge base, and other important data. To protect an organization's data and to ensure the availability of its databases, you need a solid database backup and recovery plan. Backing up databases can protect against accidental loss of data, database corruption, hardware failures, and even natural disasters. It's your job as a database administrator to make sure that backups are performed and that they're stored in a safe and secure location.

Creating a Backup and Recovery Plan

Creating and implementing a backup and recovery plan is one of your most important duties as a database administrator. Think of database backup as an insurance plan for the future—and for your job. Important data is accidentally deleted all the time. Mission-critical data can become corrupt. Natural disasters can leave your office in ruins. With a solid backup and recovery plan you can recover from any of these situations. Without one, you're left with nothing to fall back on.

Creating and implementing a backup and recovery plan takes time. You'll need to figure out what databases need to be backed up, how often the databases should be backed up, and more. To help you create a plan, consider the following:

- **What type of database are you backing up?** System and user databases often have different backup and recovery needs. For example, the master database is essential for all Microsoft SQL Server operations. If the master database fails or becomes corrupt, it takes the whole server down with it. But you don't need to back up master every hour or every half hour—as you might have to do with a critical user database that handles real-time customer transactions. You only need to backup master after you create a database, change configuration values, configure SQL logons, or perform similar activities that make changes to the database.

- **How important is the data in the database?** How you judge the data's importance can go a long way toward determining *when* and *how* you should back up the database. While you may back up a development database only once a week, you would probably back up a production database at least daily. The data's importance also drives your decision about the *type* of backup. With that development database, you'd probably do a full backup once a week. With an in-house customer order database that is updated throughout the weekday, you'd probably perform full backups twice a week and supplement this with daily differential backups and hourly backups for the transaction logs.

- **How often are changes made to the database?**   The frequency of change can drive your decision about how often the database should be backed up. Because a read-only database doesn't ordinarily change, it doesn't need to be backed up regularly. On the other hand, a database that's updated nightly should be backed up after the nightly changes are posted. A database that's updated around the clock should be backed up continually.

- **How quickly do you need to recover the data?**   It's important to consider time when you create a backup plan. For mission-critical databases, you may need to get the database back online swiftly; to do this, you may need to alter your backup plan. Instead of backing up to tape, you may want to back up to disk drives or use multiple backup devices. Both options are many times faster than restoring from a single tape device.

- **Do you have the equipment necessary to perform backup?**   You need backup hardware to perform backups. If you don't have the hardware, you can't perform backups. To perform timely backups, you may need several backup devices and several sets of backup media. Backup hardware includes a tape drive, optical drives, removable disk drives, and plain-old disk drives. Generally, tape drives are less expensive but slower than other types of drives.

- **What is the best time to schedule backups?**   You'll want to schedule backups when database usage is as low as possible. This will speed the backup process. However, in the real world you can't always schedule backups for off-peak hours. So you'll need to carefully plan when key databases are backed up.

- **Do you need to store backups off-site?**   Storing copies of backup tapes off-site is essential to the recovery of your systems in the case of a natural disaster. In your off-site storage location, you should also include copies of the software you may need to install in order to restore operations on a new system.

Backing up a database is a bit different than backing up a server or a workstation. Primarily, this is because you'll often need to combine all (or nearly all) of the available techniques to ensure that you can recover a database completely. The basic types of backups you can perform include

- **Complete database backups**   Perform a full backup of the database, including all objects, system tables, and data. When the backup starts, SQL Server copies everything in the database and also includes any needed portions of the transaction log as the backup is in progress. Because of this, you can use a complete backup to recover the complete state of the data in the database at the time the backup operation finishes.

- **Differential backups** Designed to back up data that has changed since the last complete backup. Because you store only the changes, the backup is faster and can be performed more often. As with complete backups, differential backups include needed portions of the transaction logs, which allow you to restore the database to the time when the backup operation finishes.

Tip You can only use differential backups in conjunction with complete backups, and differential backups can't be performed on the master database. Don't confuse *differential* backups with *incremental* backups. Differential backups record all changes since the last full backup (which means the size of the incremental backup grows over time). Incremental backups record changes since the most recent full or incremental backup (which means the size of the incremental backup is usually much smaller than a full backup).

- **Transaction log backups** Transaction logs are serial records of all database modifications and are used during recovery operations to commit completed transactions and to roll back uncompleted transactions. When you back up a transaction log, the backup stores the changes that have occurred since the last transaction log backup and then truncates the log, which clears out transactions that have been committed or aborted. Unlike complete and differential backups, transaction log backups record the state of the transaction log at the time the backup operation starts (not when it ends).

- **File and filegroup backups** Allow you to back up database files and filegroups rather than the entire database. This is useful with large databases where, to save time, you want to back up individual files rather than the entire database. Many factors affect file and filegroup backups. When you use file and filegroup backups, you must back up the transaction log as well. Because of this dependency, you can't use this backup technique if Truncate Log On Checkpoint is enabled. Furthermore, if objects in the database span multiple files or filegroups, you must back up all the related files and filegroups at the same time.

Once you determine the backup operations you'll use on each database and how often you'll back up each database, you can select backup devices and media that meet these requirements. The next section covers the selection of backup devices and media.

Selecting Backup Devices and Media

Many different solutions are available for backing up data. Some are fast and expensive. Others are slow but very reliable. The backup solution that's right for your organization depends on many factors, including

- **Capacity** The amount of data that you need to back up on a routine basis. Can the backup hardware support the required load given your time and resource constraints?

- **Reliability** The reliability of the backup hardware and media. Can you afford to sacrifice reliability to meet budget or time needs?
- **Extensibility** The extensibility of the backup solution. Will this solution meet your needs as your organization grows?
- **Speed** The speed with which data can be backed up and recovered. Can you afford to sacrifice speed to reduce costs?
- **Cost** The cost of the backup solution. Does the solution fit within your budget?

Capacity, reliability, extensibility, speed, and cost are the issues that will influence your choice of a backup plan. If you determine the relative value of these issues to your organization, you'll be on the right track to selecting an appropriate backup solution. Some of the most commonly used backup solutions include

- **Tape drives** Tape drives are the most common backup devices. They use magnetic tape cartridges to store data. Magnetic tapes are relatively inexpensive but aren't highly reliable. Tapes can break or stretch. They can also lose information over time. The average capacity of tape cartridges ranges from 100 MB to 2 GB. Compared with other backup solutions, tape drives are fairly slow. Still, the key selling point is the low cost of tape drives and magnetic tapes.
- **DAT drives** DAT (digital audio tape) drives are quickly replacing standard tape drives as the preferred backup devices. DAT drives use 4 mm and 8 mm tapes to store data. DAT drives and tapes are more expensive than standard tape drives and tapes, but they offer higher speed and more capacity. DAT drives that use 4 mm tapes typically can record over 30 MB per minute and have capacities of up to 16 GB. DAT drives that use 8 mm tapes typically can record more than 10 MB per minute and have capacities of up to 10 GB (with compression).

 Tip To perform faster backup and recovery operations, you can use multiple backup devices with SQL Server. For example, if it normally takes four hours to perform a full backup or restoration of the database, you can cut the backup and restoration time in half using two backup devices; with four backup devices you could fully back up or restore the database in an hour.

- **Auto-loader tape systems** Auto-loader tape systems use a magazine of tapes that create extended backup volumes capable of meeting the high-capacity needs of the enterprise. With an auto-loader system, tapes within the magazine are automatically changed as needed during the backup or recovery process. Most auto-loader tape systems use DAT tapes. The typical system uses magazines with between 4 and 12 tapes. The key drawback to these systems is the high cost.

- **Magnetic optical drives** Magnetic optical drives combine magnetic tape technology with optical lasers to create a more reliable backup solution than DAT. Magnetic optical drives use 3 ½" and 5 ¼" disks that look similar to floppies but are much thicker. Typically, magnetic optical disks have capacities of between 1 GB and 4 GB.

- **Tape jukeboxes** Tape jukeboxes are similar to auto-loader tape systems. Jukeboxes use magnetic optical disks rather than DAT tapes to offer high-capacity solutions for the enterprise. These systems load and unload disks stored internally for backup and recovery operations. The key drawback to tape jukeboxes is the high cost.

- **Removable disks** Removable disks, such as Iomega Jaz, are increasingly being used as backup devices. Removable disks offer good speed and ease of use for a single drive or single system backup. However, the disk drives and the removable disks tend to be more expensive than standard tape or DAT drive solutions.

- **Disk drives** Disk drives provide the fastest way to back up and restore databases. With disk drives, you can often accomplish in minutes what a tape drive takes hours to do. When your needs mandate a speedy recovery, nothing beats a disk drive. The drawbacks to disk drives, however, are high cost and low extensibility.

Although backup device selection is an important step in implementing a backup and recovery plan, it isn't the only step. You also need to purchase the tapes, disks, or both, that will allow you to implement your backup and recovery plan. The number of tapes, disks, or drives you need depends on

- How much data you'll be backing up
- How often you'll be backing up the data
- How long you'll need to keep additional data sets

The typical way to implement backups is to use a rotation schedule whereby you rotate through two or more sets of tapes, disks, or files. The idea is that you can increase media longevity by reducing media usage, and at the same time reduce the number of actual tapes, disks, or files you need to ensure that you have data on hand when necessary.

Best Practice For important databases, I recommend using four media sets. Use two sets for regular rotations. Use the third set for the first rotation cycle at the beginning of each month. Use the fourth set for the first rotation cycle of each quarter. This technique allows you to recover the database in a wide variety of situations.

Table 6-1 lists backup strategies you may want to use. As you can see, these backup strategies are based on the type of database as well as the type of data.

Tip The size of a database can change automatically, and master may get updated without your knowing about it. Because of this, often the best backup strategy for master is to schedule backups every other day and to rotate through several backup sets so that you can go back to several different versions of master if necessary.

Table 6-1. Backup Strategies for System and User Databases

Database Type	Details	Strategy
User	Up to the minute recovery	Run complete backups twice a week, if possible. Use nightly differential backups and back up the transaction log every 10 minutes during business hours. Do not use Truncate Log On Checkpoint, as this will make it impossible to recover some transactions. To improve backup/restore speed, use multiple backup devices whenever possible.
	Up to the hour recovery	Run complete backups twice a week, if possible. Use nightly differential backups and back up the transaction log every 30 minutes during business hours. Do not use Truncate Log On Checkpoint. To improve backup/restore speed, use multiple backup devices whenever possible.
	Recovery of daily changes	Run complete backups at least once a week. Use nightly differential backups and back up the transaction log every four hours during business hours. Do not use Truncate Log On Checkpoint.
	Read-only database	Schedule a complete backup of the database every 30 days and supplement this with an additional complete backup if the database is modified.
System	distribution	Available when you configure replication and the server is acting as a distributor. Schedule complete backups after snapshots. With transactional replication, schedule regular log backups.
	master	Run complete backups immediately after creating or removing databases, changing the size of a database, adding or removing logons, or modifying server configuration settings. Don't forget to maintain several backup sets for master.
	msdb	If you schedule jobs through the SQL Server Agent, back up this database regularly because this is where the job schedule and history is maintained and backup history is stored.
	model	Treat like a read-only database.
	tempdb	Normally doesn't need to be backed up. This database is re-created each time you start SQL Server.

Creating a Backup Device

Previous versions of SQL Server required you to configure backup devices before you could back up databases. With SQL Server 7.0, this is no longer the case, and you don't need to explicitly define backup devices. Nevertheless, backup devices do provide an easy way to ensure that you create backups that have the same filename and location time after time. With consistent names and locations, you can more easily manage the backup and recovery process.

To create a backup device using Enterprise Manager, complete the following steps:

1. Start Enterprise Manager and then access the server you want to work with.
2. Click the plus sign (+) next to the server's Management folder.
3. Right-click Backup and then, from the shortcut menu, select New Backup Device. This opens the dialog box shown in Figure 6-1.
4. In the Name field, type the name of the logical backup device. Use a short but descriptive name, such as Customer Device or Master Device, to make the device easier to work with.
5. If you've installed a tape drive and want to back up to the tape drive, select the Tape Drive Name field and then use the related drop-down list box to select the target drive.
6. If you're backing up to a file, select the File Name option button and then enter the full path to the backup file you want to associate with this device, such as E:\MSSQL\BACKUP\CUSTOMER.BAK.
7. Click OK.

With Transact-SQL, you create backup devices using SP_ADDUMPDEVICE. The syntax and usage for this command is shown in Listing 6-1. This command uses many different arguments, including *device_type*, *logical_name*, *physical_name*, *controller_type*, and *devstatus*. The *device_type* is the type of device you're

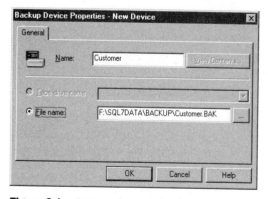

Figure 6-1. *Create a backup device to make it easier to manage backups.*

using—disk, tape, or pipe. The *logical_name* is the name of the backup device. The *physical_name* is the full path to the backup file. The controller type is 2 for a disk, 5 for a tape, and 6 for a named pipe. The *devstatus* is either *noskip,* to read ANSI tape headers, or *skip,* to skip ANSI tape headers.

Listing 6-1. SP_ADDUMPDEVICE Syntax and Usage

Syntax

```
sp_addumpdevice [@devtype =] 'device_type',
   [@logicalname =] 'logical_name',
   [@physicalname =] 'physical_name'
   [, {
      [@cntrltype =] controller_type
        |
      [@devstatus =] 'device_status'
      }
   ]
```

Usage

```
EXEC sp_addumpdevice 'disk', 'Customer', 'c:\mssql\backup\cust.bak'

EXEC sp_addumpdevice 'disk', 'Customer on Backup Server',
   '\\omega\backups\cust.bak'

EXEC sp_addumpdevice 'tape', 'Customer on Tape',
   '\\.\tape0'
```

Performing Backups

Backups are an essential part of database administration. They're so important that SQL Server provides multiple backup procedures and several backup-related wizards—all designed to help you better manage database backup and recovery. In this section, I'll look at standard backup procedures, the Backup Wizard, and the Transact-SQL backup process. The final ingredient for backups involves database maintenance plans, which you'll learn about in Chapter 12, "Database Automation and Maintenance."

Creating Backups in Enterprise Manager

In Enterprise Manager you can start the backup process using either of these techniques:

- Select the server you want to work with and then, from the Tools menu, choose Backup Database. This opens the SQL Server Backup dialog box.

- Select the server you want to work with and then, from the Tools menu, choose Wizards. This opens the Wizards dialog box. Click the plus sign (+) next to Management and then double-click Backup Wizard.

Regardless of which technique you use, the steps you follow are similar. Rather than covering the same information twice, I'll focus on the SQL Server Backup dialog box and how you can use it to perform backups in these situations:

- Creating a new backup set
- Adding to an existing backup set

You can use these techniques with the Backup Wizard as well. The key difference is that you'll need to go through a series of dialog boxes.

Creating a New Backup Set

Whenever you back up a database for the first time or start a new rotation on an existing backup set, follow these steps to create the backup:

1. Select the server you want to work with and then, from the Tools menu, choose Backup Database. This opens the SQL Server Backup dialog box shown in Figure 6-2.

2. Use the Database drop-down list box to select the database you want to back up.

3. In the Name field, type a name for the backup set you're creating. This is an ordinary, English name that'll help you tell at a glance what the backup

Figure 6-2. *Use the SQL Server Backup dialog box to start or schedule a backup. If this is the first time you're running backup, some of the backup types may be unavailable.*

contains. For example, name the first backup set for the customer database Customer Backup Set 1. Then you can add the complete, differential, and transaction log backups for this rotation to the set.

4. Type a description of the backup, such as "Set 1 contains the weekly complete, daily differential, and hourly transaction log backups."

5. In the Backup area, use the option buttons to select the type of backup. Because this is your first time running a backup on the database, some of the options may be unavailable. Don't worry, once you run a complete or differential backup, the other options should become available.

 Note The only available backup option for the master database is Database – Complete. That's because you can run only complete backups on master.

6. If a backup set exists and is listed in the Destination area, select it and click Remove.

7. Click Add to display the Choose Backup Destination dialog box shown in Figure 6-3. To use a file as the backup destination, select the File Name option button and enter the full path to the backup file, such as e:\DATA\BACKUPS\CUST.BAK or \\OMEGA\BACKUPS\CUST.BAK. To use a backup device, select the Backup Device option button and then choose the backup destination using the drop-down list box. Click OK when you're ready to continue.

8. To schedule the backup, click Schedule and then configure the backup schedule as discussed in Chapter 12, "Database Automation and Maintenance."

9. To set additional options for the backup, click the Options tab. The available options are used as follows:

- **Verify Backup Upon Completion**   Reads the entire backup and checks for errors.

- **Eject Tape After Backup**   Set to eject the tape after the backup (only valid with tape devices).

- **Remove Inactive Entries From The Transaction Log**   Cleans out entries that are no longer needed after the backup. These entries are for transactions that have been committed or rolled back. (Set by default for transaction log backups.)

 Tip   You'll usually want to perform one last log backup before trying to restore a corrupt database. When you do, you'll want to clear the option and perform the log backup without truncation. This option is the same as running BACKUP LOG NO_TRUNCATE.

Figure 6-3. *Use the Choose Backup Destination dialog box to select a file or backup device to use as the backup destination.*

- **Check Media Set Name And Backup Expiration** Ensures that you're writing to the correct tape set and that the tape expiration date has not been met.

- **Backup Set Will Expire On** When backing up to a tape device, you can check this option and then set an expiration date. This option allows the backup to overwrite the media after a specified date or period.

- **Initialize And Label Media** When backing up to tape devices, you can use this option to erase the previous contents of the media and then add a new label and description.

10. Click OK to start the backup or confirm that you want to schedule the backup. For an immediate backup, you'll see the Backup Progress dialog box, which displays a progress bar as the backup proceeds. If you opted to verify the data, the verification process starts immediately after the backup ends.

Adding to an Existing Backup Set

When you want to add to an existing backup set, complete the following steps:

1. Select the server you want to work with and then, from the Tools menu, choose Backup Database. This opens the SQL Server Backup dialog box shown previously in Figure 6-2.

2. Use the Database drop-down list box to select the database you want to back up.

3. In the Backup area, use the option buttons to select the type of backup you want to perform:

- Database – Complete
- Database – Differential
- Transaction Log
- File And Filegroup

4. A backup set should be listed in the Destination area. If one isn't, click Add to display the Choose Backup Destination and then enter the location of the existing backup. Click OK when you're ready to continue.

5. If you want to add data to the existing backup set, select the Append To Media option button.

 Real World Whether you back up to a tape or disk drive, you should use the tape rotation philosophy. Create multiple tape sets and then write to these sets on a rotating basis. With a disk drive, for example, you could create these backup files on different network drives and use them as follows:

//omega/data1drive/backups/cust_set1.bak Used on week 1, 3, 5, and so on for complete and differential backups of the customer database.

//omega/data2drive/backups/cust_set2.bak Used on week 2, 4, 6, and so on for complete and differential backups of the customer database.

//omega/data3drive/backups/cust_set3.bak Used on the first week of the month for complete backups of the customer database.

//omega/data4drive/backups/cust_set4.bak Used on the first week of the quarter for complete backups of the customer database.

Don't forget that each time you start a new rotation on a tape set, you should overwrite the existing media. For example, you would append all backups on week 1. Then, when starting the next rotation on week 3, you would overwrite the existing media for the first backup and then append the remaining backups for the week.

6. Click the Options tab to double-check the backup options. For transaction log backups, you'll usually want to select the Remove Inactive Entries From Transaction Log check box. This ensures that inactive entries are cleared out of the transaction log after a backup.

7. To schedule the backup, click Schedule and then configure the backup schedule as discussed in Chapter 12, "Database Automation and Maintenance."

8. Click OK to start the backup or to confirm that you want to schedule the backup. For an immediate backup, you'll see the Backup Progress dialog box, which displays a progress bar as the backup proceeds. If you opted to verify the data, the verify process starts immediately after the backup ends.

Using Striped Backups with Multiple Devices

Through a process called parallel striped backups, SQL Server can perform backups to multiple backup devices simultaneously. As you can imagine, writing multiple backup files at the same time can dramatically speed backup operations. The key to this speed, however, lies in having physically separate devices, such as three different tape devices or three different drives that you're using for the backup. You can't write parallel backups to a single tape device and you can't write parallel backups to the same drive.

Multiple devices used in a backup operation are referred to as a *media set*. SQL Server allows you to use from 2 to 32 devices to form the media set. These devices must be of the same type. For example, you can't create a striped backup with one backup tape device and one backup drive device.

The two main operations you'll perform are

- Creating a new media set
- Adding to an existing media set

Creating a New Media Set

To create a new media set using multiple devices, complete the following steps:

1. Select the server you want to work with and then create each of the backup devices you need in the media set as described in the section of this chapter entitled "Creating a Backup Device."

2. Open the SQL Server Backup dialog box by going to the Tools menu and choosing Backup Database. (You can't create a multiple device backup with the Backup Wizard.)

3. Follow the steps outlined in the section of this chapter entitled "Creating a New Backup Set." Repeat step 7 for each backup device you want to use in the media set.

Adding to an Existing Media Set

To add to an existing media set, complete the following steps:

1. Open the SQL Server Backup dialog box by going to the Tools menu and choosing Backup Database. (You can't create a multiple backup with the Backup Wizard.)

2. Follow the steps outlined in the "Adding to an Existing Backup Set" section of this chapter. The only change is that in step 4 you should see a list of all backup devices used in the media set. If you don't, you'll need to add them one by one using the Add button and the related Choose Backup Destination dialog box.

Transact-SQL Backup

An alternative to the backup procedures in Enterprise Manager is to use Transact-SQL BACKUP. You'll use BACKUP DATABASE to back up databases and BACKUP LOG to back up transaction logs.

Tip If you back up databases using Transact-SQL, you lose one of the biggest benefits of SQL Server—the automated recovery process. With automated recovery, you don't have to worry about which backup to apply when, which command flags to use when, and more. Furthermore, because you can schedule automated and unattended backups, you really don't need to run backups manually through SQL as often as you used to. So I recommend using the Enterprise Manager backup and restore process whenever possible.

BACKUP DATABASE has dual syntax. Listing 6-2 shows the syntax and usage for complete and differential backups. A complete backup is the default operation.

Listing 6-2. BACKUP DATABASE Syntax and Usage for Complete and Differential Backups

Syntax

```
BACKUP DATABASE {database_name | @database_name_var}
TO <backup_device> [,...n]
[WITH
   [BLOCKSIZE = {blocksize | @blocksize_variable}]
   [[,] DESCRIPTION = {text | @text_variable}]
   [[,] DIFFERENTIAL]
   [[,] EXPIREDATE = {date | @date_var}
        | RETAINDAYS = {days | @days_var}]
   [[,] FORMAT | NOFORMAT]
   [[,] {INIT | NOINIT}]
   [[,] MEDIADESCRIPTION = {text | @text_variable}]
   [[,] MEDIANAME = {media_name | @media_name_variable}]
   [[,] [NAME = {backup_set_name | @backup_set_name_var}]
   [[,] {NOSKIP | SKIP}]
   [[,] {NOUNLOAD | UNLOAD}]
   [[,] [RESTART]
   [[,] STATS [= percentage]]
]
```

Usage

```
USE master
EXEC sp_addumpdevice 'disk', 'Customer Backup Set 1',
'f:\data\backup\Cust2.dat'
BACKUP DATABASE 'Customer' TO 'Customer Backup Set 1'
```

Listing 6-3 shows the BACKUP DATABASE syntax for file and file group backups.

Listing 6-3. BACKUP DATABASE Syntax and Usage for File or Filegroup Backups

Syntax

```
BACKUP DATABASE {database_name | @database_name_var}
   <file_or_filegroup> [,...n]
TO <backup_device> [,...n]
[WITH
   [BLOCKSIZE = {blocksize | @blocksize_variable}]
   [[,] DESCRIPTION = {text | @text_variable}]
   [[,] EXPIREDATE = {date | @date_var}
        | RETAINDAYS = {days | @days_var}]
   [[,] FORMAT | NOFORMAT]
   [[,] {INIT | NOINIT}]
```

(continued)

Listing 6-3. *(continued)*
```
   [[,] MEDIADESCRIPTION = {text | @text_variable}]
   [[,] MEDIANAME = {media_name | @media_name_variable}]
   [[,] [NAME = {backup_set_name | @backup_set_name_var}]
   [[,] {NOSKIP | SKIP}]
   [[,] {NOUNLOAD | UNLOAD}]
   [[,] [RESTART]
   [[,] STATS [= percentage]]
]
```

Usage

```
USE master
EXEC sp_addumpdevice 'disk', 'Customer Backup Set 1',
'f:\data\backup\Cust2.dat'
BACKUP DATABASE Customer
     FILE = 'Customer_data',
     FILEGROUP = 'Primary',
     FILE = 'Customer_data2',
     FILEGROUP = 'Secondary'
     TO 'Customer Backup Set 1'
```

Listing 6-4 shows the syntax for BACKUP LOG. By default, this command truncates the log after the backup.

Listing 6-4. BACKUP LOG Syntax and Usage

Syntax

```
BACKUP LOG {database_name | @database_name_var}
[WITH
     { NO_LOG | TRUNCATE_ONLY }]
TO <backup_device> [,...n]
  [WITH
     [BLOCKSIZE = {blocksize | @blocksize_variable}]
     [[,] DESCRIPTION = {text | @text_variable}]
     [[,] EXPIREDATE = {date | @date_var}
          | RETAINDAYS = {days | @days_var}]
     [[,] FORMAT | NOFORMAT]
     [[,] {INIT | NOINIT}]
     [[,] MEDIADESCRIPTION = {text | @text_variable}]
     [[,] MEDIANAME = {media_name | @media_name_variable}]
     [[,] [NAME = {backup_set_name | @backup_set_name_var}]
     [[,] NO_TRUNCATE]
     [[,] {NOSKIP | SKIP}]
     [[,] {NOUNLOAD | UNLOAD}]
     [[,] [RESTART]
     [[,] STATS [= percentage]]
  ]
```

(continued)

Listing 6-4. *(continued)*
Usage

```
USE master
EXEC sp_addumpdevice 'disk', 'Customer_log1',
  'f:\data\backup\Cust_log.dat'
BACKUP LOG Customer
  TO Customer_log1
```

Performing Transaction Log Backups

Transaction logs are essential to the timely recovery of SQL Server databases. Unlike database backups, which can be complete or differential, transaction log backups are usually incremental. This means that each transaction log backup has a record of transactions only within a certain time frame. Transaction logs are always applied in sequence—with the completion time of the last complete or differential backup marking the beginning of a transaction log sequence.

Consequently, in order to restore the database you must apply each transaction logon sequence up to the point of failure. For example, if you run a complete backup at 1 P.M. and the database fails at 1:46 P.M., you would restore the last complete backup and then apply each transaction log created after that time, such as the backup at 1:15 P.M., 1:30 P.M. and 1:45 P.M. As you can see, without the incremental transaction log backups, you would lose all the transactions that took place after the 1 P.M. complete backup.

You can perform transaction log backups like any other backup. Still, there are a few details that you should know beforehand and these details are covered in the sections that follow.

Options and Commands that Invalidate Log Sequences

Although the normal backup process for transaction logs is fairly straightforward, SQL Server throws a few curveballs by providing option flags that you can set for the backup or the database, or both. The following database options prevent you from using a transaction log sequence to recover a database:

- **Truncate Log On Checkpoint**   A database option that clears out inactive entries in the transaction log on checkpoint.

- **Using Non Logged Operations**   Commands that bypass the log invalidate a log backup sequence.

- **ALTER DATABASE**   Adding or deleting files with ALTER DATABASE invalidates a backup sequence.

   Tip   As I stated earlier, the completion time of the last complete or differential backup marks the beginning of a transaction log sequence. If you use any of the previous commands and invalidate a log sequence, perform a complete or differential backup to start a new sequence.

Log Truncation Options

When you back up transaction logs, you have several options that determine how the backups are made. With SQL Server Backup in Enterprise Manager, you can use the Remove Inactive Entries From The Log option. Setting this option clears committed transactions out of the log after a log backup. The BACKUP LOG command normally clears out committed or aborted transactions after a log backup as well. However, you can override this behavior with these options:

- **TRUNCATE_ONLY**   Removes inactive entries from the log without creating a backup. This invalidates the log sequence.

- **NO_LOG**   Same as TRUNCATE_ONLY but doesn't log the BACKUP LOG command in the transaction log. This option is designed for a situation where the transaction log or its home drive is full, and you must truncate the log without writing to the log device.

- **NO_TRUNCATE**   Writes all the transaction log entries from the last backup to the point of failure. Use this option when the database is corrupt and you're about to restore it.

Tip After you use TRUNCATE_ONLY or NO_LOG, always perform a complete or differential backup. This revalidates the log sequence. Additionally, because you can grow logs automatically, you should rarely encounter a situation where you need to truncate the log without logging. The log can only run out of space if you set a maximum size or the drive(s) the log uses runs out of space.

Restoring a Database

Occasional database corruption, hardware failure, and natural disasters are facts of life, and as a database administrator you need to be able to restore the database if any of these situations occur. Even if you're an old pro at backup and restore, keep in mind that restoring a database is a bit different from restoring an operating system or recovering other types of applications. The mix of complete, differential, and transaction log backups ensures that you can get up-to-the-minute recovery of a database, but it complicates the recovery process.

In the section that follows you'll find tips and advice on troubleshooting database corruption. In the sections after that you'll find specific step-by-step procedures for restoring a database in various situations, including

- Restoring a database using backups created in Enterprise Manager
- Restoring a file or filegroup
- Restoring a database from a device
- Restoring a database to a different location
- Restoring a database using Transact-SQL

Database Corruption and Problem Resolution

All your database administration know-how comes into play in one defining moment. That's the moment when you attempt to restore a database. The techniques you use to restore a database depend on the backup options you've used and the state of the database. As you know, the backup techniques available are complete, differential, transaction log, and file/filegroups. What you may not know is how to restore a database when these techniques are combined.

Table 6-2 lists some suggested recovery strategies. These strategies show how to recover a database with various combinations of the available backup operations. If you use Enterprise Manager for backup and restore, these procedures are done for you automatically in most cases. The actual step-by-step process is covered later in the chapter.

Table 6-2. Recovery Strategies for Databases

Backup Type	Restore Process
Complete backups only	Restore the database using the last complete backup.
Complete and differential backups	Restore the last complete backup with NORECOVERY. Then restore the last differential backup with RECOVERY.
Complete and transaction log backups	Back up the current transaction log with NO_TRUNCATE. Restore the last complete backup with NORECOVERY. Apply log backups from that time forward in sequence and using NORECOVERY. Apply the last backup log using the RECOVERY option.
Complete, differential, and transaction log backups	Back up the current transaction log with NO_TRUNCATE. Restore the last complete backup with NORECOVERY and then the last differential backup with NORECOVERY. Apply log backups from that time forward in sequence and using NORECOVERY. Apply the last backup using the RECOVERY option.

All right, now you know in theory how to restore a database. But before you pull out all the stops, you should make sure the database is really corrupt and can't be recovered by other means. To troubleshoot database problems and potential corruption, complete the following steps:

1. Start with the error logs. See what types of error messages are in the logs, paying particular attention to errors that occur during database startup. Also take a look at user-related errors. If you find errors, you can look up the error numbers in the SQL Server Books Online (click Start, then Programs, then Microsoft SQL Server 7.0, and then choose Books Online) or the Microsoft Online Support Web site (SUPPORT.MICROSOFT.COM). You access the server logs through the Management folder in Enterprise Manager.

2. Check the state of the database. Every time SQL Server is started, it goes through a recovery process on each database. If the recovery process has

problems, the mode or state of the database may be abnormal. To check mode or state, use these properties of the *databaseproperty* function:

- **IsShutDown**   If set to 1, the database is shut down because of problems during startup.

- **IsEmergencyMode**   If set to 1, the database is in emergency mode, which allows a suspect database to be used.

- **IsSuspect**   If set to 1, the database is suspect, which means there is possible corruption.

- **IsInLoad**   If set to 1, the database is going through the loading process.

- **IsInRecovery**   If set to 1, the database is going through the recovery process.

3. If possible, try to use the DBCC command to further troubleshoot or repair the database. DBCC is covered in Chapter 12, "Database Automation and Maintenance."

4. If these procedures indicate a corrupt database that can't be repaired, restore the database from backup.

The *databaseproperty* function can be used as shown in Listing 6-5.

Listing 6-5. The *databaseproperty* Function Syntax and Usage

Syntax

```
databaseproperty('database','property')
```

Usage

```
select databaseproperty('Customer','IsEmergencyMode')
```

Restoring a Database from a Normal Backup

Enterprise Manager tracks all the backups you create for each database; when you need to restore a database, Enterprise Manager automatically configures the restore. You can restore a database using these default settings or fine tune the restore operation as necessary.

To restore a database, complete the following steps:

1. If you're using transaction logs and the database is still running, you should back up the current transaction log with NO_TRUNCATE. When you're using the SQL Server Backup dialog box, this means you should cancel the option labeled Remove Inactive Entries From Transaction Log before running the backup.

2. You must have exclusive access to the database. Close all active connections to the database or have users log off, or both.

3. In Enterprise Manager, select the server you want to work with and then, from the Tools menu, choose the Restore Database option. This opens the Restore Database dialog box.

4. Use the Restore As Database drop-down list box to specify which database to restore and then select the Database option button.

5. Select the database again using the Show Backups Of Database option. This option is provided to allow you to restore a database to a different location, as described in the section below entitled "Restoring a Database to a Different Location."

6. Use the First Backup To Restore option to select which backup you want to apply first. Only complete backups are available in this drop-down list box. By default, the last complete backup should be selected.

 Real World Normally, you'll want to start with the last complete backup. However, if you know that the last backup is bad or contains transactions that you don't want to apply, such as a massive table deletion, go back to a previous complete backup by selecting a different backup as the starting point.

7. If multiple backups are available, you may be able to select a point in time for the restore. For example, if you know that GOTEAM accidentally deleted the Accounts table at 12:16 P.M., you could restore the database to a point just prior to this transaction, such as 12:15:00 P.M. To use the point in time option, select the Point In Time Restore check box. This opens the Point In Time Restore dialog box shown in Figure 6-4. Select a date and time using the fields provided and then click OK.

8. The lower portion of the Restore Database dialog box provides a backup history for the selected database. The information in the history can be used as follows:

   • **Restore** Allows you to select which backup sets to restore. Default selections are based on the first backup to restore and go forward in time through differential and transaction log backups. You should rarely change the default selections.

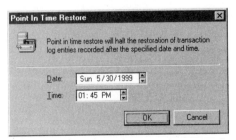

Figure 6-4. *Optionally, use the Point In Time Restore dialog box to select a point in time for the database restore operation.*

- **Type** Icons in this field are just about the only indicator of the type of backup. A backup device with a yellow database symbol behind it indicates a complete backup. A backup device with a bluish-green database symbol behind it indicates a differential backup. A backup device with a notebook symbol behind it indicates a transaction log.

- **Backup Set Date** Shows a date and time stamp for the backup entry.

- **Size** Shows the size of the backup.

- **Restore From** Shows the location of the related backup file.

- **Backup Set Name** Shows the name of the backup set.

Tip Select an entry and then click Properties to see a more detailed summary of the backup.

9. Click the Options tab to configure options for the restore operation. The Options tab is shown in Figure 6-5. The available options are used as follows:

- **Eject Tapes After Restoring Each Backup** Automatically ejects tapes from the tape drive when a restore completes. This is a time-saver if you have to deal with lots of tapes.

- **Prompt Before Restoring Each Backup** Automatically prompts after completing a successful restore and before starting the next restore. The prompt includes a Cancel button, which is useful if you want to cancel the restore operation after a particular backup is restored.

Figure 6-5. *Use the Options tab to configure options for the restore operation, as necessary.*

- **Force Restore Over Existing Database** Automatically overwrites existing database files.
- **Restore Database Files As** Allows you to change the restore location for database files.
- **Leave Database Operational** Completes the entire restore process and applies all the selected backups, which can include a complete backup, a differential backup, and multiple transaction log backups. All completed transactions are applied, and any uncompleted transactions are rolled back. When the restore process is completed, the database is returned to ready status and can be used for normal operations.
- **Leave Database Nonoperational** Essentially a manual restore that allows you to go step-by-step through the backups. SQL Server completes the entire restore process and applies all the selected backups, which can include a complete backup, a differential backup, and multiple transaction log backups. When the restore is completed, the database isn't returned to ready status and can't be used for normal operations. All transactions have not been processed, and the database is waiting for you to apply additional transaction logs. Apply these transaction logs using this mode, and then for the last transaction log set the mode to Leave Database Operational. All completed transactions are then applied, and any uncompleted transactions are rolled back.
- **Leave Database Read-Only** Essentially the same as Leave Database Nonoperational, with some exceptions. When the restore process ends, the database is in read-only mode and ready for additional transaction logs to be applied. In read-only mode, you can check the data and test the database. If necessary, apply additional transaction logs. For the last transaction log, set the mode to Leave Database Operational. All completed transactions are then applied, and any uncompleted transactions are rolled back.

 Tip With Leave Database Read-Only, SQL Server also creates an Undo file, which you can use to undo the restore operation. To commit the restore operations and the final transactions, if possible, without restoring another transaction log, you could use

```
RESTORE DATABASE Customer
    WITH RECOVERY
```

This commits final transactions (if possible), deletes the undo file, and puts the database back in operations mode. Although you may want to use WITH RECOVERY at this stage, you probably don't want to use WITH NORECOVERY because you'll undo all the changes from the restore and may end up with an empty database.

10. When you're ready to start the restore operation, click OK. Restore Database shows the progress of each backup. You can stop the restore at any time by clicking Stop. If an error occurs, you'll see a prompt with an error message. The most common error is the Database In Use error. This error occurs when you don't have exclusive access to the database, which means that someone is still connected to the database, and you can't proceed until the connection is closed.

Restoring Files and Filegroups

You can restore files and filegroups from database backups or file backups either individually, in combination with each other, or all together. If any changes were made to the files or filegroups, you must also restore all transaction log backups that were created after the files or filegroups were backed up.

Although you can usually recover individual files or filegroups, there are exceptions. If tables and indexes are created that span multiple filegroups, all the related filegroups must be restored together. Don't worry, SQL Server generates an error prior to starting the restore if a needed filegroup is missing. Further, if the entire database is corrupted, you must restore all files and filegroups in the database. In both cases you must also apply transaction log backups created after the file or filegroup backups you're restoring.

To restore files or filegroups, complete the following steps:

1. You must have exclusive access to the database. Close all active connections to the database or have users log off, or both.

2. In Enterprise Manager, select the server you want to work with and then, from the Tools menu, select the Restore Database option.

3. Use the Restore As Database drop-down list box to specify which database to restore and then select the Filegroups Or Files option button. This changes the Restore Database dialog box, as shown in Figure 6-6.

4. Select the database you're restoring again using the Show Backups Of Database drop-down list box. This option is provided to allow you to restore a database to a different location, as described in the section below entitled "Restoring a Database to a Different Location."

5. If you want to specify criteria for determining which files to use in the backup, choose Select A Subset Of Backup Sets and then click Selection Criteria. This opens the Filter Backup Sets dialog box, shown in Figure 6-7. The options of this dialog box determine which of the available backups are selected and are used as follows:

   - **Only The Backup Sets Of The Data Files On Drive**   Choose this option to restore only data files that are on a specific drive, such as F:.

   - **Only The Backup Sets Completed After**   Choose this option to filter backup sets by creation date and time.

Figure 6-6. *When you restore from files or filegroups, you have different options than with a normal backup.*

Figure 6-7. *Use the Filter Backup Sets dialog box to filter the available backup sets by drive, creation date, or filename.*

- **Only Backup Sets Of The Following Filegroups And Files** Choose this option to filter restore by filegroup and file.

6. The lower portion of the Restore Database dialog box provides a backup history for the files and filegroups in the selected database. By setting selec-

tion criteria, you remove options from the history and narrow the choices based on your filters. The information in the history can be used as follows:

- **Restore** Allows you to select which backup files to restore. No default selections are made and you must choose the files manually.

- **Type** Icons in this field indicate the type of backup. A backup device with a folder symbol behind it indicates a file backup. A backup device with a notebook symbol behind it indicates a transaction log.

- **Backup Date** Shows a date and time stamp for the backup entry.

- **Size** Shows the size of the backup.

- **File Logical Name** Shows the logical name of the file.

- **File Physical Name** Shows the complete file path for the backup entry.

Tip Select an entry and then click Properties to see a more detailed summary of the backup.

7. Select the backup files you want to restore. When you do this, Restore Database automatically selects related transaction logs that must be restored with this file.

8. Click the Options tab to configure options for the restore operation. The available options are the same as those discussed in the section of this chapter entitled "Restoring a Database from a Normal Backup."

9. When you're ready to start the restore operation, click OK. Restore Database shows the progress of each backup. You can stop the restore at any time by clicking Stop.

Restoring a Database from a Device

Restoring a database from a tape device or other backup device is different from a normal backup. This is primarily because you have to work with backup media (tapes) that may contain multiple backups, as well as multiple backup media sets (tape sets). Although you can use this procedure to restore a disk backup device, the normal backup procedure is especially designed for this purpose and is much easier to use.

To restore a database from a device, complete the following steps:

1. You must have exclusive access to the database. Close all active connections to the database or have users log off, or both.

2. In Enterprise Manager, select the server you want to work with and then, from the Tools menu, select the Restore Database option.

Figure 6-8. *When you restore from a device, you have additional options for selecting devices and accessing media.*

3. Use the Restore As Database drop-down list box to specify which database to restore and then select the From Device option button. This changes the Restore Database dialog box, as shown in Figure 6-8.

4. Click Select Devices to display the Choose Restore Devices dialog box. This dialog box is shown in Figure 6-9.

5. To restore from disk, select the Disk option button. Otherwise, select the Tape option button.

6. Click Add to choose the file or backup device for the restore operation. With multiple backup devices, repeat this step to select additional files or backup devices.

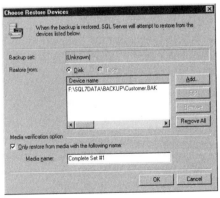

Figure 6-9. *In the Choose Restore Devices dialog box, select the restore devices and specify media criteria.*

7. When restoring from tape, you can ensure that you're backing up from the right tapes by selecting Only Restore From Media With The Following Name and then typing the name of the backup set in the Media Name field.

8. In the Backup Set field, type the number of the backup set you're restoring. If you're restoring the first backup set on the tape, type 1. For the second backup set type 2, and so on. To make sure that you've set the right backup, click View Contents and double-check the information provided.

9. To restore the backup set, select the Restore Backup Set option button, and then specify the type of backup you're restoring using these option buttons:

    - Database – Complete
    - Database – Differential
    - Transaction Log
    - File Or Filegroup

10. To read the backup information and add to backup history rather than perform a restore, select Read Backup Set Information And Add To Backup History.

11. Click the Options tab to configure options for the restore operation. The available options are almost the same as discussed in the "Restoring a Database from a Normal Backup" section of this chapter. You also have the option of reading from the tape to ensure that you have the right backup set. To do this, click Read From Media.

12. When you're ready to start the restore operation, click OK. Restore Database shows the progress of each backup. You can stop the restore at any time by clicking Stop.

Restoring a Database to a Different Location

When you restore a database to a different location, you're essentially copying the database from the backups. If you use this procedure to copy a database to a new location on the same computer, you create a copy of the database that can have separate files and a different database name. Restoring a database to a different location is exactly the same as outlined in the previous section. The key differences are as follows:

1. In the Restore As field, type a new name for the database. For example, if you're restoring the Customer database to a new location, name the copy Customer 2 or CustomerCopy.

2. When you access the Options tab, you override the default destination paths and enter new destination paths for all of the files you're restoring. Simply click in the Restore As or Move To Physical File Name field associated with a backup and then enter a new file path.

If you use this procedure to copy a database to a different computer, you can create a working copy of the database on another server. You don't need to create a new database or perform any preliminary work. The exception is that if you want to use backup devices on the destination server, you should set these up beforehand. Also, before you begin the restore, you should ensure that the destination computer is using the same code page, sort order, Unicode collation, and Unicode locale as the source server. If these configuration settings aren't identical, you won't be able to run the database on the destination server.

Creating a Standby Server

The notion of restoring a backup to a different computer can be extended to create a standby backup server that can be brought online if the primary server fails. To do that, complete the following steps:

1. Install SQL Server on a new server system using an identical configuration. This means that the destination server should use the same code page, sort order, Unicode collation, and Unicode locale as the source server.

2. Copy all of the databases on the primary server to this new system by specifying a different restore location in the Restore Database dialog box.

3. Maintain the copies of the databases by periodically applying the transaction log backups from the primary to the standby.

4. You may want to leave the standby server in Standby mode so that the database is read-only. This allows users to access the database but not make any changes.

If one or more databases on the primary server fail for any reason, you can make the corresponding databases on the standby available to users. However, before you do this, you should synchronize the primary and the standby by completing the following steps:

1. On the standby server, apply any transaction log backups created on the primary server that haven't been applied yet. You must apply these backups in the proper time sequence.

2. Create a backup of the active transaction log on the primary server and apply this backup to the database on the standby server. This ensures up-to-the-minute synchronization. Be sure to recover the database or specify that the database should be put in operational mode after this backup is applied.

 Tip If you need to make the standby appear to be the primary, you may need to take the primary off the network and rename it. Then rename the standby so that it appears to be the primary.

3. After you restore the primary server to working condition, any changes to the standby's databases need to be restored to the primary server. Otherwise, those changes are lost when you start using the primary server again.

Note Standby servers aren't the same as virtual servers created with the Microsoft SQL Server Failover Support. Standby servers store a second copy of databases on their hard drives. Virtual servers use a single copy of databases that is accessed from a shared disk.

Transact-SQL Restore

You can also restore databases using Transact-SQL. The commands you'll use are RESTORE DATABASE and RESTORE LOG. RESTORE DATABASE has dual syntax. Listing 6-6 shows the syntax and usage for a complete restore. The option WITH RECOVERY is the default mode.

Listing 6-6. RESTORE DATABASE Syntax and Usage for a Complete Restore

Syntax

```
RESTORE DATABASE {database_name | @database_name_var}
[FROM <backup_device> [,...n]]
[WITH
  [DBO_ONLY]
  [[,] FILE = file_number]
  [[,] MEDIANAME = {media_name | @media_name_variable}]
  [[,] MOVE 'logical_file_name' TO 'operating_system_file_name']
    [,...n]
  [[,] {NORECOVERY | RECOVERY | STANDBY = undo_file_name}]
  [[,] {NOUNLOAD | UNLOAD}]
  [[,] REPLACE]
  [[,] RESTART]
  [[,] STATS [= percentage]]
]
```

Usage

```
RESTORE DATABASE Customer
  FROM Customer_1
  WITH NORECOVERY

RESTORE DATABASE Customer
  FROM Customer_1
  WITH FILE = 2
```

Usage

```
RESTORE DATABASE Customer
  FROM TAPE = '\\.\tape0'
```

Usage

```
RESTORE DATABASE Customer
  FROM Customer_1
```

(continued)

Listing 6-6. *(continued)*

```
   WITH NORECOVERY,
      MOVE 'CustomerData1' TO 'F:\mssql7\data\NewCust.mdf',
      MOVE 'CustomerLog1' TO 'F:\mssql7\data\NewCust.ldf'
RESTORE LOG Customer
   FROM CustomerLog1
   WITH RECOVERY
```

With RESTORE DATABASE you can also restore files and filegroups. The related syntax and usage is shown in Listing 6-8.

Listing 6-8. RESTORE DATABASE Syntax and Usage for File and Filegroup Restore

Syntax

```
RESTORE DATABASE {database_name | @database_name_var}
   <file_or_filegroup> [,...n]
[FROM <backup_device> [,...n]]
[WITH
   [DBO_ONLY]
   [[,] FILE = file_number]
   [[,] MEDIANAME = {media_name | @media_name_variable}]
   [[,] NORECOVERY]
   [[,] {NOUNLOAD | UNLOAD}]
   [[,] REPLACE]
   [[,] RESTART]
   [[,] STATS [= percentage]]
]
```

Usage

```
RESTORE DATABASE Customer
   FILE = 'Customerdata_1',
   FILE = 'Customerdata_2',
   FILEGROUP = 'Primary'
   FROM Customer_1
   WITH NORECOVERY
RESTORE LOG Customer
   FROM CustomerLog1
```

Listing 6-9 shows how you can use RESTORE LOG.

Listing 6-9. RESTORE LOG Syntax and Usage

Syntax

```
RESTORE LOG {database_name | @database_name_var}
[FROM <backup_device> [,...n]]
[WITH
   [DBO_ONLY]
```

(continued)

Listing 6-9. *(continued)*

```
    [[,] FILE = file_number]
    [[,] MEDIANAME = {media_name | @media_name_variable}]
    [[,] {NORECOVERY | RECOVERY | STANDBY = undo_file_name}]
    [[,] {NOUNLOAD | UNLOAD}]
    [[,] RESTART]
    [[,] STATS [= percentage]]
    [[,] STOPAT = {date_time | @date_time_var}]
]
```

Usage

```
RESTORE DATABASE Customer
    FROM Customer_1, Customer_2
    WITH NORECOVERY
RESTORE LOG Customer
    FROM CustomerLog1
    WITH NORECOVERY
RESTORE LOG Customer
    FROM CustomerLog2
    WITH RECOVERY, STOPAT = 'Dec 11, 1999 3:30 PM'
```

Restoring the Master Database

The master database is the most important database on SQL Server. This database stores information about all the databases on the server, server configuration, server logons, and other important information. If master gets corrupted, operations on the server may grind to a halt, and you'll have to recover master using one of two techniques.

If you can start SQL Server, you can restore master from backup much like you would any other database. To do this, complete the following steps:

1. You can only back up master using a complete backup. As a result, no differential or transaction log backups will be available. This means you may not be able to restore master exactly as it was before the failure, and that you should normally use the Recovery Complete state of Leave Database Operation.

2. When you finish restoring the master database, you may need to manually apply any changes made since the last complete backup.

3. After you check the server and verify that everything is okay, make a complete backup of master.

If you can't start SQL Server and you know master is the cause of the problem, you can restore master by completing the following steps:

1. Run the REBUILD MASTER utility discussed in Chapter 2.

2. Once you rebuild master and get SQL Server back online, you can restore the last backup of master to return the server to its most current state.

3. Because Rebuild Master rebuilds the msdb and model databases, you may need to restore these databases from backup as well.

4. Re-create any backup devices, if necessary.

5. Reenter logons and other security settings, if necessary.

6. Restore distribution, if necessary.

7. Restore or attach user databases, if necessary.

8. Restore other server configuration settings, if necessary.

As you can see from the step-by-step procedure, restoring master can take a lot of time and work, which is why regularly backing up master is so important. When you finish recovering the server, be sure to make a complete backup of the master database.

Chapter 7

Importing and Exporting Data

In the old days, bulk copy program (BCP) was just about the only tool Microsoft SQL Server administrators could use to move data around. BCP is extremely fast and has a minimal overhead, but it also has a very rigid (and sometimes unforgiving) syntax. Then along came Data Transformation Services (DTS), an improved method for importing and exporting data between heterogeneous data sources. Whether you want to move data from a legacy system on a one-time basis or continually move data back and forth for data warehousing, DTS should be your first choice. With DTS, you don't need to struggle with BCP anymore. DTS is extremely flexible and surprisingly fast, and you can use the technology to copy and transform data to or from any OLE DB or ODBC data source.

Understanding DTS

DTS is designed to move data accurately and efficiently as well as to convert or transform data between heterogeneous data sources. You can use DTS when you want to

- Move data between heterogeneous systems, such as from Oracle to SQL Server or vice versa.

- Move data between SQL Servers with different code page, sort order, Unicode collation, and Unicode locale settings.

- Move data from Microsoft Access or Microsoft Excel to SQL Server or vice versa.

- Extract data; transform the data by performing column mappings, filling in missing values, and so on; and then import the data on the destination system.

Tip The DTS Wizard can run the import/export process between any of the available data sources. You don't have to set SQL Server as either the source or the destination. For example, you can use the DTS Wizard to copy data from a text file to an Excel spreadsheet.

The key components of DTS are database drivers, wizards, packages, and other support tools.

DTS and Database Drivers

OLE DB and ODBC drivers are a key part of DTS. Without these drivers, you couldn't communicate with other systems. SQL Server provides native OLE DB and ODBC drivers for

- SQL Server
- Oracle
- Microsoft OLAP Services
- Microsoft Internet Publishing
- Microsoft Access and Excel
- ASCII text files
- Other ODBC data sources

The text file driver is the catchall for import and export procedures. If you don't have a native driver for your legacy database and you can't use the generic ODBC driver, you can usually export the data to a text file and then import it into SQL Server. You can go from SQL Server to a legacy system using the same technique.

DTS Wizards

At the heart of DTS, you'll find a set of wizards—the DTS Import Wizard, the DTS Export Wizard, and the plain old DTS Wizard. All three wizards do the exact same thing and have the same interface. The key differences are in the first dialog box, which describes the DTS process you're starting, and in how you start the wizards. With those two exceptions, you use the wizards in exactly the same way.

DTS Packages

You use the DTS wizards to create DTS packages. Packages are simply sets of tasks for importing, transforming, and exporting data that can be reused or scheduled to run as often as needed. Packages can be placed in COM-structured system files, stored on the local server, or shared in the Microsoft Repository. You then run packages directly from Enterprise Manager or with the DTSWIZ command-line utility. Within DTS packages, you'll find

- **Connections**   Store information about the source or destination of data. In a connection, you specify the data provider to use (such as the Microsoft OLE DB Data Provider for SQL Server) the server to which you want to connect, the logon to use for the connection, and the database to work with for the import/export operation. In DTS Package Designer, you select connections using the Data menu.
- **Tasks**   Set the operations that need to be performed within the package. Tasks can consist of ActiveX scripts, SQL scripts, SQL queries, commands to transfer SQL Server objects, data-driven queries, bulk insert commands, and external processes to execute. You can even have DTS send e-mail when a package completes.

- **Workflow procedures** Set when and how a particular task should be executed, such as on completion, on failure, or on success. For example, you could schedule a task that sends e-mail on failure or on success.
- **Data transformation procedures** Set the step-by-step transformation process for the data. Also referred to as Data Pumps.

Other DTS Tools

Other tools available for DTS are

- **DTS Designer** A tool for developing and maintaining packages. With DTS Designer, you have complete control over every step of the transformation process. After you create a package in a DTS wizard, you can use DTS Designer to modify the package and to set additional tasks, workflow, and other procedures.
- **DTS COM objects** Extensible components for integrating DTS functionality into external applications and scripts. A powerful scripting utility is integrated into DTS Designer.

Creating Packages with the DTS Wizards

Creating a DTS package is one of the most complex tasks you'll perform as a database administrator. Although the DTS wizards, fortunately, are designed to help you build DTS packages without a lot of fuss, the process is still involved. To help reduce complexity, I'll divide the creation process into stages and then examine each stage individually. The stages used to create DTS packages are

- Stage 1: Source and Destination Configuration
- Stage 2: Copy, Query, or Transfer
- Stage 3: Formatting and Transformation
- Stage 4: Save, Schedule, and Replicate

To get started with DTS, start one of the DTS wizards and then click the Next button to advance to the Source selection page. You start the import and export wizards in Enterprise Manager by completing the following steps:

1. Start Enterprise Manager and then access the server you want to work with.
2. Right-click the Database Transformation Services folder and then select All Tasks. Then select either Import Data or Export Data.

You don't need to start Enterprise Manager to run the DTS Wizard. Instead, you start the DTS Wizard from the menu by completing the following steps:

1. Access the Microsoft SQL Server 7.0 menu by selecting Start and then Programs.
2. Select Import And Export Data.

You can also run the DTS Wizard from the command line by entering

dtswiz

If necessary, you can specify setup options through the command line as well. You can use these options to preconfigure information needed for the source or for the destination connection (but not both). To configure source information you use the /i switch and then enter additional options. For example, you could set the source server, user, password, and database using the following command:

dtswiz /i /szeta /usa /pgorilla /dcustomer

To configure the destination information, you use the /x switch and then enter additional options, such as

dtswiz /x /somega /usa /pgorilla /dcustomer2

The DTSWIZ options are shown in Listing 7-1, and they are defined in Table 7-1.

Listing 7-1. DTSWIZ Syntax

Syntax

```
dtswiz [/f<filename>] [{/i or /x}] [/s<servername>]
[/u<username>] [/p<password>] [/d<database>] [/r<providername>]
[/y] [/n] [/?]
```

Table 7-1. dtswiz Switches Defined

Switch	Definition
/i	Sets import operation and configures source with other options
/x	Sets export operation and configures destination with other options
/f<filename>	Sets the file name to output the package to
/s<servername>	Sets server name
/u<username>	Sets user name for SQL Login id
/p<password>	Sets password for SQL Login id
/d<database>	Sets database
/r<providername>	Sets data provider name
/y	Hides system databases
/n	Sets Windows NT authentication
/?	Displays syntax and usage help

Stage 1: Source and Destination Configuration

In Stage 1 you choose the source and destination for the import/export operation. If you started a DTS wizard and clicked Next, you should be on the Choose A Data Source page. At this stage, you should complete the following steps:

1. Use the Source drop-down list box to select the source for the import/export operation. SQL Server provides native drivers for OLE DB and ODBC data sources. Select the data source that matches the type of file, application, or database you want to use as the source. For example, if you're copying from an Excel 5.0 spreadsheet, you would choose Microsoft Excel 5.0.

2. Fill in any additional information required to establish a connection to the source. The source you select determines what additional information you need to supply. Then click Next.

3. Use the Destination drop-down list box to select the destination for the import/export operation.

4. Fill in any additional information required to establish a connection to the destination. As with the source, the destination you select determines what additional information you need to supply.

5. Click Next to go on to Stage 2: Copy, Query, or Transfer.

If choosing a source and destination were that easy, it would be a snap. But sometimes it isn't clear what additional information you need to provide. Basically, this is because there are several types of sources and destinations that you can select. These sources include

- File-based data connections
- DSN connections through ODBC drivers
- Server-based connections to databases other than SQL Server
- Server-based connections to SQL Server
- Text files

The sections that follow take a closer look at each of these connection categories.

File-Based Data Connections

File-based data connections are used with applications and databases that are file-based. You'll use this type of connection with dBase, Microsoft Access, Microsoft Excel, and Paradox. With file-based connections, you use a dialog box similar to the one shown in Figure 7-1. You need to enter the following information:

- **File Name**   The full file or Uniform Naming Convention (UNC) path to the source or destination file, such as //omega/data/excel/cust.xls

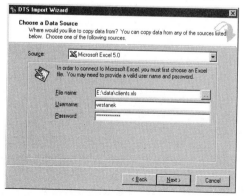

Figure 7-1. *With file-based connections, you need to specify the full path to the source/destination file and give authentication information, if necessary.*

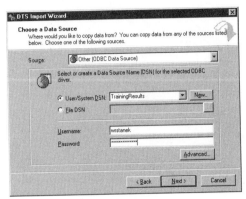

Figure 7-2. *With DSNs, you need to specify the type and name of the DSN to use as well as to supply authentication information.*

- **Username** A valid username for accessing the source or destination file
- **Password** A valid password for accessing the source or destination file

DSN Connections Through ODBC Drivers

Data source name (DSN) connections are used with most databases that use ODBC drivers. You'll use this type of connection with dBase VFP, Microsoft Fox Pro, Microsoft Visual Fox Pro, and other ODBC data sources. With DSN connections, you use a dialog box similar to the one shown in Figure 7-2. You configure the DSN connection by completing the following steps:

1. With user or system DSNs, select the User/System DSN option button and then use the drop-down list box to select any of the available DSNs. User and system DSNs must be on the local system.

2. With file DSNs, select the File DSN option button and then enter the full path to the DSN. File DSNs can be located anywhere on the network.

3. If you need to create a new user, system, or file DSN, click New and then use the Create New Data Source Wizard to create a new DSN. Afterward you may need to enter additional setup options.

4. Type a username and password that can be used to access the data source.

5. Click Advanced to set advanced options for the driver/provider you're working with.

Server-Based Connections to Databases Other than SQL Server

You use server-based data connections to connect to databases other than SQL Server. You'll use this type of connection with Oracle, Microsoft OLE DB Provider for Internet Publishing, and Microsoft OLE DB Provider for OLAP Services. You configure server-based connections much like a file-based connection, except you provide a *server* name instead of a *file* name.

Figure 7-3. *Connecting to SQL Server is different from other types of connections.*

Note With Oracle, the Oracle client and networking components must be installed on the system running SQL Server. If these components aren't installed, you won't be able to use the OLE DB provider.

Server-Based Connections to SQL Server

You can connect to SQL Server using an ODBC driver or an OLE DB provider. Either way, the options you have are the same as those shown in Figure 7-3, and you can configure the connection by completing the following steps:

1. Use the Server drop-down list box to select the SQL Server for the connection. The (local) option lets you choose the local system as the source or destination. Because remote procedure calls (RPCs) are used to determine available servers, the server you want to use may not be listed. In this case, click Refresh or just type in the server name.

2. Select an authentication method. Type a username and password, if necessary.

3. Use the Database drop-down list box to select a database to work with.

4. Click Advanced to set advanced options for the driver/provider you're working with.

Importing and Exporting Text Files

You can use text files as a data source or destination. When you do, you must provide additional information about the input or output formatting. In either case, the steps are similar, and I'll examine the import data source process in the following example:

1. From the DTS Wizard, choose the Text File option. Then enter the full filename or UNC path to the file you want to work with.

Tip If the file is in use, you'll get an error message. Click OK and then select the file again. (This forces the DTS Wizard to try to read the file again. Otherwise, you won't see the results of the formatting.)

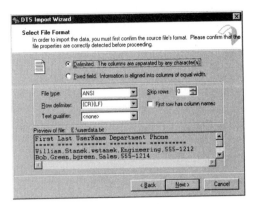

Figure 7-4. *After you enter the file information, you need to specify the file format.*

2. After you enter the text file information, click Next. You'll see the dialog box shown in Figure 7-4.

3. Specify how the file is delimited. If the file has fixed-width columns, select the Fixed Field option button. If the columns are delimited with commas, tabs, semicolons, or other unique characters, select the Delimited option button.

4. Select the file type using the File Type drop-down list box. The file must be formatted as ASCII, OEM (original equipment manufacturer), or Unicode. For importing, OEM normally refers to the native SQL Server format.

5. Specify the end-of-row delimiter using the Row Delimiter drop-down list box. The available options are

   - {CR} {LF} for carriage return and line feed
   - {CR} for carriage return only
   - {LF} for line feed only
   - Semicolon
   - Comma
   - Tab
   - Vertical bar for the | character
   - None

6. Use the Text Qualifier drop-down list box to specify the qualifier for text as either Double Quote ("), Single Quote ('), or None.

7. If the first row contains column headers, select First Row Has Column Names.

 Tip Column headers make it easier to import data. If the file doesn't contain column names, you may want to click the Cancel button, add the column names to the first line, and then restart the import/export procedure.

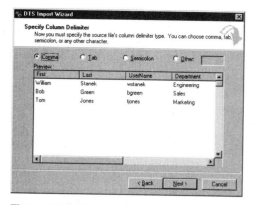

Figure 7-5. *Select a delimiter and then double-check the formatting of the file. If something is wrong, make changes before you proceed to the next stage.*

8. To skip rows at the beginning of a file, use the Skip Rows field to set the number of rows to skip.

Note If you indicated that the first row contains column names, the first row is read and the specified number of rows is skipped.

9. Click Next.

10. If the file is delimited, the next screen allows you to select the delimiter as either a comma, a tab, a semicolon, or another character. Use the option buttons provided to make your selection. If you choose Other, enter the characters that form the delimiter as well. As shown in Figure 7-5, the Preview area shows the data format for the options you've chosen in this dialog box and the previous dialog box.

Tip If you notice data elements out of place, you can click the Back button to reconfigure the previous dialog box. You may also need to modify the source file. In this case, click the Cancel button, modify the file, and then restart the DTS Wizard.

11. If you selected fixed-width, you'll need to tell the DTS Wizard where columns start and end. Vertical lines indicate the start and end of columns. Add column markers by clicking in the Preview area to create a column marker. Remove column markers by double-clicking them. Move column markers by clicking them and dragging them to a new position.

12. Click Next when you're ready to select the destination for the import/export operation. After selecting the destination, you'll go on to Stage 2.

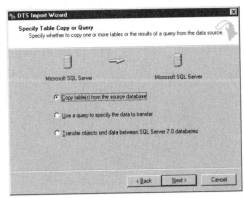

Figure 7-6. *Determine whether to copy tables, build a query, or transfer objects.*

Stage 2: Copy, Query, or Transfer

With most import or export procedures, the next stage involves specifying tables to copy, building a query, or selecting objects to transfer. You'll select the operation using the dialog box shown in Figure 7-6, and then you'll proceed as described in the sections that follow.

Specifying Tables to Copy

If you want to copy tables to the destination, you'll need to select which tables you want to copy. When a text file is the data source, selecting which table to use is easy—there's only one table available. With other data sources, you'll need to select the tables you want to work with. In either case, the dialog box you use is the one shown in Figure 7-7.

When selecting tables, complete the following steps:

1. In the Specify Table Copy Or Query dialog box, select the Copy Table(s) From The Source Database option button and then click Next.

2. Select a table by clicking its entry and then preview the data the table contains by clicking Preview.

3. When you find a table you want to copy, place a check in the related Source Table column.

4. By default, the destination name of the table is set to be the same as the source table name. If you want to change the table name, edit the corresponding value in the Destination Table column.

5. If you want to manipulate the row values in a table, select it and then click the corresponding button in the Transform column. Transforming row values is covered in Stage 3.

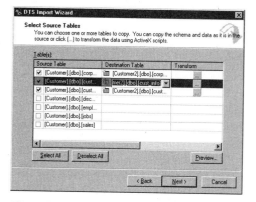

Figure 7-7. *Specifying which tables you want to copy.*

Building a Query

Another way to select data for exporting is to build a query and execute it against the source file, spreadsheet, or database. Regardless of the type of data source, you build the query in the same way by completing the following steps:

1. In the Specify Table Copy Or Query dialog box, select the Use a Query To Specify The Data To Transfer option button and then click Next.

2. In the Type SQL Query dialog box you can

   * Type a query directly in the text box provided and then parse it to check for accuracy using the Parse button.

   * Click Query Builder to build a query using the Query Builder utility.

Tip You could also create a query in your favorite query builder, then paste the results into the Type SQL Query dialog box.

3. Query Builder provides the easiest alternative, so click Query Builder. This displays the Select Columns dialog box shown in Figure 7-8.

4. Select columns for the query using the following techniques:

   * **Select all the columns in a table** Click the table name in the Source Tables list box and then choose the add button (>).

   * **Add individual columns** Click the plus sign (+) next to a table name in the Source Tables list box. This displays the columns in the table. Now select a column by clicking on it and then choose the add button (>).

   * **Remove a column from the Selected Columns list box** Click on it and then choose the remove button (<).

Figure 7-8. *Select the columns you want to query.*

- **Remove all selected columns from the Selected Columns list box** Click the remove all button (<<).
- **Change the order of selected columns** Click the column you want to reorder and then use the Move Up or Move Down button to change the column order.

5. Click Next when you're ready to continue. You can now select the sort order for columns using the dialog box shown in Figure 7-9. The buttons provided are used as follows:

- > Add the selected column.
- >> Add all remaining columns using their current order.
- < Remove a column from the Sorting Order list box
- << Remove all columns from the Sorting Order list box.
- **Move Up** Change the order of a selected column by moving it up the list.

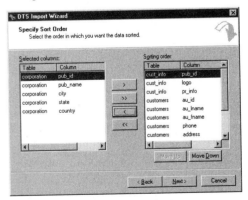

Figure 7-9. *Set the sort order for the data.*

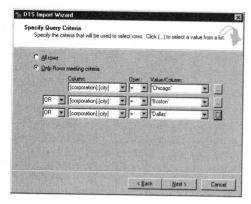

Figure 7-10. *Select the columns you want to work with and the values to search for. Use the And/Or operation to determine how to apply multiple query parameters. Use the build button (...) to the right of the query criteria to see the available values for the selected column.*

- **Move Down** Change the order of a selected column by moving it down the list.

6. Set the query criteria. To choose all rows in the selection, select the All Rows option button. To set specific query criteria, select the Only Rows Meeting Criteria option button and then use the fields provided to set the query criteria. Figure 7-10 shows an example.

7. The result of the Query Builder procedure is a complete SQL statement that you can use to select data for exporting.

8. Click the Parse button to ensure that the query runs. If necessary, rebuild the *query* or *remove* statements causing errors.

9. Click Next to continue. The next dialog box you'll see is the Select Source Table(s) dialog box discussed in the section of this chapter entitled "Specifying Tables to Copy."

10. The default table name is Results. Click in the Destination Table column to set a new name for the destination table.

11. Click the button in the Transform column to manipulate the data before writing it to the destination.

Selecting Objects to Transfer

The only time you can select objects to transfer is when copying between SQL Server databases. You select objects to transfer by completing the following steps:

1. In the Specify Table Copy Or Query dialog box, select the Transfer Objects And Data Between SQL Server 7.0 Databases option button and then click Next. This displays the Select Objects To Transfer dialog box shown in Figure 7-11.

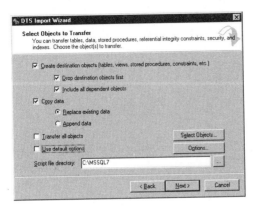

Figure 7-11. *Select the objects you want to transfer.*

2. The options of the Select Objects To Transfer dialog box are used as follows:

- **Create Destination Objects** When selected, creates objects at the destination (if necessary) and allows you to determine what happens to existing objects as well as whether dependent objects are transferred.

- **Drop Destination Objects First** Drops existing objects from the destination database.

- **Include All Dependent Objects** Ensures that dependent objects are transferred even if they aren't explicitly selected.

- **Copy Data** When selected, copies data along with the source objects. When cleared, only the objects are created at the destination.

- **Replace Existing Data** If you choose to copy data, you can replace all existing data for the selected objects by selecting this option button.

- **Append Data** If you choose to copy data, you can add data from the source objects to the current data in the destination database by selecting this option.

- **Transfer All Objects** When selected, transfers all objects from the source to the destination. Cancel this option and then click Select Objects to select individual objects.

- **Use Default Options** Select this option to use the default transfer options. To configure the options manually, clear this check box and then click Options.

- **Script File Directory** Sets the directory for scripts created when you select the Generate Scripts In Unicode option in the Advanced Options dialog box.

3. Click Next to continue Stage 4, skipping Stage 3.

Stage 3: Formatting and Transformation

Transformation is the process of manipulating the source data and formatting it for the chosen destination. The way you transform and format data depends on the destination you've chosen. With most types of files, databases, and spreadsheets, you go through a column mapping and transformation process. But if you've chosen a text file as the destination, you must also specify the format of the output file. Because the formatting options are essentially the same as those used for importing, I won't cover them here and will instead refer you to the "Importing and Exporting Text Files" section of this chapter.

Unless you specify otherwise, the DTS Wizard sets default mapping for all selected tables. This default mapping

- Specifies that every column in the source table is copied
- Maps to the original column name, data type, nullability, size, precision, and scale to the destination table
- Appends the source data to the destination table and creates the destination table if it doesn't exist

You can override the default mappings by completing the following steps:

1. The Select Source Tables dialog box lists the results of your query or all of the available tables in the source database, spreadsheet, or file that you've selected. If you've selected a particular table, you'll find a button in the Transform column. Click this button to open the Column Mappings And Transformations dialog box shown in Figure 7-12.

2. Click the Column Mappings tab and then set the general transfer options as follows:

- **Create Destination Table** Creates the destination table before copying source data. If the destination table exists, you must

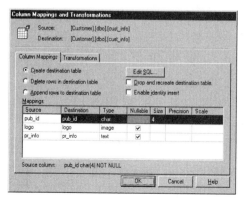

Figure 7-12. *Use the Column Mappings tab to map individual values in the selected table's columns.*

select Drop And Recreate Destination Table. Otherwise, an error will occur.

- **Delete Rows In Destination Table**   Deletes all rows in the destination table before copying the source data. Indexes and constraints on the destination table remain.

- **Append Rows To Destination Table**   Inserts the source data into the destination table rather than overwriting existing data. This option doesn't affect existing data, indexes, or constraints in the destination table.

Note   Rows may not necessarily be appended to the end of the destination table. To determine where rows are inserted, use a clustered index on the destination table.

- **Edit SQL**   Choose this button to modify the default *Create Table* statement generated by the DTS wizard.

- **Drop And Recreate Destination Table**   Drops and re-creates the destination table before attempting to copy data into it, which permanently deletes all existing data and indexes.

Tip   If the table exists at the destination, you must drop and re-create it to map new column values to the destination table. Otherwise, you can only map source columns to different destination columns.

- **Enable Identity Insert**   Allows explicit values to be inserted into the identity column of a table. This option is only available on SQL Server and only if an identity column is detected.

3. After you set the general transfer options, use the fields in the Mappings list box to determine how values are mapped from the source to the destination. The fields of this list box are all set to default values based on the source column. If you want to override these values for a new table or if you're dropping and recreating an existing table, you can modify these values. The Mapping fields are used as follows:

- **Source**   Sets the source column to map to a destination column. If you choose <ignore>, the source data isn't copied. Entering <ignore> can result in an error if there is no DEFAULT value and the destination is defined as NOT NULL.

- **Destination**   Click in this column and then select an existing column name or type a new column name for the destination table. Use the <ignore> option if the destination column should not be created.

Note   If the destination column already exists and you choose <ignore>, the source data isn't copied into this column.

- **Type**   Select a data type for the Destination column. If you select a different data type than the source column, the data is converted to the new data type during the transfer.

Note   Make sure you select a valid conversion option. The DTS Wizard won't let you truncate data, and if you try to, an error occurs.

- **Nullable**   Select this check box if the destination allows null values.
- **Size**   Sets the length of the destination column. This value is only applicable for the char, varchar, nchar, nvarchar, binary, and varbinary data types.

Note   Setting the size smaller than the length of the source data can result in data truncation. If this happens, the DTS Wizard will generate an error and won't complete the transfer.

- **Precision**   Sets the maximum number of decimal digits, including decimal places. For decimal and numeric data types only.
- **Scale**   Sets the maximum number of digits to the right of the decimal point. This value must be less than or equal to Precision and applies to decimal and numeric data types only.

4. Once you complete the mappings, you can fine-tune the transformation. Click the Transformation tab. As shown in Figure 7-13, the DTS Wizard now lets you

- Copy source columns directly to destination columns and set advanced flags for the transformation.
- Transform information as it's copied to the destination using a script.

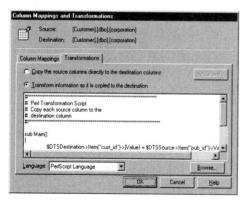

Figure 7-13. *With the Transformations tab you can set transformation options or use a script for the transformation.*

5. To copy source columns directly, select the Copy The Source Columns Directly To The Destination Columns option button. By default, all possible conversions are allowed. If you want to limit the conversions to exact matches, click the Advanced button and then select Require Exact Match Between Source And Destination. If you want to configure the conversion, click the Advanced button, select the Custom Transformation Flags option button, and then configure the conversion options.

6. To use a script for the transformation, select Transform Information As It Is Copied To The Destination. Next, use the Language drop-down list box to select your preferred scripting language. You can choose Microsoft JScript, Microsoft VBScript, PerlScript, and related encoding or an XML Script Engine. When you make a selection, the default script is converted to your chosen scripting language. You can then add to the default script as necessary or click the button to find and import a script you've created in another application.

7. Click OK and then repeat this process for other tables you want to transform.

8. When you're ready to continue, click Next.

Stage 4: Save, Schedule, and Replicate

The end of the road is in sight, really! At this stage, you specify when to use the package you've created and whether the package should be saved for future use. Now you should be on the Save, Schedule And Replicate Package dialog box shown in Figure 7-14. To use this dialog box, complete the following steps:

1. Use the options under the When heading to specify when the DTS package is executed. You can use any combination of the available options, including

   - **Run Immediately** Run the package now.

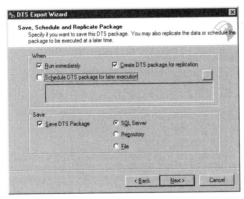

Figure 7-14. *Now that you've configured the package, you can run it and save it for future use.*

- **Create DTS Package For Replication**   Set up replication between the source and destination using the package you just created.

- **Schedule The DTS Package For Later Execution**   Set up a schedule for when this package should run.

2. Use the options under the Save heading to save the package for future use. If you want to save the package for use later, you should select the Save DTS Package check box and then specify where the package should be saved. The available locations are

   - **SQL Server**   Saves as a local package
   - **Repository**   Saves to the Microsoft Repository where the package can be shared with other servers
   - **File**   Saves as a file

3. When you're finished configuring run and save options, click Next.

4. If you've opted to save the package, the next dialog box lets you set the save location (see Figure 7-15). The options are slightly different depending on the save location you previously selected.

5. Type a name and description of the package using the Name and Description fields, respectively. The name should be unique for the target location.

6. To password-protect the package and prevent unauthorized users from working with it, type an owner password and a user password in the fields provided. Anyone with the owner password can design, schedule, and execute the package. Anyone with the user password can only schedule or execute the package.

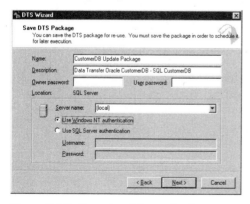

Figure 7-15. *Provide additional information needed to save the package to a local or remote system.*

7. If you want to copy the package to the local package or remote repository area of a remote server, select the destination server. Use the Server Name drop-down list box or type the server name directly. Select an authentication mode and type a username and password as needed.

8. Click Next and then Finish. If you've elected to run the package immediately, SQL Server runs the package. As each step is completed (or fails), the status is updated. If an error occurs, you can double-click its entry to view a detailed description of the error. Errors may halt execution of the package and if they do, you'll need to redesign the package using DTS Designer or re-create the package using one of the DTS wizards.

Working with DTS Packages

SQL Server stores DTS packages as local packages, repository packages, and file-based packages. Packages are managed through Enterprise Manager or through the DTSRUN command-line utility.

Examining, Running, and Scheduling Packages

In Enterprise Manager you can examine, run, or schedule packages you've created by completing the following steps:

1. Start Enterprise Manager and then access the server you want to work with.

2. Click the plus sign (+) next to the server's Data Transformation Services folder.

3. You can now perform the tasks described below.

- **View local packages**   To view local packages on the selected server, click the Local Packages entry in the left pane. As shown in Figure 7-16, local packages are then listed in the right pane.

- **View repository packages**   To view packages in the server's repository, click the Repository Packages entry in the left pane.

- **View metadata**   To access the repository's metadata, click the Metadata entry in the left pane.

- **Run a package**   To run a local or repository package, right-click its entry in the right pane and select Execute Package from the shortcut menu.

- **Schedule a package to run**   To schedule a local or repository package, right-click it and select Schedule Package from the shortcut menu. Then configure the package as a recurring job using the Edit Recurring Job dialog box. Scheduling is covered in Chapter 12, "Database Automation and Maintenance."

- **Modify a package's design**   To modify a package's design, right-click it and select Design Package from the shortcut menu. This starts the DTS Designer.

Figure 7-16. *Packages are accessed through the Data Transformation Services folder.*

- **View or modify file packages** To view or modify packages stored in files, right-click on the Data Transformation Services folder, select All Tasks on the shortcut menu, then click Open Package. Use the Select File dialog box to select the package.

Managing Packages from the Command Line

To manage packages from the command line, you can use DTSRUN. This utility works with all package types. By default, DTSRUN executes the specified package, but you can also use the utility to delete or overwrite packages. You delete local or repository packages to drop them from SQL Server. You overwrite file-based packages to empty their associated file. The syntax and usage for DTSRUN is shown as Listing 7-2.

Listing 7-2. DTSRUN Syntax and Usage

Syntax

```
dtsrun /~S ServerName [{/~U UserName] [/~P Password] or [/E]}]
/~N PackageName [/~M PackagePassword] [/~G PackageGuidString]
[/~V PackageVersionGuidString] [/~F StructuredStorageUNCfilename]
[/~R RepositoryDatabaseName]
```

By default, DTSRUN executes the package. You can change this behavior with these options:

```
/!X <Do not execute; retrieve Package to /F filename>
/!D <Do not execute; drop package from SQL Server>
/!Y <Do not execute; output encrypted command-line>
/!C <Copies command-line to Windows clipboard (may be used with /
!Y and /!X)>
```

Usage

```
dtsrun /~S"zeta" /~U"sa" /~P"gorilla" /~N"DTS Customer"
```

 Note   The tilde (~) is optional. If you use the tilde, the parameter is specified as hexidecimal text with an encrypted value.

Understanding BCP

The bulk copy program (BCP) offers a command-line alternative to Data Transformation Services. The Transact-SQL counterpart to BCP import is BULK INSERT. You'll find that BULK INSERT has a similar syntax when used for importing data. To learn more about BCP, let's examine

- Basics
- Syntax
- Permissions
- Modes
- Importing data
- Exporting data

BCP Basics

Although BCP has been around for some time, it may remain a favorite of database administrators for a while longer because of its great performance and minimal overhead. You'll find that import and export processes tend to be very fast and that BCP uses very little memory to operate. BCP doesn't have a graphical user interface (GUI) and is best used in two situations:

- To import data from a text file to a single SQL Server table or view
- To export data to a text file from a single SQL Server table or view

When transferring data to or from SQL Server, BCP uses ODBC. This is a change from previous versions that communicated with SQL Server through the DB-Library.

 Tip   With ODBC datetime, smalldatetime and money datatypes are treated differently than with DB-Library. You'll find that the datetime format is now yyyy-mm-dd hh:mm:ss rather than mmm dd yyy hh:mm (AM/PM) and the money format now has no commas with four digits after the decimal rather than commas and two digits after the decimal.

Note When importing with BCP, columns with computed values and timestamps are ignored. SQL Server can automatically assign values. To do this, use a format file to specify that the computed values or timestamp columns in the table should be skipped; SQL Server then automatically assigns values for the column. During export, computed values and timestamps are handled like other values.

BCP Syntax

Before exploring how to use BCP, let's look at the command syntax, which, as you can see from Listing 7-3, is fairly extensive. BCP switches are case and order sensitive. You must use them in the exact manner expected. If you don't, you'll have problems.

Listing 7-3. BCP Syntax and Usage

Syntax

```
bcp {[[dbname.][owner].]{tablename | viewname } "query"} {in |
out | queryout | format} datafile [switch1 [parameter1]] [switch2
[parameter2]]
[switchN [parameterN]]
```

Usage

```
bcp pubs..customer out customers.txt -c -U sa -P"guerilla"
bcp pubs..customer in customers.txt -f customers.fmt -U sa
-P"guerilla"
```

Table 7-2 provides a summary of key BCP parameters.

Table 7-2. Key Parameters Used with BCP

Parameter	Description
dbname	The name of the database. This parameter is optional and if it's not supplied, the user's default database is used.
owner	The owner of the table or view being used. Use the .. syntax for a general owner, such as pubs..authors instead of pubs.dbo.authors.
tablename	The name of the table or view to access. Use the # or ## syntax to copy a temporary table.
viewname	The name of the destination view when copying data into SQL Server; the source view when copying data from SQL Server.
query	A Transact-SQL statement that generates a result set. Using double quotation marks and specifying the queryout parameter are mandatory with this option.
in	Specifies an import process.

(continued)

Table 7-2. *(continued)*

Parameter	Description
out	Specifies an export process.
format	Sets the creation of a format file. You must set the name of the format file with the -f switch and also specify the format for this file with -n, -c, -w, or -6.
queryout	Must be used when exporting output from an SQL query or stored procedure.
datafile	The name of the file for importing or the name of the file to create when exporting. This can include the full file path.

BCP also supports a wide variety of switches. These switches and their associated parameters are summarized in Table 7-3.

Table 7-3. Switches Used with BCP

Switch	Description
-6	Uses datatypes as per DB-Library and SQL Server 6.0 rather than ODBC and SQL Server 7.0.
-a packetsize	Sets the number of bytes in a network packet. Default is 4096 on Windows NT and 512 for MS-DOS. The valid range is 512 to 65,535 bytes.
-b batchsize	The number of rows to transfer in the batch. Each batch is copied to the server as one transaction. By default all rows are copied in a single batch. Do not use with the -h ROWS_PER_BATCH option.
-c	Character data mode (ASCII text) for transfers to and from non-SQL Server products.
-C codepage	Code page being used by the import file. Only relevant when the data contains *char*, *varchar*, or *text* columns with character values greater than 127 or less than 32. Use the code page value ACP with ANSI ISO 1252 data, RAW when no conversion should occur, OEM to use the client's default code page, or type a specific code page value, such as 850.
-e errfile	Stores error messages in the specified error file.
-E	Uses identify values. Otherwise, identity values are ignored and automatically assigned new ones.
-F firstrow	Sets the number of the first row to use.
-f formatfile	Sets the name and path to a BCP format file. The default file name is BCP.FMT.
-h "load hints"	Used to set load hints: ROWS_PER_BATCH, KILOBYTES_PER_BATCH, TABLOCK, CHECK_CONSTRAINTS, and ORDER.
-i inputfile	Sets the name of a response file, containing responses to the command prompt questions for each field when performing a bulk copy using interactive mode.

(continued)

Table 7-3. (*continued*)

Switch	Description
-k	Preserves null values.
-L lastrow	Sets the last row to use.
-m maxerrors	Sets the maximum number of errors that can occur before terminating BCP. The default is 10.
-N	Sets native export for noncharacter data and Unicode character export for character data.
-n	Sets native data mode, which is SQL Server–specific.
-o outfile	Sets file to redirect output of BCP during unattended operation.
-P password	Password to use to log on.
-q	Uses quoted identifiers.
-R	Enables regional format copy for currency, date, and time data.
-r rowterminator	Sets the row terminator.
-S servername	Sets the SQL Server name.
-t fieldterminator	Sets the field terminator.
-T	Uses a trusted connection.
-U username	Sets the username for logon.
-v	Displays the BCP version.
-w	Sets wide character (Unicode) mode.

BCP Permissions and Modes

Although any user can run BCP, only users with appropriate permissions can access SQL Server and the specified database objects. When you run BCP, you can set logon information using the -U and -P switches. For unattended operations, using these switches is essential to ensure that permissions are granted appropriately. To import data into a table, the user needs INSERT permission on the target table. To export data from a table, the user needs SELECT permission for the source table.

BCP can use three different modes:

- **Character mode**   Used when you want to import or export data as ASCII text. The switch to set this mode is -c.

- **Native mode**   Used when you want to import or export data in native format. The switch to set this mode is -n or -N.

- **Wide mode**   Used when you want to import or export data as Unicode text. The switch to set this mode is -w.

The character and wide modes are best when copying to a non-SQL Server product. Use native mode when you're copying data between SQL Server tables. These modes all have their strengths and weaknesses.

With character or wide mode files, you can view the contents and make sure that you have the right data set, but for imports you must also tell SQL Server how this data is formatted. You can do this through interactive prompts or by using a format file containing the responses to these prompts. With native mode, on the other hand, there's also a trade-off. You can't view the contents of native data files, but you don't have to specify data formatting information when importing files either.

Importing Data with BCP

With BCP you can import data in two ways. You can start an interactive session or you can set the necessary responses in a format file. The following example shows how you could start an interactive import.

```
bcp pubs..customer in customers.txt -c
```

To specify a format file, you use the -f flag, such as

```
bcp pubs..customer in customers.txt -w -f customers.fmt
```

In an interactive session, BCP prompts you for information needed to complete the import or export process. BCP starts an interactive session when either of the following situations occur:

- You import an ASCII or Unicode file without using a format file.
- You export without setting the mode.

The interactive session allows you to customize the BCP process much as you do with a format file. In fact, before you try to create a format file, you should run BCP in interactive mode and then choose to have BCP create the necessary format file for you. This operation will give you a good idea of how to configure the format file.

For each column in a table you're importing, you'll see the following prompts during an interactive session:

```
Enter the file storage type of field [char]:
Enter prefix-length of field [0]:
Enter length of field [5]:
Enter field terminator [none]:
```

 Tip To skip a column in an import file, type **0** for the prefix length, **0** for the field length, and **none** for the terminator type. You can't skip a column when exporting data.

These prompts ask you to type various kinds of information, and in every case the default value for the current column is shown in brackets. At the end of the interactive session, you'll be asked if you want to save your responses in a

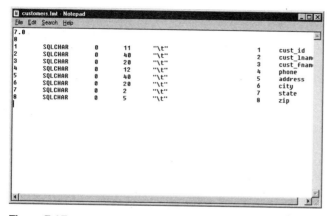

Figure 7-17. *Format files are written in ASCII text and can be viewed in Notepad or any other text editor.*

format file. If you answer Y, you can type the name of the format file when prompted, such as

```
Do you want to save this format information in a file? [Y/N]
Host filename [bcp.fmt]: customers.fmt
```

You can then use the format file for other BCP sessions by setting the -f switch as specified earlier. Figure 7-17 shows a sample format file. Because the format file has a rigid syntax that must be followed, I recommend creating a sample file to get started. Each line in the file contains information fields that determine how data should be imported. These lines tell you the following information:

- The first line sets the version of BCP used. Here the version is 7.0.

- The second line sets the number of columns in the table you're importing. In the example the table contains eight columns.

- Subsequent lines set the formatting of each column in the table from the first column to the last column.

The lines defining table columns are broken down into fields with each field setting a different input parameter. Normally, these fields are separated with spaces. The number of spaces doesn't really matter—provided there is at least one space. BCP treats one or more spaces as a field separator. File format fields operate in the following manner:

- Field 1 sets the column number you're describing from the data file.

- Field 2 sets the file storage type, which is simply the datatype of the column.

- Field 3 sets the prefix length for compacted data. A value of zero specifies that no prefix is used.

- Field 4 sets the field length, which is the number of bytes required to store the datatype. Use the default value provided whenever possible.

- Field 5 sets the field terminator. By default, BCP separates all fields but the last one with tabs (\t) and separates the last field with a carriage return and line field (\r\n).

- Field 6 sets the table column number in the database. For example, a value of 1 says the column corresponds to the first column in the database.

- Field 7 sets the table column name.

Exporting Data with BCP

When you export data, BCP creates a data file using the name you specify. With non-native files (ASCII and Unicode text), the columns in this file are separated with tabs by default, with the last column having a carriage return and line feed. You specify a tab as a terminator with \t, and carriage return and line feed with \r\n. In a format file, a tab can be an actual tab character or a series of five or more spaces.

As with importing data, you can handle data export interactively. For example, if you start an export session without specifying appropriate logon information, you're prompted for this information. In the following example you export a table to a file called customers.txt and use semicolons as the delimiter.

```
bcp pubs..customer out customers.txt -c -t;
```

BCP Scripts

A BCP script is simply a batch file or a Microsoft Windows Script Host file containing BCP commands. Listing 7-4 shows examples of how you could run BCP using various scripting options. If you don't know how to use batch files or Windows Script Host, a great resource is the *Windows NT Scripting Administrator's Guide.*

Listing 7-4. Using BCP in a Script

sched-export.bat

```
@echo off
@if not "%OS%"=="Windows_NT" goto :EXIT
bcp pubs..customer out customers.txt -c -t, -Usa -P"guerilla"
:EXIT
```

sched-export.vbs

```
'Nightly Bulk Copy export for the customers table
'Writes output to cust.txt and errors to err.txt
Set ws = WScript.CreateObject("WScript.Shell")
ret = ws.Run("bcp pubs..customers out cust.txt -c -t, -Usa
-Pguerilla -eerr.txt",0,"TRUE")
```

(continued)

Listing 7-4. *(continued)*
sched-export.js

```
\\Nightly Bulk Copy export for the customers table
\\Writes output to cust.txt and errors to err.txt
var ws = WScript.CreateObject("WScript.Shell");
ret = ws.Run("bcp pubs..customers out cust.txt -c -t, -Usa
-Pguerilla -eerr.txt",0,"TRUE")
```

After you create a script file for the BCP command, you can schedule it as a task to run on your system. To schedule these scripts to run every night at midnight, you could use the following commands.

```
AT 00:00 /every:M,T,W,Th,F,S,Su " sched-export.bat"
AT 00:00 /every:M,T,W,Th,F,S,Su "cscript //B sched-export.js"
AT 00:00 /every:M,T,W,Th,F,S,Su "cscript //B sched-export.vbs"
```

More Info For more information on scheduling tasks, try *Microsoft* *Windows NT Server 4.0 Administrator's Pocket Consultant* or *Microsoft Windows 2000 Administrator's Pocket Consultant.*

Bulk Insert

A Transact-SQL command for importing data into a database is BULK INSERT. You can use BULK INSERT in much the same way as you do BCP. In fact, most of the parameters for BULK INSERT are the same as those used with BCP—they just have a different syntax. This syntax is shown as Listing 7-5.

Listing 7-5. BULK INSERT Syntax and Usage

Syntax

```
BULK INSERT [['dbname'.]['owner'].]{'tablename' FROM datafile}
[WITH
(
[ BATCHSIZE [= batch_size]]
[[,] CHECK_CONSTRAINTS]
[[,] CODEPAGE [= 'ACP' | 'OEM' | 'RAW' | 'code_page']]
[[,] DATAFILETYPE [=
{'char' | 'native'| 'widechar' | 'widenative'}]]
[[,] FIELDTERMINATOR [= 'field_terminator']]
[[,] FIRSTROW [= first_row]]
[[,] FORMATFILE [= 'format_file_path']]
[[,] KEEPIDENTITY]
[[,] KEEPNULLS]
[[,] KILOBYTES_PER_BATCH [= kilobytes_per_batch]]
```

(continued)

Listing 7-5. *(continued)*

```
[[,] LASTROW [= last_row]]
[[,] MAXERRORS [= max_errors]]
[[,] ORDER ({column [ASC | DESC]} [,...n])]
[[,] ROWS_PER_BATCH [= rows_per_batch]]
[[,] ROWTERMINATOR [= 'row_terminator']]
[[,] TABLOCK]
)
]
```

Usage

```
BULK INSERT pubs..customers FROM 'c:\data\customer.txt'

BULK INSERT pubs..customers FROM 'c:\cust.txt' with
 (DATAFILETYPE = 'char',
  FORMATFILE='c:\cust.fmt')
```

In order to use BULK INSERT, you must set the database properties option Select Into/Bulk Copy. To set this option, open the Properties dialog box for the database you want to work with, choose the Options tab, and then select the Select Into/Bulk Copy check box.

Chapter 8
Distributed Data and Remote Servers

Networking environments are becoming more and more complex. Organizations that, in the past, may have had a single Microsoft SQL Server are now finding that they need additional servers or that they need to integrate their existing server with other heterogeneous data sources. SQL Server 7.0 provides several features for integrating SQL Server databases with other SQL Server databases and with other data sources, including distributed data, remote servers, and replication. This chapter focuses on remote servers and distributed data. Replication is covered in the next chapter.

Remote servers are a legacy feature of SQL Server that allows you to connect SQL Servers and execute stored procedures on these servers. Distributed data, on the other hand, is a new feature for SQL Server 7.0 that includes support for distributed queries, distributed transactions, and remote stored procedure execution. These distributed data features are handled through linked servers, which can be SQL Servers or non-SQL Servers.

Working with Remote Servers

Previous versions of SQL Server supported remote server configurations, and SQL Server 7.0 supports this feature for backward compatibility only. Through a remote server, a client connected to one server can run a stored procedure on another server without having to establish another connection. The originating server handles the client's request and passes it to the remote server. The remote server then executes the referenced stored procedure and returns any results to the originating server, which in turn passes those results to the client.

Remote server connections can only be established with other SQL Servers. You can't connect to other database servers, such as Oracle. If you have existing applications that use remote server connections, you can configure remote servers and use these remote servers as you have with previous versions of SQL Server. However, if you're creating new applications, you should use the new distributed data features of SQL Server 7.0. You'll find that these new features are much more versatile.

Note Previous versions of SQL Server used remote servers for replication. SQL Server 7.0 doesn't handle replication in this way. Instead, it uses linked servers to set up replication.

Setting Up Remote Servers in Enterprise Manager

Remote servers are configured in pairs. You must make each server recognize the other as a remote server. You must also explicitly permit remote connections to each server in the pair. After you've configured the necessary connections, users logging on to either server in the pair can execute stored procedures remotely.

Tip If you have an existing application that uses remote servers, you may need to check the data services gateway setup. The only Open Data Services gateways supported by SQL Server 7.0 are those that ship with SQL Server 7.0. If you aren't using this version, you'll need to recompile the Open Data Services with the header (SRV.H) and library (OPENDS60.LIB) files that ship with SQL Server 7.0. Trying to call SQL Server 7.0 with an older version of the gateway usually results in one of the following errors:

Error 7399, Level 16, State 1 OLE DB provider 'SQLOLEDB' reported an error. A provider-specific error occurred.

Error 7304, Level 16, State 1 Could not create a new session on OLE DB provider 'SQLOLEDB'. Reported an error.

Error 7303, Level 16, State 1 Unable to initialize data source object of OLE DB provider 'SQLOLEDB'.

You must configure each server in the pair to accept remote connections. You configure this SQL Server property setting as discussed in the section of Chapter 2 titled "Configuring Remote Server Connections." Don't forget to stop and start the SQL Server service on each server.

Next, you must configure each server in the pair to accept the other as a remote server. To do this, complete the following steps:

1. Start Enterprise Manager and then access the first server in the pair.
2. Click the plus sign (+) next to the server's Security folder.
3. Right-click the Remote Servers entry and, from the shortcut menu, choose New Remote Server. This opens the dialog box shown in Figure 8-1.
4. In the Name field, type the name of the second server in the pair.
5. To enable the remote server to execute stored procedures on the current server using remote procedure calls, select the RPC check box.

6. Next, determine how logins are used on the current server. Logins can be configured in one of these ways:

   - To map remote logins to a local login with the same name, select Map All Remote Logins To and then select <Same Name> on the related drop-down list box.

   - To map all remote logins to a single SQL Server login ID, select Map All Remote Logins To and then use the related drop-down list box to select the login ID you want to use for remote connections.

   - To map each remote login to a separate SQL Server login ID, select Map Remote Logins To Different Local Logins. Then specify how the remote logins should be mapped. For example, to map the remote login genUser to the local login currUser, you would type webUser in the Remote Login Name field and currUser in the Local Login Name field. Repeat this process for each individual login you want to configure.

7. By default, all logins are trusted, which means users aren't prompted for a password to access the remote server. If you want to prompt users for a password, select the Check Password check box for each type of login or login ID you want to verify.

8. Click OK and then repeat the process on the second server in the pair.

Figure 8-1. *Configure each remote server in the pair through the Remote Server Properties dialog box.*

Setting Up Remote Servers Using Stored Procedures

Remote server pairs can also be configured with *sp_addserver* and *sp_configure*. You use *sp_addserver* to add remote server connections and *sp_configure* to allow remote server connections. The syntax and usage for *sp_addserver* is shown in Listing 8-1.

Listing 8-1. *sp_addserver* Syntax and Usage

Syntax

```
sp_addserver [@server =] 'server'
  [,[@local =] 'local']
  [,[@duplicate_ok =] 'duplicate_OK']
```

Usage

```
EXEC sp_addserver Pluto, local
EXEC sp_addserver Zeta
```

The following example shows how you could configure the SQL Servers Zeta and Pluto as remote servers. Use this example as a starting point to configure your own server pair.

On Zeta, you would run the following SQL commands:

```
EXEC sp_addserver Zeta, local
EXEC sp_addserver Pluto
EXEC sp_configure 'remote access', 1
RECONFIGURE
GO
```

Then you would stop and restart the MSSQL Server service on Zeta. Afterward, you would configure Pluto for remote server connections to Zeta as follows:

```
EXEC sp_addserver Pluto, local
EXEC sp_addserver Zeta
EXEC sp_configure 'remote access', 1
RECONFIGURE
GO
```

 Note You drop remote servers using the *sp_dropserver* stored procedure. The syntax and usage for this procedure is shown later in the chapter as Listing 8-7.

Then you would stop and restart the MSSQL Server service on Pluto. Now you can configure logins on the servers. You map remote logins to local logins using *sp_addremotelogin*. The syntax and usage for *sp_addremotelogin* is shown in Listing 8-2.

Listing 8-2. *sp_addremotelogin* Syntax and Usage

Syntax

```
sp_addremotelogin [@remoteserver =] 'remoteserver'
  [,[@loginame =] 'login']
  [,[@remotename =] 'remote_name']
```

Usage

```
EXEC sp_addremotelogin 'Pluto'
EXEC sp_addremotelogin 'Omega', 'BILLS', 'WRSTANEK'
```

You map remote logins to local logins with the same name by completing the following steps:

1. Execute this command on Zeta:

   ```
   EXEC sp_addremotelogin 'Pluto'
   ```

2. Then execute this command on Pluto:

   ```
   EXEC sp_addremotelogin 'Zeta'
   ```

You map all users to a single user ID by completing the following steps:

1. Execute this command on Zeta:

   ```
   EXEC sp_addremotelogin 'Pluto', 'remUser'
   ```

2. Then execute this command on Pluto:

   ```
   EXEC sp_addremotelogin 'Zeta', 'remUser'
   ```

You've just mapped all remote logins to the remUser login ID.

You can also map each remote login to a separate SQL Server login ID. For example, if you wanted to map the GOTEAM login on Pluto to GEORGEJ on Zeta, you would use the following command:

```
EXEC sp_addremotelogin 'Pluto', 'GEORGEJ', 'GOTEAM'
```

By default, remote logins are configured to check passwords, and users may be prompted for a password. To set up a trusted login and disable password checking, use the *sp_remoteoption* stored procedure after configuring the login. Listing 8-3 shows the syntax and usage of *sp_remoteoption*.

Listing 8-3. *sp_remoteoption* Syntax and Usage

Syntax

```
sp_remoteoption [[@remoteserver =] 'remoteserver']
  [,[@loginame =] 'loginame']
  [,[@remotename =] 'remotename']
  [,[@optname =] 'optname']
  [,[@optvalue =] 'optvalue']
```

(continued)

Listing 8-3. (continued)
Usage

```
EXEC sp_remoteoption 'Pluto', 'GEORGEJ', 'GOTEAM', trusted, true
```

Executing Remote Stored Procedures

You execute remote stored procedures in much the same way as any other stored procedure. The key difference is that you use a prefix to specify where the stored procedure is to be executed. For example, if you wanted to execute the *totalRevenues* stored procedure on a remote server's Customer database, you could use the following Transact-SQL command:

```
EXECUTE Pluto.Customer.dbo.totalRevenues 'December'
```

Or

```
EXECUTE Pluto.Customer..totalRevenues 'December'
```

Here, Pluto is the name of the remote server, Customer is the database name, and totalRevenues is a user-defined stored procedure.

Working with Linked Servers and Distributed Data

Before you use distributed data, you must configure the linked servers you want to use. These servers depend on OLE DB providers to communicate with one another. Through OLE DB, you can link SQL Servers to other SQL Servers as well as to other data sources.

Linked servers are a new feature in SQL Server 7.0. You use linked servers to handle distributed queries, distributed transactions, remote stored procedure calls, and replication. Basically, queries and transactions are distributed when they make use of two or more servers. For example, if a client is connected to one server and starts a query that accesses a database on another server, the query is distributed. On the other hand, if the same client queries two different databases on the same server, the query is considered a local query and is handled internally. The same is true for transactions that span two or more databases on the same server.

Using Distributed Queries

When you execute a distributed query, SQL Server interprets the command and then breaks it down for the destination OLE DB provider using rowset requests. A rowset is a type of database object that enables OLE DB data providers to support data with a tabular format. As their name implies, rowset objects represent a set of rows and columns of data. After creating the rowset objects, the OLE DB provider calls the data source, opens the necessary files, and returns the requested information as rowsets. SQL Server then formats the rowsets as result sets and adds any applicable output parameters.

Note With SQL-92 user connections must have the ANSI_NULLS and ANSI_WARNINGS options before they can execute distributed queries. Be sure to configure these options, if necessary. For more information, see the section of Chapter 2 titled, "Configuring User and Remote Connections."

You can create ad hoc distributed queries by creating your own rowsets. To do this, you use the *Openrowset* function. When you do this, you don't need to use linked servers and can use the *Openrowset* function in place of a table in a query as long as you pass parameters that identify the OLE DB data source and provider.

You use the *Openrowset* function in the same way as you use virtual tables. Simply replace the virtual table reference with an *Openrowset* reference. Listing 8-4 shows the syntax and usage of *Openrowset*.

Listing 8-4. *Openrowset* **Syntax and Usage**

Syntax

```
OPENROWSET('provider_name'
   {'datasource';'user_id';'password' 'provider_string'},
   {[catalog.][schema.]object 'query'})
```

Usage

```
SELECT cu.*
   FROM OPENROWSET('SQLOLEDB','Pluto';'netUser';'totem12',
'customer.dbo.customers')
   AS au

SELECT o.*
   FROM OPENROWSET('Microsoft.Jet.OLEDB.4.0','C:\
northwind.mdb';'Admin';'',  'Orders')
   AS o
```

Using Distributed Transactions

Distributed transactions are transactions that use distributed queries or remote procedure calls. As you might expect, distributed transactions are a bit more involved than distributed queries. This is primarily because you need a mechanism that ensures that transactions are uniformly committed or rolled back on all the linked servers. For example, if you start a transaction that updates databases on three different servers, you want to ensure that the transaction is committed when successfully completed or that the transaction is rolled back if an error occurs. In this way, you ensure the integrity of the databases involved in the distributed transaction.

Each server involved in a distributed transaction is known as a *resource manager*. Resource managers coordinate transactions through a transaction manager such as the Microsoft Distributed Transaction Coordinator (MS DTC). You can use other transaction managers just as long as they support the X/Open XA specification for distributed transaction processing. For more information on MS DTC, see the section entitled "Using MS DTC" later in the chapter.

You handle distributed transactions in much the same manner as local transactions. Applications start distributed transactions in one of three ways:

- Explicitly, by using BEGIN DISTRIBUTED TRANSACTION
- Implicitly, by executing a distributed query within a local transaction
- Implicitly, by calling a remote stored procedure within a local transaction

At the end of the transaction, the application requests that the transaction be either committed or rolled back. To ensure that the transaction is handled properly on all servers, even if problems occur during the transaction, the transaction manager uses a commit process with two phases:

- **Phase 1: The prepare phase**   In this phase, the transaction manager sends a prepare command to all the resource managers involved in the transaction. The resource managers perform any necessary preparatory tasks and then report their individual success or failure to the transaction manager. If all the resource managers are ready to commit, the transaction manager broadcasts a commit message and the transaction enters phase 2, the commit phase.

- **Phase 2: The commit phase**   In this phase, the resource managers attempt to commit the transaction. Each resource manager then sends back a success or failure message. If all the resource managers report success, the transaction manager marks the transaction as completed and reports this to the application. If a resource manager fails in either phase, the transaction enters a pending state that must be resolved before the transaction can continue. Otherwise, the transaction is rolled back.

Permitted Commands

SQL Server applications manage distributed transactions either through Transact-SQL or through the SQL Server database application programming interface (API). SQL Server itself supports distributed transactions using the ITransactionLocal (local transaction) and ITransactionJoin (distributed transactions) OLE DB interfaces as well as the rowset objects discussed previously. If an OLE DB provider doesn't support ITransactionJoin, then only read-only procedures are allowed for that provider. Similarly, the types of queries you can execute on a linked server depend on the OLE DB provider you're using.

With distributed queries and transactions, you can use most data manipulation language (DML) commands, such as SELECT, INSERT, UPDATE, and DELETE. You can't, however, use data definition language (DDL) commands, such as CREATE, DROP, or ALTER. If you need to use DDL commands on linked servers, you may want to create stored procedures and then execute these stored procedures remotely, as necessary. More specifically, OLE DB providers that support the

ITransactionLocal and ITransactionJoin interfaces are subject to the following constraints:

- Queries with the standard form of SELECT list *from* clause *where* clause are allowed. However, SELECT INTO new_table isn't allowed when the new_table refers to a remote table. Also, SELECT statements can't contain an *order by* clause when specifying a large object (LOB) column from a remote table as a list item.

- INSERT, UPDATE, and DELETE statements are allowed against remote tables in most cases. However, columns with large object data types, such as image, can't be referenced with UPDATE or INSERT if the OLE DB provider is instantiated outside the SQL Server process.

- Remote tables can be updated or deleted through cursors defined in distributed queries, provided that the remote table is specified in the UPDATE or DELETE statement such as *update remote_table where current of cursor_name*.

- STATIC, INSENSITIVE, and KEYSET cursors can usually reference remote tables. No other type of cursor can reference a remote table.

- READTEXT, WRITETEXT, and UPDATETEXT statements aren't supported against remote tables.

- IS NULL and IS NOT NULL predicates can't reference LOB columns in a remote table.

- GROUP BY ALL isn't allowed in a distributed query.

- No DDL statements are allowed against linked servers.

- No other database-level operations or statements are allowed on linked servers.

Note The Microsoft OLE DB Provider for SQL Server supports the ITransactionLocal (local transaction) and ITransactionJoin (distributed transactions) OLE DB interfaces only on a table that has a unique index. Because of this, *Update* and *Delete* statements are permitted against a remote table in another SQL Server only when the table has a unique index.

Managing Linked Servers

To work properly, distributed queries and transactions depend on linked servers. To configure the linked servers you want to work with, you register their connection and data source information in SQL Server. Afterward, you can reference the linked server using a single logical name. If you don't need to link to a server anymore, you can remove the linked server connection.

Adding Linked Servers

If you want a server to be able to use distributed queries, distributed transactions, or remote procedure calls (or all three), you must configure linked server connections to other servers. For example, if clients that access a server named Zeta make distributed queries to Pluto and Omega, you'll want to configure Pluto and

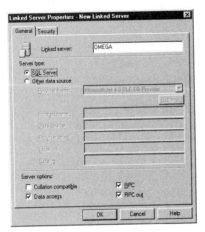

Figure 8-2. *In the Linked Server Properties dialog box, choose SQL Server or configure another data source, and then set Linked Server options and security.*

Omega as linked servers on Zeta. If clients that connect to Pluto make distributed queries to Zeta and Omega, you'll want to configure Zeta and Omega as linked servers on Pluto.

To add a linked server, complete the following steps:

1. Start Enterprise Manager and then access the server you want to configure.

2. Click the plus sign (+) next to the server's Security folder.

3. Right-click the Linked Servers entry and, from the shortcut menu, choose New Linked Server. This opens the dialog box shown in Figure 8-2.

4. In the Linked Server field, type the name of the linked server to create.

5. If you're linking to a SQL Server, select the SQL Server option button.

6. If you're linking to a different data source, select the Other Data Source option button and then configure the data source using the input fields provided. Fields that are unavailable can't be configured for the selected provider. The available fields are summarized in Table 8-1, and can be used as follows:

   - **Provider Name** Use the drop-down list box to select the name of the OLE DB provider to use when communicating with the specified linked server.

   - **Product Name** Sets the server product name for the OLE DB data source.

   - **Data Source** Sets the OLE DB data source, which is used to initialize the OLE DB provider.

   - **Provider String** Sets a provider-specific connection string that identifies a unique data source.

Figure 8-3. *Use the Provider Options dialog box to set options for OLE DB providers to configure or disable features, such as nested queries.*

- **Location** Sets the location of the database for the OLE DB provider.
- **Catalog** Sets the catalog to use when connecting to the OLE DB provider.

Real World The most commonly used option combinations are provider name and data source. For example, if you're configuring a linked server for a Microsoft Access database or a Microsoft Excel spreadsheet, you would select Microsoft Jet 4.0 OLE DB Provider and then set the data source name. With Oracle, you would select Microsoft OLE DB Provider For Oracle and then set the data source name.

7. If you're using a data source other than SQL Server, you can configure options for the OLE DB provider. Click Options and then use the dialog box shown in Figure 8-3 to configure provider options.

8. Next, configure server-specific settings using these check boxes in the Server Options area:

- **Collation Compatible** Set this option to enable SQL Server to send comparisons on character columns to the provider. Otherwise, SQL Server evaluates comparisons on character columns locally. Only set this option when the linked server has the same character set and sort order as the local server.

Note Collation compatible controls sort order settings. If you don't select this option, SQL Server uses the local sort order. This affects the order of result sets and should be noted when developing SQL Server applications or configuring clients.

- **Data Access** Set this option to enable the linked server for distributed query access.
- **RPC** Set this option to enable RPC from the linked server.
- **RPC Out** Set this option to enable RPC to the linked server.

9. Click OK to create the linked server. Next, you'll need to configure security settings for the linked server. You may also need to configure MS DTC. For details, see "Using MS DTC" in this chapter.

The corresponding Transact-SQL command for adding linked servers is *sp_addlinkedserver*. You use this stored procedure as shown in Listing 8-5.

Listing 8-5. *sp_addlinkedserver* Syntax and Usage

Syntax

```
sp_addlinkedserver [@server =] 'server' [, [@srvproduct =] 'product_name']
    [, [@provider =] 'provider_name'] [, [@datasrc =] 'data_source']
    [, [@location =] 'location'] [, [@provstr =] 'provider_string']
    [, [@catalog =] 'catalog']
```

Usage

```
EXEC sp_addlinkedserver
    'Pluto',
    'Microsoft.Jet.OLEDB.4.0',
    'OLE DB Provider for Jet',
    'D:\data\sales.mdb'
GO
```

Table 8-1 provides a summary of parameter values you can use when configuring various OLE DB providers. The table also shows the *sp_addlinkedserver* parameter values to use for each OLE DB provider. Because some providers have different configurations, there may be more than one row for a particular data source type.

Table 8-1. Parameter Values for Configuring OLE DB Providers

OLE DB Provider	Provider Name	Product Name	Data Source	Other
Microsoft OLE DB Provider for SQL Server		SQL Server		
Microsoft OLE DB Provider for SQL Server	SQLOLEDB	SQL Server	Network name of SQL Server	Set Catalog to database name (optional).

(continued)

Table 8-1. *(continued)*

OLE DB Provider	Provider Name	Product Name	Data Source	Other
Microsoft OLE DB Provider for Oracle	MSDAORA	Any	SQL*Net alias for Oracle database	
Microsoft OLE DB Provider for Jet	Microsoft. Jet.OLEDB. 4.0	Any	Full pathname of Jet database file.	
Microsoft OLE DB Provider for Jet	Microsoft. Jet.OLEDB. 4.0	Any	Full pathname of Excel file	Set provider string to Excel 5.0.
Microsoft OLE DB Provider for ODBC	MSDASQL	Any	System DSN of ODBC data source	
Microsoft OLE DB Provider for ODBC	MSDASQL	Any		Set provider string to the ODBC connection string.
Microsoft OLE DB Provider for Indexing Service	MSIDXS	Any	Indexing Service catalog name	

Configuring Security for Linked Servers

You use linked server security to control access and to determine how local logins are used. By default, new linked servers are set to have no security context when a user login isn't defined. This blocks access to all logins not explicitly mapped to the linked server.

To change the security settings for a linked server, complete the following steps:

1. Start Enterprise Manager and then access the local server that contains the linked server definitions you want to work with.

2. Click the plus sign (+) next to the server's Security folder, and then click the plus sign (+) next to the Linked Servers entry. You should now see an entry for each linked server you created on the currently selected server.

3. Right-click the icon for the linked server you want to configure and then choose Properties.

4. In the Linked Servers Properties dialog box, click the Security tab, as shown in Figure 8-4.

5. Use the option buttons and fields in the top portion of the Security tab to set a default security context for all users who don't have a specific login setting for the linked server. These options are used as follows:

   • **No Security Context Will Be Used**   This option blocks access to all logins not explicitly mapped to the linked server.

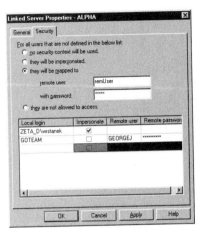

Figure 8-4. *Access to linked servers is controlled by mapping logins and by setting default security information for all other users.*

- **They Will Be Impersonated** Logins not explicitly mapped to the linked server use their current login and password to connect to the linked server. Access is denied if the login and password don't exist on the linked server.

- **They Will Be Mapped To** Logins not explicitly mapped to the linked server will use the login and password provided in the Remote User and Remote Password fields.

- **They Are Not Allowed To Access** Users without logins aren't allowed access to the linked server.

6. Next, map local logins to remote logins, as necessary, using the following fields:

- **Local Login** This field sets the ID of a local login that can connect to the linked server.

- **Impersonate** Select this check box to use the local login ID to connect to the linked server. The local login ID must exactly match a login ID on the linked server.

Note If you select the Impersonate check box, you can't map the local login to a remote login.

- **Remote User** Sets the remote user to which the local login ID maps on the linked server.

- **Remote Password** Sets the password for the remote user. If not provided, the user may be prompted for a password.

7. When you're finished configuring logins, click OK.

The related Transact-SQL command for configuring logins is *sp_addlinkedsrvlogin*. You can use this stored procedure as shown in Listing 8-6.

Listing 8-6. *sp_addlinkedsrvlogin* **Syntax and Usage**

Syntax

```
sp_addlinkedsrvlogin [@rmtsrvname =] 'rmtsrvname'
  [,[@useself =] 'useself']
  [,[@locallogin =] 'locallogin']
  [,[@rmtuser =] 'rmtuser']
  [,[@rmtpassword =] 'rmtpassword']
```

Usage

```
EXEC sp_addlinkedsrvlogin 'Pluto', 'true'
EXEC sp_addlinkedsrvlogin 'Pluto', 'false', NULL, 'remUser', 'tangent23'
EXEC sp_addlinkedsrvlogin 'Pluto', 'false', 'Domain\GOTEAM', 'GEORGEJ', 'tango98'
```

Deleting Linked Servers

If you don't need a linked server anymore, you can delete it by completing the following steps:

1. Start Enterprise Manager and then access the local server that contains the linked server definition you want to delete.

2. Click the plus sign (+) next to the server's Security folder and then click the plus sign (+) next to the Linked Servers entry. You should now see an entry for each linked server you created on the local server.

3. Right-click the icon for the linked server you want to remove and then choose Delete. When prompted to confirm the action, choose Yes.

The Transact-SQL command to drop linked servers is *sp_dropserver*. You can use this stored procedure as shown in Listing 8-7.

Listing 8-7. *sp_dropserver* **Syntax and Usage**

Syntax

```
sp_dropserver [@server =] 'server'
  [, [@droplogins =]{'droplogins' | NULL}]
```

Usage

```
sp_dropserver 'Pluto', 'droplogins'
```

Using MS DTC

On SQL Server, three key components are required for distributed transactions to be handled properly:

- **Resource managers** You must configure resource managers, which are the linked servers used in the distributed transactions. For details, see the earlier section of this chapter entitled "Managing Linked Servers."
- **MSDTC service** The MSDTC service must be running on all servers handling distributed transactions. If it's not, distributed transactions won't work properly.
- **Transaction manager** The transaction manager coordinates and manages distributed transactions. The transaction manager on SQL Server is the MS DTC.

 Note The MS DTC can be used by applications other than SQL Server. You should note which applications are using MS DTC in addition to SQL Server if you try to analyze MS DTC performance.

The sections that follow explore using the MSDTC service and administering the transaction manager.

Running the MSDTC Service

The MSDTC service must run on each server that handles distributed transactions, and you'll usually want the service to start automatically when the system starts. This ensures that the distributed transactions are executed as expected. Using SQL Server Service Manager, you can control the MSDTC service just as you do other SQL Server-related services. For details, see the section of Chapter 3 entitled "Managing SQL Server Service with Service Manager."

You can also start and stop the MSDTC service in Enterprise Manager. To do this, complete the following steps:

1. Start Enterprise Manager and then access the server that you want to configure.
2. Click the plus sign (+) next to the server's Support Services folder and then right-click Distributed Transaction Coordinator.
3. To start the MSDTC service, from the shortcut menu, select Start.
4. To stop the MSDTC service, from the shortcut menu, select Stop.

Administering the Transaction Manager

The transaction manager for SQL Server is administered through the MS DTC Admin Console. To start the MS DTC Admin Console, select Start, then Programs, then Microsoft SQL Server 7.0, and finally MS DTC Administrative Console. As

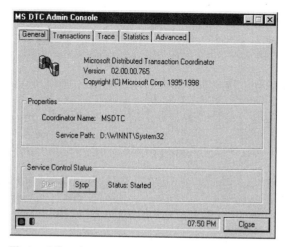

Figure 8-5. *The MS DTC Admin Console lets you track distributed transactions, check statistics, manage logs, and more.*

Figure 8-5 shows, the MS DTC Admin Console has several tabs that provide quick access to options that perform key administration tasks. In the sections that follow, I'll use a task-oriented approach to explain how to use the various options to manage the MS DTC.

Checking MS DTC Version and Properties

The current version and properties of MS DTC are shown in the General tab. The key properties are

- **Version** The version number of the MS DTC being used on the server
- **Coordinator Name** The service handling transactions, which is normally MSDTC
- **Service Path** The path for the related service, which is normally <%SystemRoot%>\System32

You can also use the General tab to start and stop the MSDTC service.

Viewing Transaction Statistics

The Statistics tab provides a quick summary of transaction statistics, such as the current number of active transactions and the total number of transactions committed. You can use the statistics to monitor the performance of MS DTC.

Cumulative statistics (referred to as aggregate statistics) represent statistics gathered since the MSDTC service was last started. By default, statistics are updated once every five seconds. You can change this setting by using the Display Refresh slider in the Advanced tab.

Tip Gathering statistics too frequently can degrade MS DTC performance on a busy server. To improve MS DTC performance, you may want to set the frequency of the display refresh to its lowest setting—infrequently.

Tracing Transactions

The Trace tab allows you to troubleshoot problems you may be experiencing with distributed transactions and the MS DTC. The type of information shown in the Trace tab depends on the trace level set in the Advanced tab, and it can include informational messages, warnings, errors, and other messages. Messages are shown according to severity, source, and message text.

 Tip By default, informational messages, warnings, and errors are shown in the trace tab. This setting is great in a development environment or when you're trying to troubleshoot problems. However, tracing too many messages can degrade MS DTC performance. To improve performance, you may want to lower the trace level.

Viewing Current Transactions

Current transactions are accessible in the Transactions tab. Transactions shown will have one of the following states:

- **Active** The transaction has been started and the Resource Managers are working with it.
- **Aborting** The transaction is aborting and will be rolled back.
- **Aborted** The transaction is aborted and has been rolled back.
- **Preparing** The application has submitted a prepare request.
- **Prepared** The enlisted resource managers and MS DTC have agreed to prepare.
- **Notifying Committed** The transaction is ready to be committed and MS DTC is notifying enlisted resource managers of this.
- **Committed** The transaction has been successfully committed.
- **Force Abort** An In-Doubt transaction has been manually aborted.
- **Force Commit** An In-Doubt transaction has been manually committed.
- **In-Doubt** The transaction is initiated and prepared by a different server or the MS DTC managing the transaction is unavailable.
- **Only Failed To Notify** The transaction has been committed and all connected resource managers have been notified; resource managers that aren't connected haven't been notified.

By default, transactions are shown in a summary list. You can reconfigure the transaction view by completing the following steps:

1. Right-click anywhere within the transaction view window, and then select View.

2. From the shortcut menu, choose the type of view you want to use, from these choices:

- **Large Icon**   To display large icons with current transactions.
- **Small Icon**   To display small icons with current transactions.
- **Details**   To display summary details with current transactions.
- **List**   To display a summary list of current transactions.

You can view properties of a transaction as well. To do this, complete the following steps:

1. Right-click the transaction you want to examine.
2. From the shortcut menu, choose Properties. This opens the Transaction Properties dialog box.

Manually Resolving Transactions

Although MS DTC is responsible for managing transactions, sometimes you may need to resolve transactions manually. For example, if a linked server is offline and you have an In-Doubt transaction that's causing resources to be locked and unavailable to other processes, you may need to manually resolve the transaction. You may also need to resolve the transaction if it's in the Only Failed To Notify state. Here, the transaction has been committed but some of the resource managers haven't been notified of the successful completion because they can't be contacted.

You manually resolve transactions through the Transactions tab in the MS DTC Admin Console. Before you do this, however, you need to trace the transaction through the parent nodes. Doing this tells you the status of the transaction on the parent. To trace and resolve a transaction, complete the following steps:

1. In the Transactions tab in the MS DTC Admin Console, right-click the transaction you want to examine.
2. Choose Properties from the shortcut menu. If the transaction has a parent node, the Properties dialog box should list the linked server that's managing the transaction. Otherwise, you should see the identifier NoParent. This tells you that the current server is managing the transaction.
3. Access the linked server acting as the parent and check the transaction state through the related MS DTC Admin Console. You can resolve transactions by committing them, aborting them, or forgetting them. On the parent, try to resolve the transaction as follows:

   - If the transaction doesn't appear on the parent node, it's been aborted, and you can abort the transaction on the original server that you checked in step 1.
   - If the transaction is listed in the Only Failed To Notify state, the transaction has been committed. Commit the transaction on the original server you checked in step 1.
   - If the status reads In-Doubt, you must look at the transaction properties and then continue to the next parent node listed.

Continue this procedure until you find the top-level parent and learn whether the transaction has been aborted or committed. When you know the status of the transaction, commit or abort the transaction on the child nodes (the servers below the parent).

4. After you resolve the transaction by committing or aborting it, you can forget the transaction with the Only Failed To Notify status on the parent.

5. To forget, commit, or abort a transaction, right-click the transaction in the Transactions tab and then select Resolve. This opens a shortcut menu with Commit, Abort, and Forget options. Use the appropriate option.

Configuring Advanced Settings

MS DTC properties can be configured through the Advanced tab of the MS DTC Admin Console. As shown in Figure 8-6, the Advanced tab has three sliders that control key property settings: Display Refresh, Transactions Shown, and Trace.

The Display Refresh slider controls how often statistics, transactions, and trace information is updated in MS DTC. The more frequently information is updated, the more accurate it is. However, frequent updates also require more system resources to maintain. The slider position controls the update interval as follows:

- Every 20 seconds = Infrequently
- Every 10 seconds
- Every 5 seconds = the default
- Every 3 seconds
- Every second = Frequently

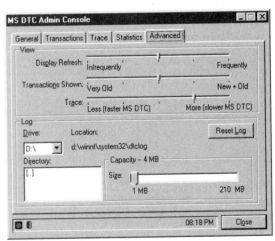

Figure 8-6. *Use the Advanced tab to configure MS DTC property and log settings.*

The Transactions Shown slider controls how long transactions must be active before they are shown in the MS DTC Admin Console. It also controls how long old transactions are maintained. The default interval is 30 seconds, but you can use the slider to set a new interval as follows:

- 5 minutes = Very Old
- 1 minute
- 30 seconds = the default
- 10 seconds
- 1 second = New + Old

The Trace slider controls the amount and type of messages displayed in the Transactions tab. The slider goes from Less (faster MS DTC) to More (slower MS DTC). As the values indicate, the more messages you display, the slower MS DTC performs. You can set the slider to any of the following values:

- No trace messages = Less (Faster MS DTC)
- Only errors
- Errors and warnings
- Errors, warnings, and informational messages = the default
- All trace messages = More (Slower MS DTC)

Tip To improve performance of MS DTC, you'll usually want to set Display Refresh to Infrequently, Transactions Shown to Very Old, and Trace to Less (Faster MS DTC). This sets most properties at or near their minimum values. For troubleshooting or debugging, you'll want to increase these values temporarily.

Configuring and Managing the MS DTC Log

MS DTC maintains a log of all transactions. By default, the maximum size of this log is set to 4 MB and the log is located in the file <%SystemRoot%>\System32\ DTCLOG\MSDTC.LOG. Administrative tasks you may need to perform on the log include

Clearing out the log If the log is full or just needs to be cleared out, you can clear it out by completing the following steps:

1. Start the MS DTC Admin Console.
2. Check the Transaction tab and make sure that there are no unresolved transactions. If there are unresolved transactions, wait until they are resolved (or perform the task after hours).
3. Access the General tab and then click Stop. This stops the MSDTC service.
4. Access the Advanced tab and then click Reset Log.
5. Access the General tab and then click Start. This starts the MSDTC service.

Tip A full or invalid MS DTC log may prevent the MSDTC service from starting. To recover, clear out the log.

Changing the size of the log If the log frequently gets full, you may want to change the size of the MS DTC log. To do this, complete the following steps:

1. Start the MS DTC Admin Console.
2. Check the Transaction tab and make sure that there are no unresolved transactions. If there are unresolved transactions, wait (or perform the task after hours).
3. Access the General tab and then click Stop. This stops the MSDTC service.
4. In the Log area of the Advanced tab, you'll find a slider called Size. Use this slider to change the size of the log and then click Reset Log.
5. Access the General tab and then click Start. This starts the MSDTC service.

Moving the log If SQL Server uses distributed transactions frequently, the default location of the log is less than optimal. While you can't change the name of the log file, you can change its location. To do that, complete the following steps:

1. Start the MS DTC Admin Console.
2. Check the Transaction tab and make sure that there are no unresolved transactions. If there are unresolved transactions, wait (or perform the task after hours).
3. Access the General tab and then click Stop. This stops the MSDTC service.
4. Access the Advanced tab.
5. Use the Drive drop-down list box and the Directory list to select a new location and then click Reset Log.
6. Access the General tab and then click Start. This starts the MSDTC service.

Data Replication

Data replication allows you to distribute data from a source database to one or more destination databases. The source and destination databases can be on other Microsoft SQL Servers or on other databases, as long as an OLE DB provider is available for each destination database. You have precise control over when replication occurs, what data is replicated, and how other aspects of replication are handled. For example, you can configure replication to happen continuously or periodically. Before covering how to implement replication, let's look at why you'd want to use replication and review its key concepts.

An Overview of Replication

You use replication to copy data on one server and distribute it to other servers. If you need to create a copy of a database on a one-time basis, you don't need replication and instead should copy the database as discussed in Chapter 4, under "Manipulating Databases," or Chapter 6, under " Restoring a Database to a Different Location." If you need to copy and transform data on a periodic basis, you don't need replication either, and instead should use the Data Transformation Services (DTS) that were discussed in Chapter 7. Some reasons to use replication include:

- To create multiple instances of a database so that you can distribute the workload. For example, if you have a central database that is updated regularly, you may want to push changes out to departmental databases as they occur. Employees can then access data through these departmental databases instead of trying to connect to the central database.

- To move specific data sets from a central server and distribute them to several other servers. For example, you would use replication if you had a central database and needed to distribute sales data to all the databases in the company's department stores.

- To synchronize (merge) changes to remote databases with a central database. For example, if the sales team uses remote laptops, you may need to create a copy of data for their sales region on the laptop. Later, a salesperson in the field may add information or make changes while disconnected from the network. These modifications will need to be copied back to the central database.

Replication is designed to be extremely versatile to meet the needs of a wide variety of environments. Replication architecture is broken down into several different processes, procedures, and components, each of which is used to tailor replication for a given situation. The replication architecture includes

- **Replication components** The server and data components used in replication
- **Replication agents** Applications that assist in the replication process
- **Replication variants** The types of replication you can configure

Replication Components

Before working with replication, you'll need to know the key terms and how they're used. Servers in the replication model can have one or more of the following roles:

- **Publisher** Publishers are servers that make data available for replication to other servers. Publishers also track changes to data and maintain other information about source databases. Each data grouping has only one publisher.
- **Distributor** Distributors are servers that distribute replicated data. Distributors store the distribution database, metadata, historical data, and (for transactional replication) transactions. Each data grouping has only one publisher.
- **Subscriber** Subscribers are the destination servers for replication. These servers store the replicated data and receive updates. Subscribers can also make changes to data. Data can be published to multiple subscribers.

The actual data being published for replication are referred to as *articles* and *publications*. Articles are the basic unit for replication and can consist of a table, a subset of a table, or a stored procedure. Publications are collections of articles that subscribers can receive. Articles can contain

- An entire table
- Only certain columns from a table, obtained by using a vertical filter
- Only certain rows from a table, obtained by using a horizontal filter
- A table subset containing certain rows and columns
- A stored procedure

 Note In SQL Server 6.5 you could publish a single article. In SQL Server 7.0, this feature is maintained for backward compatibility, but its use is discouraged. Instead, you should associate articles with a publication and then publish the publication.

You can't publish any of the following for replication:

- The model, tempdb, and msdb databases
- System tables in the master database

In the publication and subscription model, replication involves the following steps:

1. Selecting a replication type and model
2. Performing any necessary preliminary tasks
3. Configuring a distributor and enabling publishers, publication databases, and subscribers
4. Creating a publication
5. Creating subscriptions to the publication

Replication Agents

SQL Server uses various helper applications to assist in the replication process. These applications are called replication agents and include

- **Snapshot agent** Creates snapshots of data. It includes schema and data, which are stored for distribution. The snapshot agent is also responsible for updating status information in the distribution database. The snapshot agent runs on the distributor. Each published database has its own snapshot agent that runs on the distributor and connects to the publisher. Snapshot agents are used with all types of replication.

- **Distribution agent** Responsible for applying data from snapshot replication or transactions from transaction replication to subscribers. The distribution agent can run on the distributor or on subscribers. This agent isn't used with merge replication.

- **Merge agent** Used to synchronize changes that occur after the initial snapshot is created. If any conflicts occur when the changes are being synchronized, the conflicts are resolved using the rules set with the conflict resolver. Depending on the configuration, merge agents run on the publisher or on subscribers. Merge agents are only used with merge replication.

- **Log reader agent** Moves transactions marked for replication from the transaction log on the publisher to the distributor. Each database that's published using transactional replication has its own log reader agent that runs on the distributor and connects to the publisher. Log reader agents are only used in transactional replication.

Replication Variants

SQL Server supports several different types of replication. These replication variants are

- **Snapshot replication** Takes a snapshot of current data and replaces the entire copy of the data on one or more subscribers. With subsequent snapshots, the entire copy of the data is again distributed to subscribers. While exact copies are a strong point of snapshot replication, this technique increases the amount of overhead and traffic on the network. Another weak point of snapshot replication is that it runs only on a periodic basis, which usually means subscribers don't have the most current information.

- **Transactional replication**   Uses transactions to distribute changes. When replication is first started, a snapshot of the data is sent to subscribers. After that, selected transactions in the publisher's transaction log are marked for replication and then distributed to each subscriber separately. Snapshots are then taken on a periodic basis to ensure that the databases are synchronized. Distributed transactions are used to ensure that incremental changes are applied consistently. A benefit of transactional replication is that you replicate individual transactions rather than an entire database. Transactional replication can also occur on a continuous or periodic basis, which makes the procedure more versatile than snapshot replication by itself.

- **Merge replication**   Allows subscribers to make changes to replicated data independently. Later, you can merge these changes into all of the related source and destination databases. Merge replication doesn't use distributed transactions and can't guarantee transactional consistency. Instead, merge replication uses a conflict resolver to determine which changes are applied.

In snapshot and transactional replication, subscribers normally don't change data. However, you can add an option that allows subscribers to make changes and then immediately update the publisher. The publisher then replicates these changes to other subscribers. This is called the Immediate-Updating Subscribers option.

You can also set replication options for stored procedures. When you include stored procedures as articles in a snapshot publication, SQL Server replicates the entire stored procedure from the publisher to the subscribers. Changes caused by the execution of those stored procedures are replicated with new snapshots. With transactional replication, on the other hand, you can replicate execution of the stored procedure rather than replicate the changes that the execution causes. By sending an execute command rather than data changes, you reduce the amount of data that needs to flow across the network and improve the performance of SQL applications.

If you replicate the execution of stored procedures, you have two configuration settings. You can use *standard* procedure execution, or you can use *serialized* procedure execution. With standard procedure execution, procedure execution is replicated to all subscribers, even if those procedures are executed in different transactions. Because multiple transactions may be executing at a particular time, subscribers' data can't be guaranteed to be consistent with the publisher's. With serialized stored procedures, procedures are executed in sequence as long as they are referenced within serialized transactions. If the procedures are executed outside of serialized transactions, changes to the data are replicated instead. This behavior guarantees that the subscribers' data is consistent with the publisher's.

Planning for Replication

As you've seen, the replication architecture is fairly extensive. The reason is to ensure that the architecture is versatile enough to meet the needs of just about any replication situation. Unfortunately, this versatility also makes replication tricky to configure. To make the replication go more smoothly, you should do a bit of planning, which involves selecting a specific replication model and performing any necessary preliminary tasks before you start configuring replication.

Replication Models

The key decision you make when you select a replication model involves the physical layout of the publisher, distributor, and subscriber databases. Replication models you may want to use are

- **Central publisher model**   A central publisher maintains the publisher and distributor databases on the same server, with one or more subscribers configured on other servers. The advantages of this model are manageability and ease of maintenance. The disadvantages are the extra workload and resource usage on the publication server.

Tip   The central publisher model is the most commonly used replication model. Unfortunately, you'll often find that the extra load on the publication server hampers server performance. To reduce the server load, you'll want to put the distributor on its own server. Keep in mind, though, that doing so won't entirely eliminate the workload on the publication server. The publisher and distributor still need to communicate, and they still need to pass data back and forth.

- **Central publisher with remote distributor model**   A remote distributor maintains the publisher and distributor databases on different servers, with one or more subscribers configured on other servers. The advantage of this model is that you distribute the workload. The disadvantage is that you have to maintain an additional server.

- **Central subscriber model**   A central subscriber is a single subscriber database that collects data from several publishers. For example, if you have ServerA, ServerB, and ServerC, ServerA and ServerB would act as central publishers and ServerC would act as the central subscriber. Now, when updates are distributed from ServerA and ServerB, they are collected on ServerC. A central subscriber could then republish the combined data to other servers. To use this model, all tables used in replication must have a unique primary key. Otherwise, the replication model won't work properly.

- **Publishing subscriber model**   A publishing subscriber relays the distribution of data to other subscribers, and it can be used with any of the other models. For example, if you have two geographically separated sites, a publisher could replicate data to servers at site A and then have a publishing subscriber at site B that distributes the data to servers at site B.

Preliminary Replication Tasks

After selecting the replication type and model you want to use, you prepare for the replication by performing preliminary tasks. Key tasks you should consider are described, according to replication type, in the sections that follow.

Preparing for Snapshot Replication

With snapshot replication, the data being replicated is copied in full to data files on the distributor. These snapshot files are the same size as the data you're replicating and are stored in the SQL Server Repldata folder by default. You should make sure that the drive on which the replication data is stored has enough free space. For example, if you're using snapshot replication to distribute publication A with 5 MB of data, publication B with 42 MB, and publication C with 9 MB, you'll need at least 56 MB of free space.

Replication timing is another important consideration in snapshot replication. When the snapshot agent creates a snapshot of a published table, the agent locks the entire table while it bulk copies the data from the publisher to the distributor and as a result, users can't update any data in the table until the lock is released. To reduce the impact on operations, you should carefully schedule when replication occurs. Some actions that may help include

- Identifying times when operations are at their lowest levels or users don't need write access to the tables you're replicating
- Identifying times when snapshots must be made and scheduling users to do work that doesn't require write access to the tables you're replicating

Preparing for Transactional Replication

Because transactional replication builds on the snapshot replication model, you'll want to prepare for both snapshot and transactional replication. With transactional replication, an initial snapshot is sent to the distributor and this snapshot is then updated on a periodic basis, like once a week. In between snapshots, transactions are used to update subscribers. These transactions are logged in the distributor's database and are cleared out only after a new snapshot is created.

Transaction logs for published databases are extremely important to successful replication. As long as replication is enabled, pending transactions can't be cleared out of a published database until they have been passed to the distributor. Because of this, you may need to increase the size of a published database's transaction log. Furthermore, if the publisher can't contact the distributor or the log reader agent isn't running, transactions will continue to build up in the publisher's transaction logs.

With transactional replication, all published tables must have a declared primary key. You can add a primary key to an existing table using the ALTER TABLE statement (see Chapter 11). Additionally, if a publication uses text or image data types, you must make sure that you keep these limitations in mind:

- With WRITETEXT and UPDATETEXT statements, you must use the WITH LOG option on tables that are published for replication. You can't use the WITH

NO_LOG option. While WRITETEXT is supported with any compliant database, UPDATETEXT is supported only on subscribers that are running SQL Server version 6.0 or later. Further, you must retrieve text pointers immediately prior to executing the UPDATETEXT or WRITETEXT statement in a transaction.

- The MAX TEXT REPL SIZE SQL Server configuration option controls the maximum byte size of the text and image data that can be replicated. Operations that exceed this limit will fail. Set the maximum text replication size with the *sp_configure* system stored procedure.

Preparing for Merge Replication

With merge replication, all published tables must have primary keys. If a table contains foreign keys or is used in validation, you must include the reference table in the publication. Otherwise, update operations that add new rows will fail because SQL Server can't find the required primary key. Additionally, merge replication doesn't support timestamp columns, and you must remove the timestamp column from any table you want to publish. Timestamps are generated automatically and are guaranteed to be unique only in a specific database.

Like transactional replication, merge replication has a few limitations when it comes to text and image columns. You must explicitly update text and image columns with an UPDATE statement. If you use WRITETEXT or UPDATETEXT to update text columns, you must follow the WRITETEXT or UPDATETEXT statement with a dummy UPDATE statement within the same transaction. Otherwise, the changes may not be distributed.

Distributor Administration

As the name indicates, you use distributors to distribute replicated data. When you work with distributors, the core set of administration tasks you'll perform includes setting up a new distributor, updating an existing distributor, and deleting distributors.

Setting Up a New Distributor

Setting up a new distributor is the first major step in configuring replication. Before you get started, you should

- Select a replication type—either snapshot, transactional, or merge.
- Select a replication model, such as the central publisher model.
- Perform any necessary preliminary tasks. To meet certain limitations, you may need to update clients and applications that modify published databases directly.

When you're ready to proceed, configure the distributor by completing the following steps:

1. Start Enterprise Manager and then select the server you want to use as the distributor.

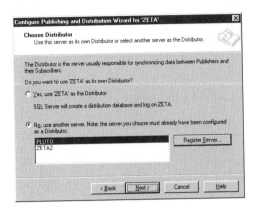

Figure 9-1. *Use the Configure Publishing And Distribution Wizard to config-ure replication. As shown here, the first step is to select a distributor.*

2. Select the Tools menu and then choose Replication. On the submenu, select Configure Publishing And Distribution. This starts the Configure Publishing And Distribution Wizard.

3. Click Next to move past the Welcome screen. As shown in Figure 9-1, you can now select a distributor.

4. To set up the current server as a central publisher, choose Yes, Use <ServerName> As The Distributor. The distribution database and log are created for you.

5. Next, as shown in Figure 9-2, you can let the wizard configure the remaining setup options for you by selecting No, Use The Following Default Settings option button. Afterward, click Next and then click Finish. Skip the remaining steps.

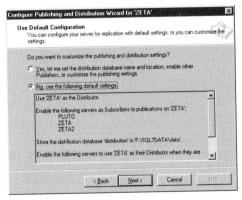

Figure 9-2. *Choose Yes to configure the distribution options yourself or No to use the default options shown.*

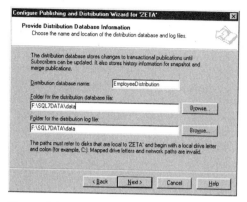

Figure 9-3. *Configure the distribution database name and the location of data and log files.*

6. To configure the options yourself, choose the Yes option and then continue with the configuration.

7. Now provide information for the distribution database using the dialog box shown in Figure 9-3. Enter a name for the distribution database and then set folder locations for the corresponding data and log files. You can't use mapped network drives.

Note Be sure to use a descriptive name for the database, such as EmployeeDistribution or EmpDistr.

8. Next, as shown in Figure 9-4, use the buttons or check boxes provided to enable or disable publishers that can use this distribution database. Only registered servers are shown. If you want to register a new server, click Register Server.

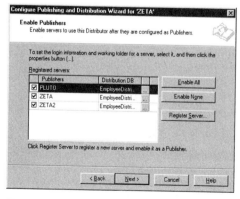

Figure 9-4. *Enable publishers and set server properties, if necessary.*

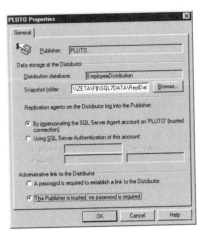

Figure 9-5. *You can set additional properties for each publisher using the distribution database. Use this dialog box to configure the available options.*

9. To the right of registered server entries, you'll see a button with three dots (...). Click this button to set publisher options for the related server. As Figure 9-5 shows, you have the following options available:

- **Data Storage At The Distributor** Sets the location of the folder used to store snapshots. The Snapshot folder is stored on the distribution database and can be in a different location for each publisher that uses the distribution database.

- **Replication Agents On The Distributor Log Into The Publisher** Determines how replication agents on the distributor log into the publisher. Select the By Impersonating The SQL Server Agent Account option button to use a trusted connection. Otherwise, select the Using SQL Server Authentication Of This Account option button and then type the necessary username and password.

- **Administrative Link To The Distributor** Determine whether the selected publisher is trusted. If you want the selected publisher to link to the distributor without needing a password, choose This Publisher Is Trusted. If you want to ensure that a password is required, choose A Password Is Required To Establish A Link To The Distributor. (This option is only available if the selected publisher and distributor are located on different servers.)

10. When you have finished enabling publishers, click Next. As shown in Figure 9-6, you can now enable publication databases for replication. Select entries under the Trans column to enable a database for snapshot or transactional replication, or both. Select entries under the Merge column to enable a database for merge replication. Click Next when you're ready to continue.

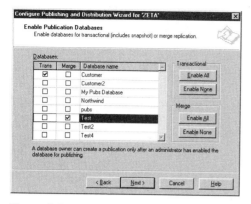

Figure 9-6. *Enable publication databases. Database owners can create publications only after you enable the database for publishing.*

Tip To enable a publication database for any type of replication, select the corresponding Trans and Merge check boxes.

11. Enable subscribers to the distribution database as shown in Figure 9-7. Again, only registered servers are shown. If you want to register a new server, click Register Server.

12. To the right of registered server entries, you'll see a button with three dots (...). Click this button to set subscriber options for the related server. The Properties dialog box has two tabs:

- **General** Use these options to add a description for the subscriber and to determine how replication agents link to the subscriber. Select the option named By Impersonating The SQL

Figure 9-7. *Enable subscribers and set their properties, if desired.*

Server Agent Account to use a trusted connection. Otherwise, select Using SQL Server Authentication Of This Account and then type the necessary username and password.

* **Schedules** Use these options to configure when distribution and merge agents run. You can configure these agents to run continuously, which ensures that updates are made continuously, or at specific times, which limits updates to specific time intervals. For detailed information on scheduling jobs, see Chapter 12, "Database Automation and Maintenance."

 Note While agents can run updates continuously, the updates are not immediate. There is always some latency with replication.

13. When you're ready to continue, click Next, and then click Finish to complete the configuration. The progress of each step of the configuration process is shown in a dialog box. If the process completes successfully, click OK. If errors occur, you'll need to resolve them before you can complete the configuration.

 Note The distributor must run the SQL Server Agent service. This service should be configured to run automatically. If it isn't, you'll see an error prompt. Click Yes to configure the service to start automatically. Otherwise, click No (but you'll need to remember to start the service each time you restart the distributor).

14. On the distributor, a Replication Monitor is added to the folder list in Enterprise Manager. To learn how to work with this SQL Server feature, see Chapter 10, "Monitoring and Profiling SQL Server."

15. Configure publications and subscriptions as explained later in this chapter under "Enabling Publishers, Publication Databases, and Subscribers."

Creating Distribution Databases

When you configure a new distributor, you can set up a new distribution database, as discussed in the section of this chapter entitled "Setting Up a New Distributor." If you've already configured a distributor, you can create additional distribution databases by completing the following steps:

1. Start Enterprise Manager and then select the distribution server.

2. Select the Tools menu and then choose Replication. On the submenu, choose Configure Publishing, Subscribers, And Distribution. This opens the Publisher And Distributor Properties dialog box shown in Figure 9-8.

3. In the Distributor tab, click New. You can now configure the distribution database.

Figure 9-8. *The Publisher And Distributor Properties dialog box controls all the distributor options. You can use it to create new distribution databases and to perform many other administration tasks.*

4. Enter a name for the distribution database and then set folder locations for the corresponding data and log files. You can't use mapped network drives.

5. Use the options in the Transaction Retention and History Retention areas to determine how long transactions and performance history are retained for the distribution database.

6. Click OK to create the distribution database.

Enabling Publishers, Publication Databases, and Subscribers

Distributors can only work with servers and databases that are enabled for their use. You can enable publishers, publication databases, and subscribers when you create a new distributor or by completing the following steps:

1. Start Enterprise Manager and then select the distribution server.

2. Choose the Tools menu and then click Replication. On the submenu, choose Configure Publishing, Subscribers, And Distribution. This opens the Publisher And Distributor Properties dialog box shown previously in Figure 9-8.

3. To enable publishers, choose the Publishers tab and then configure publishers as discussed in steps 8–9 in the section of this chapter entitled "Setting Up a New Distributor."

4. To enable publication databases, choose the Publication Databases tab. Then select entries under the Trans column to enable a database for snapshot or transactional replication (or both) or select entries under the Merge column to enable a database for merge replication.

5. To enable subscribers, choose the Subscribers tab and then configure subscribers as discussed in steps 11–12 in the "Setting Up a New Distributor" section of this chapter. If you want to use a subscriber that isn't listed, click New Subscriber. You can then choose the type of subscriber you want to work with and configure the subscriber, as necessary. The types of subscribers you can choose from are

- SQL server database
- Microsoft Jet 4.0 database (Microsoft Access)
- ODBC data source
- OLE DB data source

 Tip Jet 4.0 databases and OLE DB data sources must be registered as linked servers on the distributor. If they aren't, click Add to create a new linked server. Linked servers are covered in Chapter 8. Additionally, ODBC data sources must be configured as Data Source Names (DSNs) on the distributor. If the data source you want to use isn't available, use the ODBC Data Sources Control Panel utility to create a DSN.

Deleting Distribution Databases

You can delete distribution databases by completing the following steps:

1. Start Enterprise Manager and then select the distribution server.
2. Choose the Tools menu and then click Replication. On the submenu, choose Configure Publishing, Subscribers, And Distribution. This opens the Publisher And Distributor Properties dialog box.
3. In the Distributor tab, select the distribution database you want to delete and then click Delete.

 Note Before you can delete a distribution database, you must remove all publications and disable all the publishers using the distribution database.

Disabling Publishing and Distribution

Through Enterprise Manager's Disable Publishing And Distribution Wizard, you can disable publishing and distribution. When you disable publishing

- All publications on the selected server are dropped.
- All subscriptions to the affected publications are dropped.
- The server is disabled as a distributor.

You can disable publishing and distribution by completing the following steps:

1. Start Enterprise Manager and then select the distribution server.

2. Choose the Tools menu and then click Replication. On the submenu, choose Disable Publishing. This starts the Disable Publishing And Distribution Wizard.
3. Select Next and then choose Yes, Disable Publishing.
4. Click Next and then click Finish.

Creating and Managing Publications

Once you've configured a distributor and enabled publishers, publication databases, and subscribers, you can create publications. Afterward, you'll need to manage the publications as you would any other SQL Server resource.

Creating Publications

The easiest way to create publications is to use Enterprise Manager. To do this, complete the following steps:

1. In Enterprise Manager select the server you want to use as the publisher.
2. Choose the Tools menu and then choose Replication. On the submenu, choose Create And Manage Publications. This opens the dialog box shown in Figure 9-9.
3. Choose the database where you want to create the publication and then click Create Publication. This starts the Create Publication Wizard. Click Next to skip the Welcome dialog box.

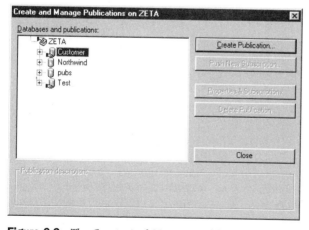

Figure 9-9. *The Create And Manage Publications dialog box is used whenever you administer publications. To create a new publication, choose the database containing the publication and then click Create Publication.*

4. The first time you create a publication in a particular database, you'll have to do everything from scratch. Choose the type of replication you want to use for the publication. The options are

- **Snapshot publication**   Creates a publication setup for snapshot replication
- **Transactional publication**   Creates a publication setup for transactional replication
- **Merge publication**   Creates a publication setup for merge replication

5. The next time you create a publication in a particular database, you'll have the option of using an existing publication as a publication template. To use a template, choose the Yes option and then select the existing publication to use as a template. Now all the default options are based on the existing publication you've selected (but you can't change the publication type).

6. If you're creating a snapshot or transactional publication, continue using the steps listed in the following section, "Snapshot and Transactional Publications."

7. If you're creating a merge publication, continue using the steps listed in the section below entitled "Merge Publications."

Snapshot and Transactional Publications

Snapshot and transactional publications are the two most commonly used types of publications. Once you've started a new publication, you can create a snapshot or transactional publication by completing the following steps:

1. The next dialog box allows you to determine whether immediate-updating subscribers are used. Immediate-updating subscribers use the MS DTC service to update the publisher directly without going through the distributor. Choose Yes, Allow Immediate-Updating Subscribers or No, Do Not Allow Immediate-Updating Subscribers.

2. Click Next to continue. You can now select the tables that are to be replicated, as shown in Figure 9-10. To display stored procedures, select the Include Stored Procs check box and then confirm that you may want to replicate stored procedures.

 Note   Tables without primary keys can't be published for transactional replication, and you'll see a key with an X through it in the Specify Articles dialog box. Additionally, if you've selected the Immediately-Updating Subscriber option, you may see a prompt telling you that a timestamp column will be added to selected tables. Timestamps are needed to synchronize updates.

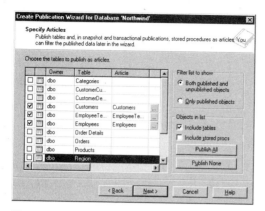

Figure 9-10. *Select tables to replicate as articles in the publication. With snapshot and transactional replication, you can also select stored procedures.*

3. When you select a table or a stored procedure, you'll see a Properties button. Click this button to configure property settings for the related article. The available options depend on the replication type and you may see one or more of the following tabs:

- **General** Allows you to configure basic options and is available for all replication types. You can set the article name and description, enter a new destination name for the table or stored procedure, and enter a new owner for the resource.

- **Snapshot** Sets options for snapshots, which are used with all replication types. You can set options that control what happens when a table exists at the subscriber already, whether indexes are copied, whether user-defined data types are converted to base data types, and whether referential integrity is included with primary keys.

- **Commands** With transactional replication, controls whether INSERT, UPDATE, and DELETE commands are replaced by customized stored procedures. By default, these commands are replaced and the necessary stored procedures are created automatically when synchronizing with subscribers.

4. After you select tables or stored procedures, or both, to use in the publication, click Next. Type a name and description of the publication and then click Next again.

5. You can now determine whether default or custom properties are used. You'll usually want to use custom properties, so select the Yes option and then click Next. If you click No, the wizard uses the default options shown and clicking Next takes you to the final step of the process.

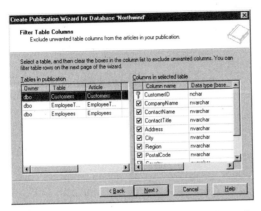

Figure 9-11. *Select columns to exclude from the publication.*

6. If you want to filter data, choose the Yes option. Otherwise, choose No and skip steps 7–8.

7. To filter table data, you choose a table in the left pane and then select or clear check boxes for columns in the right pane, as shown in Figure 9-11. By clearing a check box, you're excluding the related column from replication. Repeat this step for each table that you want to filter and then click Next.

8. Now add row filter clauses using SQL statements, if desired. Choose a table's Properties button and then enter a *where* clause for the corresponding *Select * From TableName* statement. Sample *where* clauses are shown in Figure 9-12. Click Next when you're ready to continue.

9. Determine whether anonymous subscriptions are allowed. Choose the Yes option to allow them. Otherwise, choose the No option. Anonymous subscrib-

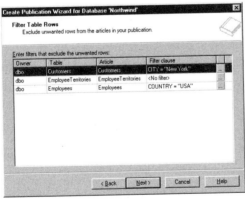

Figure 9-12. *You can also filter table rows using* where *clauses. To see a list of available column values, click Cancel and then click Back to go back to the previous wizard dialog box.*

ers reduce the amount of administration you have to do. They allow any server to receive replicated data without your having to store information about the server in the distribution database.

Note With anonymous subscribers, only pull subscriptions are allowed. To learn more about pull subscriptions, see the "Subscribing to a Publication" section of this chapter.

10. The next step lets you set the snapshot schedule. By default, snapshots are made once a day. To change this schedule, click Change and then set a new schedule.

11. With transactional replication, you can create a snapshot immediately by selecting Create First Snapshot Immediately.

12. Click Next and then click Finish. You'll see a dialog box that shows the progress of the creation process. If it's successful, the publication is shown in the Create And Manage Publication dialog box, and you can now manage subscriptions and publication options.

Merge Publications

Once you've started a new publication, you can create a merge publication by completing the following steps:

1. The next dialog box allows you to specify the type of subscribers you'll be using. If all subscribers are SQL Servers, select All Subscribers Will Be Running SQL Server. Otherwise, select the other option button.

Note The title of the second button varies depending on the type of subscribers you've enabled. Regardless of what the button label says, the purpose of the button is the same—to allow you to use non-SQL Servers as subscribers.

2. Click Next to continue. You can now select tables that are to be replicated, as shown previously in Figure 9-10.

3. When you select a table, you'll see a Properties button. Select this button to configure property settings for the related article. The following tabs are available:

   - **General** Allows you to set the article name and description, type a new destination name for a table or stored procedure, and type a new owner for the resource.

   - **Snapshot** Allows you to set options that control what happens when a table exists at the subscriber already, whether indexes are copied, whether user-defined data types are converted to base data types, and whether referential integrity is included with primary keys.

   - **Resolver** Lets you use a resolver other than the default one provided with SQL Server.

4. Click Next to continue. All tables that use merge replication must have a unique identifier column with a unique index. If any of the tables you've selected are missing these elements, you'll see a prompt telling you these elements will be created automatically. Click OK.

5. Type a name and a description of the publication and then click Next again.

6. You can now determine whether default or custom properties are used. In most cases, you'll want to use custom properties, so select the Yes option and then click Next. If you click No, the wizard uses the default options shown and clicking Next takes you to the final step of the process.

7. If you want to filter data, choose the Yes option. Otherwise, choose No and skip steps 8–9.

8. Data filtering is handled in one of two ways. You can use a dynamic filter that allows individual subscribers to receive different sections of the published data, or you can use a static filter and all subscribers will receive the same data. For dynamic filters, choose Yes, Enable Dynamic Filters. Otherwise, choose No, I Will Use Static Filters.

9. Use the Table to Filter drop-down list box to select the table you want to filter. Then enter a *where* clause for the corresponding *Select * From TableName* statement. Repeat this step for each table that you want to filter. Click Next when you're ready to continue.

10. Determine whether anonymous subscriptions are allowed. Choose the Yes option to allow them. Otherwise, choose the No option. Anonymous subscribers reduces the amount of administration you have to do. They allow any server to receive replicated data without your having to store information about the server in the distribution database.

 Note With anonymous subscribers, only pull subscriptions are allowed. To learn more about pull subscriptions, see the "Subscribing to a Publication" section of this chapter.

11. The next step lets you set the snapshot schedule. By default, snapshots are made once a day. To change this schedule, click Change and then set a new schedule.

12. To create the initial snapshot immediately, select Create First Snapshot Immediately.

13. Next, as shown in Figure 9-13, you can extend the row filters to other tables by using JOIN filters. From the list in the Filtered Table column, select a table with an existing filter. Then, from the list in the Table To Filter column, select a second table to be filtered. Afterward, click the related properties button (...) to enter a JOIN clause to use as the filter. Repeat this step to create additional filters.

14. To delete a JOIN, click <Delete Join> in the list shown in the Filtered Table column.

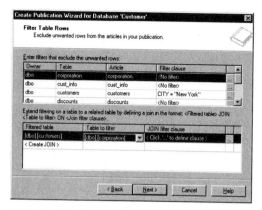

Figure 9-13. *Extend filters to other tables using a JOIN clause.*

15. Click Next and then click Finish. You'll see a dialog box that shows the progress of the creation process. If it was successful, the publication is shown in the Create And Manage Publication dialog box, and you can now manage subscriptions and publication options.

Updating a Publication

You can change the properties of publications any time you like. To change them, complete the following steps:

1. In Enterprise Manager, select the publisher you want to configure.
2. Choose the Tools menu and then click Replication. On the submenu, choose Create And Manage Publications.
3. In the Create And Manage Publications dialog box, click the plus sign (+) next to the publication database. You should see a list of publications for this database.
4. Select the publication you want to work with and then click the Properties & Subscriptions button.
5. You can now use the Properties dialog box to configure all the publication options discussed previously in the "Creating Publications" section.

Controlling Subscription Access to a Publication

All publications have access control lists (ACLs). For publications, access control lists determine which logons can be used by pull and immediate-updating subscribers to access the publication. By default, only the database owner (DBO) and administrators have subscription access to the publication. To add or remove users, complete the following steps:

1. In Enterprise Manager, select the publisher you want to configure.

2. Choose the Tools menu and then click Replication. On the submenu, choose Create And Manage Publications.

3. In the Create And Manage Publications dialog box, click the plus sign (+) next to the publication database. You should see a list of publications for this database.

4. Select the publication you want to work with and then click the Properties & Subscriptions button.

5. Choose the Publication Access List tab. Use the buttons provided to add or remove logons.

Deleting a Publication

When you're finished using a publication, you can delete it to free up resources that it's using. But before you do this, you may want to create a script that allows you to recreate the publication automatically if you have to. To create a script and then delete the publication, complete the following steps:

1. In Enterprise Manager, select the publisher (the server publishing the publication).

2. Choose the Tools menu and then click Replication. On the submenu, choose Create And Manage Publications.

3. In the Create And Manage Publications dialog box, click the plus sign (+) next to the publication database. You should see a list of publications for this database.

4. Select the publication you want to work with and then click the Properties & Subscriptions button.

5. Choose the Scripts tab the select the Create This Publication option button under Script Options.

6. Choose Save and then save the script to an .sql file, which can be executed in Query Analyzer.

 Tip In Query Analyzer, you can access scripts by clicking the Load SQL Script button on the toolbar and then entering the location of the script.

7. Double-click OK, and then, in the Create And Manage Publications dialog box, click the Delete Publication button. When prompted, choose Yes.

Subscribing to a Publication

The final step in the replication process is having servers subscribe to the publication. You can do this using *push* or *pull* subscriptions. With push subscriptions, the publisher is responsible for replicating all changes to subscribers without subscribers asking for the changes. You'll usually use push subscriptions when you need to send changes to subscribers immediately, or when you want to schedule updates on a periodic basis. Because the publisher initiates the replication, push subscriptions also offer more security than pull subscriptions. Making the publisher responsible for replicating changes, however, increases overhead on the publisher and may not be the ideal subscription model for a server that is experiencing heavy workloads.

With pull subscriptions, subscribers request periodic updates of all changes from the publisher. You'll usually use pull subscriptions when you have a large number of subscribers or when you need to reduce overhead on the publisher. You'll usually want to use pull subscriptions for independent mobile users as well. A single publication can support a mixture of push and pull subscriptions.

A special type of pull subscription, called an anonymous subscription, can also be used. With an anonymous subscription, the publisher and distributor don't maintain subscription information. Instead, the subscriber is responsible for maintaining and synchronizing the subscription, which increases the load on the subscriber but reduces the load on the publisher and distributor. Accordingly, anonymous subscriptions are most useful when you have a large number of subscribers or when you allow subscriptions using the Internet.

Note You create anonymous subscriptions to publications just like pull subscriptions. If the publication is enabled for anonymous subscriptions and the server is not registered as a subscriber, the Pull Subscription Wizard creates an anonymous subscription automatically.

Creating Pull Subscriptions

Pull subscriptions are initiated by the subscriber. You configure pull subscriptions by completing the following steps:

1. In Enterprise Manager, access the subscriber you want to configure.
2. Choose the Tools menu and then click Replication. On the submenu, choose the Pull Subscription To option. This opens the Pull Subscription To dialog box.
3. Choose the Pull New Subscription button. This starts the Pull Subscription Wizard.
4. Click Next to access the dialog box shown in Figure 9-14. Select one publication from the listed servers and then click Next again.
5. Select an existing database in which to create the subscription or choose New Database to create a new database for the subscription. Click Next when you're ready to continue.
6. Determine whether the subscription database should be initialized. Choose the Yes option to initialize the schema and data. Choose the No option if you're updating an existing database with the same schema.

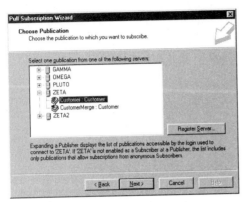

Figure 9-14. *Access the Publisher and select a publication. Click Register Server if you don't see the server you want to use.*

7. Set the distribution agent schedule using one of the following options:

- **Continuously** Select this option to continuously check for updates on the publisher.

- **Using The Following Schedule** Select this option and then click the Change button to set a periodic schedule, such as once an hour.

- **No Schedule** Select this option if you want to update the subscription database manually.

8. Determine whether required services should be started. To start a service, if necessary, select the check box to the left of the service name. Services that aren't started automatically will need to be started manually for the subscription to work.

9. Check the setup and click the Finish button when you're ready to create the pull subscription.

Managing Pull Subscriptions

To update, maintain, or delete a pull subscription, complete the following steps:

1. In Enterprise Manager, access the subscriber you want to configure.

2. Choose the Tools menu and then click Replication. On the submenu, choose the Pull Subscription To option. This opens the Pull Subscription To dialog box.

3. Select the pull subscription you want to work with.

4. To change subscription properties, click Properties and then use the Properties dialog box to reconfigure the subscription.

5. To reinitialize the snapshot in the subscription database, choose the Reinitialize Subscription button.

6. To delete the subscription, choose the Delete Subscription button.

Creating Push Subscriptions

The publisher initiates and configures push subscriptions by completing the following steps:

1. In Enterprise Manager, access the publisher you want to configure.

2. Choose the Tools menu and then click Replication. On the submenu, choose the Push Subscription To Others option. This opens the Create And Manage Publications dialog box.

3. Click the plus sign (+) next to the publication database and then select a publication.

4. Choose the Push New Subscription button. This starts the Push Subscription Wizard.

5. Click Next to access the dialog box shown in Figure 9-15. Select one or more Subscribers for the publication. Currently enabled servers are listed in the Enabled Subscribers group.

6. Type the name of the destination database on the subscriber. Click the Browse Databases button to select an existing database. Or choose Browse Databases and then choose New Database to create a new database on the subscriber. Click Next when you're ready to continue.

7. Set the distribution agent schedule using one of the following options:

   - **Continuously**   Select this option to have the publisher send updates continuously.

   - **Using The Following Schedule**   Select this option and then click the Change button to set a periodic schedule, such as once an hour.

8. Determine whether the subscription database should be initialized. Choose the Yes option to initialize the schema and data. Choose the No option if you're updating an existing database with the same schema.

Figure 9-15. *Select the subscribers for the publication.*

9. If you choose Yes to initialize the database, you can start the process immediately by selecting Start The Snapshot Agent To Begin The Initialization Process Immediately.

10. Determine whether required services should be started. To start a service, if necessary, select the check box to the left of the service name. Services that aren't started automatically will need to be started manually for the subscription to work.

11. Check the setup and click Finish when you're ready to create the push subscription.

Managing Push Subscriptions

To update, maintain, or delete a push subscription, complete the following steps:

1. In Enterprise Manager, access the publisher you want to configure.

2. Choose the Tools menu and then click Replication. On the submenu, choose the Push Subscription To Others option. This opens the Create And Manage Publications dialog box.

3. Click the plus sign (+) next to the publication database and then select a publication.

4. Choose Properties & Subscriptions and then select the Subscriptions tab.

5. Select the push subscription you want to work with.

 Note Although pull subscriptions are listed in this tab, you can't manage properties of pull subscriptions using this technique. Instead, follow the steps outlined in the "Managing Pull Subscriptions" section of this chapter.

6. To change subscription properties, click Properties and then use the Properties dialog box to reconfigure the subscription.

7. To reinitialize the snapshot of the subscription database, choose the Reinitialize Subscription button.

8. To delete the subscription, choose the Delete Subscription button.

Configuring Replication Agents

All replication agents have options that you can set to customize their behavior. You can set agent profiles that control the exact behavior of the agent as well as agent properties that control other configuration settings.

Setting Agent Profiles

Profile settings are useful for updating agents to work with slow connections, configure verbose logging, and more. You set a profile for any of the available agents by completing the following steps:

1. In Enterprise Manager, access the distributor whose agents you want to configure.

2. Choose the Tools menu and then click Replication. On the submenu, choose Configure Publishing, Subscribers, And Distribution.

3. Choose Agent Profiles.

4. Click the tab for the type of agent you want to work with.

5. Select an existing profile using the option buttons in the Default column.

6. Create a new profile by selecting Copy and then configuring the Replication Agent Profile dialog box.

7. To force all existing distribution agents to use the new profile, select Change All Existing Agents To Use The Selected Profile.

8. Click OK.

Setting Agent Properties

The snapshot agent and the distribution agent are the key agents you'll want to set properties for. To change property settings for the snapshot agent, complete the following steps:

1. In Enterprise Manager, access the distributor whose agent you want to configure.

2. Choose the Tools menu and then click Replication. On the submenu, choose the Push Subscription To Others option. This opens the Create And Manage Publications dialog box.

3. Click the plus sign (+) next to the publication database and then select a publication.

4. Choose Properties & Subscriptions and then select the Status tab.

5. Choose Agent Properties and then use the related Properties dialog box to configure the agent.

To change property settings for the distribution agent, complete the following steps:

1. In Enterprise Manager, access the subscriber whose agent you want to configure.

2. Choose the Tools menu and then click Replication. On the submenu, choose the Pull Subscription To option. This opens the Pull Subscription To dialog box.

3. Select the pull subscription you want to work with.

4. In the General tab, choose Distribution Agent Properties and use the related Properties dialog box to configure the agent.

Part IV

Performance, Optimization, and Maintenance

This part covers administration tools you'll use to enhance and maintain Microsoft SQL Server 7.0. Chapter 10 provides the essentials for working with server logs, monitoring SQL Server performance, and solving performance problems. In Chapter 11, you'll learn techniques for creating, managing, and optimizing tables and indexes. Chapter 12 explores database automation and maintenance. You'll learn how to configure alerts, schedule jobs, create maintenance plans, and resolve database consistency problems.

Chapter 10

Monitoring and Profiling Microsoft SQL Server 7.0

Monitoring server performance, tracking user activity, and troubleshooting errors are essential parts of database administration, and Microsoft SQL Server includes several tools you can use to perform these tasks. Performance Monitor, the standard Microsoft Windows NT tool for monitoring servers, has updated counters for SQL Server. These counters allow you to track many different server resources and activities. SQL Server Profiler, an analysis and profiling tool, allows you to trace server events. Other tools and resources are also available, such as stored procedures and the SQL Server logs.

Monitoring Server Performance and Activity

Monitoring SQL Server isn't something you should do haphazardly. You need to have a clear plan—a set of goals that you hope to achieve. Let's look at some reasons you may want to monitor SQL Server and the tools you can use to do this.

Why Monitor SQL Server?

Troubleshooting SQL Server performance problems is a key reason for monitoring. For example, users may be having problems connecting to the server, and you may want to monitor the server to troubleshoot these problems. Here, your goal would be to track down the problem using the available monitoring resources and then to solve it.

Another common reason for wanting to monitor SQL Server is to improve server performance. To achieve optimal performance, you need to minimize the time it takes for users to see the results of queries and maximize the total number of queries that the server can handle simultaneously. You do this by

- Resolving hardware issues that may be causing problems. For example, if slow disk drives are delaying queries, work on improving disk input/output (I/O).

- Monitoring memory and CPU usage and taking appropriate steps to reduce the load on the server, as necessary. For example, other processes running on the server may be using memory and CPU resources needed by SQL Server.

- Cutting down the network traffic load on the server. With replication, for example, configure remote stored procedure execution rather than transmitting large data changes individually.

Unfortunately, there are often trade-offs to be made when it comes to resource usage. For example, as the number of users accessing SQL Server grows, you may not be able to reduce the network traffic load, but you may be able to improve server performance by optimizing queries or indexing.

Getting Ready to Monitor

Before you start monitoring SQL Server, you may want to establish baseline performance metrics for your server. To do this, you measure server performance at various times and under different load conditions. You can then compare the baseline performance with subsequent performance to determine how SQL Server is performing. Performance metrics that are well above the baseline measurements may indicate areas where the server needs to be optimized or reconfigured.

After you establish the baseline metrics, you should formulate a monitoring plan. A comprehensive monitoring plan involves the following steps:

1. Determine which server events should be monitored to help you accomplish your goal.
2. Set filters to reduce the amount of information collected.
3. Configure monitors and alerts to watch the events.
4. Log the event data so that it can be analyzed.
5. Analyze the event data and replay the data as necessary to find a solution.

These procedures are examined later in the chapter under "Monitoring SQL Server Performance." While you should develop a monitoring plan in most cases, there are times when you may not want to go through all these steps to monitor SQL Server. For example, if you want to check current user activity levels, you may not want to use Performance Monitor and may want to run the stored procedure *sp_who* instead. Or you may simply want to examine this information in the Current Activity window in Enterprise Manager.

Monitoring Tools and Resources

The primary monitoring tools you'll use are Windows NT Performance Monitor and SQL Server Profiler. Other resources for monitoring SQL Server include

- **SQL Server error logs**   Use information in the error logs to troubleshoot SQL Server problems.
- **Windows NT event logs**   Use information in the event logs to troubleshoot system-wide problems, including SQL Server and SQL Server Agent problems.
- **Enterprise Manager Current Activity window**   This provides information on current users, processes, and locks.
- *sp_helpdb*   This stored procedure displays information about databases.

- *sp_helpindex*   This stored procedure reports information about indexes on a table.

- *sp_lock*   This stored procedure shows information concerning object locks.

- *sp_monitor*   This stored procedure shows key SQL Server usage statistics, such as CPU idle time and CPU usage.

- *sp_spaceused*   This stored procedure shows an estimate of disk space used by a table or database.

- *sp_who*   This stored procedure shows a snapshot of current SQL Server users and processes.

- **DBCC statements**   Use this set of commands to check SQL Server statistics, to trace activity, and to check database integrity.

Beyond log files and Transact-SQL statements, you'll find a set of built-in functions that return system information. Table 10-1 provides a summary of key functions and their usages. The values returned by these functions are cumulative from the time SQL Server was last started.

Table 10-1. Built-in Functions for Monitoring SQL Server Performance and Activity

Function	Description	Example
@@connections	Returns the number of connections or attempted connections	select @@*connections* as 'Total Login Attempts'
@@cpu_busy	Returns CPU processing time in milliseconds for SQL Server activity	select @@*cpu_busy* as 'CPU Busy', getdate() as 'Since'
@@idle	Returns SQL Server idle time in milliseconds	select @@*idle* as 'Idle Time', getdate() as 'Since'
@@io_busy	Returns I/O processing time in milliseconds for SQL Server	select @@*io_busy* as 'IO Time', getdate() as 'Since'
@@pack_received	Returns the number of input packets read from the network by SQL Server	select @@pack_received
@@pack_sent	Returns the number of output packets written to the network by SQL Server	select @@pack_sent
@@packet_errors	Returns the number of network packet errors for SQL Server connections	select @@packet_errors
@@total_errors	Returns the number of disk read/write errors encountered by SQL Server	select @@*total_errors* as 'Total Errors', getdate() as 'Since'
@@total_read	Returns the number of disk reads by SQL Server	select @@*total_read* as 'Reads', getdate() as 'Since'
@@total_write	Returns the number of disk writes by SQL Server	select @@*total_write* as 'Writes', getdate() as 'Since'

Working with Server Logs

Server logs are your primary resource for tracking SQL Server errors. SQL Server writes events to the SQL Server error logs and to the Windows NT application log. Both logs can be used to track messages related to SQL Server. However, there are some things you should know:

- Some events are not logged in the application log and you can control the logging of most noncritical events through the Manage SQL Server Messages dialog box in Enterprise Manager. To display this dialog box, select the Manage SQL Server Messages option from the Tools menu.

- Only the application log provides additional information on all applications running on the server, and only the application log provides features for filtering events based on type. For example, you can filter events so that only error and warning messages are displayed.

- If you start the MSSQLServer service from the command prompt, events are logged to the SQL Server error log and to standard output. No events are recorded in the Windows NT application log.

Examining the SQL Server Error Logs

The SQL Server logs store information, warnings, errors, and auditing messages pertaining to SQL Server activity. New logs are created when you start the MSSQLServer service or when you run the *sp_cycle_errorlog* stored procedure. When a new log is created, the current log is cycled to the archive. SQL Server maintains up to six archived logs.

You can view the SQL Server error logs in Enterprise Manager or through a text editor. In Enterprise Manager, you access the error logs by completing the following steps:

1. Start Enterprise Manager and then access the server whose logs you want to examine.

2. Click the plus sign (+) next to the server's Management folder, then double-click the SQL Server Logs entry.

3. The current log is shown with the label Current.

4. Archived logs are shown with the label Archive # N, such as Archive # 1.

5. To view the properties of an error log entry, double-click it.

To access the error logs in a text editor, complete the following steps:

1. Start the text editor and then use its Open dialog box to access the SQL Server Log folder. Normally, this folder is located with your SQL Server data files. For example, if you placed your data files in f:\sql7data, the Log folder would be created in f:\sql7data\log.

2. Open the log you want to examine. The current log file is named Errorlog with no file extension. The most recent log backup has the extension .1, the second most recent has the extension .2, and so on.

Examining the Windows NT Application Log

You access the Windows NT application log by completing the following steps:

1. Access the Start menu, select Programs, select Administrative Tools (Common), and then select Event Viewer.

2. From the Log menu, choose Application. This opens the application log, as shown in Figure 10-1.

The entries in Event Viewer's main window provide a quick overview of when, where, and how an event occurred. To obtain detailed information on an event, double-click its entry. A summary icon that tells you the event type precedes the date and time of the event. Event types include

- **Informational** An informational event that's generally related to a successful action.

- **Success audit** An event related to the successful execution of an action.

- **Failure audit** An event related to the failed execution of an action.

- **Warning** A noncritical error that provides a warning. Details for warnings are often useful in preventing future system problems.

- **Critical error** A critical error, such as the failure of a service to start.

Date	Time	Source	Category	Event	User	Computer
6/22/99	10:08:02 PM	LicenseService	None	202	N/A	ZETA
6/22/99	3:53:38 PM	MSSQLServer	ODS	17052	N/A	ZETA
6/22/99	3:53:38 PM	MSSQLServer	ODS	17052	N/A	ZETA
6/22/99	3:53:38 PM	Userenv	None	1000	N/A	ZETA
6/22/99	3:52:58 PM	hpmon	None	1050	N/A	ZETA
6/22/99	3:52:58 PM	hpmon	None	1002	N/A	ZETA
6/22/99	1:41:11 PM	IISInfoCtrs	None	1003	N/A	ZETA
6/22/99	1:41:11 PM	IISInfoCtrs	None	1003	N/A	ZETA
6/22/99	1:41:11 PM	IISInfoCtrs	None	1003	N/A	ZETA
6/22/99	1:41:11 PM	IISInfoCtrs	None	1003	N/A	ZETA
6/22/99	1:41:11 PM	IISInfoCtrs	None	1003	N/A	ZETA
6/22/99	1:41:11 PM	IISInfoCtrs	None	1003	N/A	ZETA
6/22/99	1:41:11 PM	IISInfoCtrs	None	1003	N/A	ZETA
6/22/99	1:23:35 PM	IISInfoCtrs	None	1003	N/A	ZETA
6/22/99	1:23:35 PM	IISInfoCtrs	None	1003	N/A	ZETA
6/22/99	10:58:35 AM	IISInfoCtrs	None	1003	N/A	ZETA
6/22/99	10:58:35 AM	IISInfoCtrs	None	1003	N/A	ZETA
6/22/99	10:42:47 AM	MSSQLServer	ODS	17052	N/A	ZETA
6/22/99	10:42:47 AM	MSSQLServer	ODS	17052	N/A	ZETA
6/22/99	10:42:46 AM	Userenv	None	1000	N/A	ZETA
6/22/99	10:42:03 AM	hpmon	None	1050	N/A	ZETA
6/22/99	10:42:03 AM	hpmon	None	1002	N/A	ZETA
6/22/99	12:54:26 AM	MSSQLServer	ODS	17052	N/A	ZETA
6/22/99	12:54:26 AM	MSSQLServer	ODS	17052	N/A	ZETA
6/22/99	12:54:25 AM	Userenv	None	1000	N/A	ZETA
6/22/99	12:53:26 AM	hpmon	None	1050	N/A	ZETA
6/22/99	12:53:26 AM	hpmon	None	1002	N/A	ZETA
6/22/99	12:31:13 AM	SQLServerAgent	Alert Engine	312	N/A	ZETA
6/22/99	12:31:13 AM	SQLServerAgent	Alert Engine	318	N/A	ZETA

Figure 10-1. *The Windows NT application log.*

In addition to the date, time, and icon, the summary and detailed event entries provide the following information:

- **Source**   The application, service, or component that logged the event
- **Category**   The category of the event, which is sometimes used to further describe the related action
- **Event**   An identifier for the specific event
- **User**   The user account that was logged on when the event occurred
- **Computer**   The computer name where the event occurred
- **Description**   In the detailed entries, this provides a text description of the event
- **Data**   In the detailed entries, this provides any data or error code output by the event

Warnings and critical errors are the two key types of events that you'll want to examine closely. Whenever these types of events occur and you're unsure of the cause, double-click the entry to view the detailed event description. If you want to see only warnings and errors, you can filter the log by completing the following steps:

1. From the View menu, select the Filter Events option. This opens the dialog box shown in Figure 10-2.
2. Clear the following check boxes: Information, Success Audit, and Failure Audit.
3. Select the Warning and Error check boxes.
4. Click OK. You should now see a list of warning and error messages only. Keep in mind that these messages are for all applications running on the server and not just SQL Server.

Figure 10-2. *You can filter events so that only warnings and errors are displayed.*

Understanding Error Messages

SQL Server error messages are cryptic and difficult to read if you don't understand the formatting. All messages logged by SQL Server have

- **An error number that uniquely identifies the error message**   System error numbers have one to five digits. System errors are numbered from 1 to 50,000. User-defined errors start at 50,001.

- **A severity level that indicates how critical the message is**   Severity levels go from 1 to 25. Messages with a severity level of 10 are informational messages. Severity levels from 11 to 16 are generated by users and can be corrected by them. Severity levels from 17 to 25 indicate software or hardware errors that you should examine.

- **An error state number that indicates the source of the error**   Error state numbers have one to three digits and a maximum value of 127. Normally, state numbers indicate the line number in the SQL Server code that generated the message.

- **A message that provides a brief description of the error**

The following message shows a MAPI login failure that was logged in the application log:

```
Error: 17903, Severity: 18, State: 1
1999-06-22 15:53:38.52 ods   MAPI login failure.
```

Normally, the corresponding entry in the SQL Server error log is written as two entries. These entries have the same date and time stamp. The first entry shows the error information:

```
Error: 17903, Severity: 18, State: 1
```

The second entry shows the error message:

```
MAPI login failure
```

Monitoring SQL Server Performance

Windows NT Performance Monitor is the tool of choice for monitoring SQL Server performance. Performance Monitor graphically displays statistics for the set of performance parameters you've selected for display. These performance parameters are referred to as counters.

When you install SQL Server on a system, Performance Monitor is updated with a set of counters for tracking SQL Server performance parameters. These counters can also be updated when you install services and add-ons for SQL Server. For example, when you configure replication on a server, the Replication Monitor window is added to Enterprise Manager, and Performance Monitor is again updated with a set of objects and counters for tracking replication performance.

Performance Monitor creates a graph depicting the various counters you're tracking. The update interval for this graphic is configurable but by default is set to three seconds. As you'll see when you work with Performance Monitor, the tracking information is most valuable when you record the information in a log file and when you configure alerts to send messages when certain events occur or when certain thresholds are reached, such as when a database log file gets close to running out of free space.

The sections that follow examine key techniques you'll use to work with Performance Monitor.

Note Performance Monitor is not available with Microsoft Windows 95/98 desktop installations.

Starting Performance Monitor

Performance Monitor can be started in several different ways. You can

- Select the Performance Monitor option from the Administrative Tools menu.
- Select the Performance Monitor option from the MS SQL Server 7.0 menu.
- In Enterprise Manager, right-click the Replication Monitor entry and then, from the shortcut menu, select Performance Monitor.

The technique you use to start Performance Monitor depends on the tasks you want to accomplish. If you start Performance Monitor from the Administrative Tools menu, no default counters are configured. On the other hand, if you start Performance Monitor using either of the other options, default counters are configured automatically for tracking. These counters show the SQL Server defaults or the replication defaults, depending on how the monitor is started.

Choosing Counters to Monitor

The Performance Monitor only displays information for counters you're tracking. Over a hundred SQL Server counters are available—and if you've configured replication, there are even more. These counters are organized into object groupings. For example, all lock-related counters are associated with the *SQLServer:Lock* object.

To select which counters you want to monitor, complete the following steps:

1. Start Performance Monitor. As Figure 10-3 shows, any default counters are shown in the lower portion of the Performance Monitor window.
2. Performance Monitor has several different views. Make sure you're in Chart view. From the View menu, select the Chart option.
3. To delete a default counter, click its entry in the lower portion of the Performance Monitor window and then press Delete.

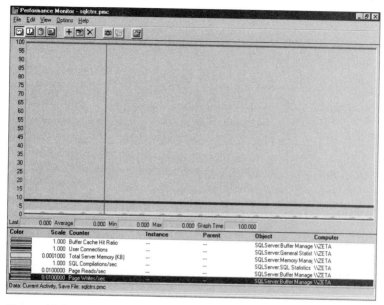

Figure 10-3. *Counters are listed in the lower portion of the Performance Monitor window.*

4. To add counters, from the Edit menu, select the Add To Chart option. This displays the Add To Chart dialog box shown in Figure 10-4. The key fields are

- **Computer**   Enter the UNC name of the SQL Server you want to work with, such as \\ZETA. Click the select computer button, shown with an ellipsis (...), to view a list of computers you have access to over the network.

- **Object**   Select the type of object you want to work with, such as *SQLServer:Locks*.

Note   Creating a huge table containing a list of all the available objects and counters really isn't practical. The easiest way to learn what you can track is to explore the objects and counters available in the Add To Chart dialog box. Select an object in the Object field, click the Explain >> button, and then scroll through the list of counters for this object. Read the description of the selected counter in the Counter Definition area.

- **Counter**   Select one or more counters for the current object. For example, you could select Lock Requests/sec, Lock Timeouts/sec, and Number of Deadlocks/sec.

Figure 10-4. *Select the counters you want to monitor.*

- **Instance**   Select one or more counter instances to monitor. For example, you could select instances of the Lock Requests/sec counter for databases, pages, and tables.

Tip   Don't try to chart too many counters or counter instances at once. You'll make the display too difficult to read and you'll use system resources—namely, CPU time and memory—that may affect server responsiveness.

5. When you've selected all the necessary options, click Add to add the counters to the chart. Repeat this process as necessary to add other performance parameters.

6. Click Done when you're finished.

Creating and Managing Performance Monitor Logs

You can use performance monitor logs to track the performance of SQL Server, and you can replay them at a later date. As you set out to work with logs, keep in mind that the parameters you track in log files are recorded separately from the parameters you're charting in the Performance Monitor window. You can configure log files to update counter data automatically or manually. With automatic logging, a snapshot of key parameters is recorded at specific time intervals, such as every 10 seconds. With manual logging, you determine when snapshots are made.

To create and manage performance monitor logging, complete the following steps:

1. Start Performance Monitor. Switch to Log view by going to the View menu and selecting the Log option. As shown in Figure 10-5, the Log view provides a summary of any current logging information as well as the status of any log file you're using.

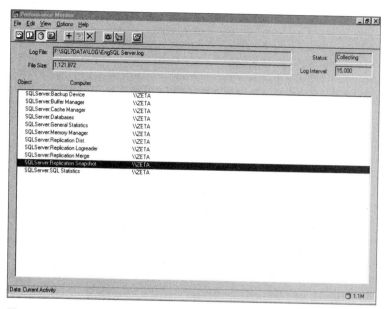

Figure 10-5. *The Log view shows current logging information and log file status.*

2. You log performance data using objects rather than individual counters. This allows you to set the counters you want to chart later. Performance data for any current objects configured for logging are shown in the main area of the Log view.

3. To stop logging an object, select its entry in the Log view window and press Delete.

4. To add logging for an object, from the Edit menu, select the Add To Log option. This opens the Add To Log dialog box, shown in Figure 10-6.

5. In the Computer field, type the name of the server whose performance you want to track. Then select one or more objects to log. Click Add to add the object(s). Repeat this step as necessary to configure other computers or objects for logging.

6. Click Done when you're finished selecting resources to log.

7. Next, select a log file and determine how logging is handled. From the Option menu, select Log and then configure the Log Options dialog box.

8. Select a destination folder for the log using the Save In selection list and then type a log file name in the File Name field.

9. For manual logging, select the Manual Update option button. Then choose Start Log to create the first log snapshot. Afterward, you can create additional snapshots of data by clicking the Update Counter Data button on the toolbar.

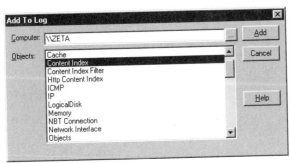

Figure 10-6. *Type the name of the server whose performance you want to track and then select the objects you want to log.*

10. For automatic logging, select the Periodic Update option button and then specify an update interval for the log, such as every 30 seconds. Afterward, choose Start Log to start the logging operation.

 Tip Log files can grow very quickly. If you plan to let Performance Monitor log data for an extended period, be sure to place the log file on a drive with lots of free space. Remember, the more frequently you update the log file, the higher drive space and CPU resource usage will be on the system. To reduce the drain on resources, set a less frequent update interval, such as every 120 seconds.

11. You can stop logging at any time. From the Option menu, select Log; then, in the Log Options dialog box, click Stop Log.

Replaying Performance Monitor Logs

When you're troubleshooting problems, you'll often want to log performance data over an extended period of time and analyze the data later. To do this, complete the following steps:

1. Start Performance Monitor and then configure automatic logging as detailed in the previous section of this chapter, "Creating and Managing Performance Monitor Logs."

2. Load the log file in Performance Monitor when you're ready to analyze the data. To do this, from the Option menu, select Data From. This opens the Data From dialog box. Select the Log File option button and then enter the file path to the log file you want to use. Click OK.

3. Counters for the objects you've logged are available for charting. Select the counters you want to display, as specified in the section of this chapter entitled "Choosing Counters to Monitor."

Configuring Alerts for Performance Counters

You can configure alerts to notify you when certain events occur or when certain performance thresholds are reached. These alerts can be sent out as network messages and as events that are logged in the Windows NT application log. You can also configure alerts to start applications.

You can configure alerts based on performance counters in Enterprise Manager and in Performance Monitor. The core set of alert functions is essentially the same in both utilities. But Enterprise Manager does provide more features, such as automated job execution on alerts and e-mail/pager notification. To add alerts in Enterprise Manager, see the section of Chapter 12 entitled "Managing Alerts."

To add alerts in Performance Monitor, complete the following steps:

1. Start Performance Monitor and then access the Alert view by going to the View menu and selecting Alert.

2. As shown in Figure 10-7, open the Add To Alert dialog box by going to the Edit menu and selecting Add To Alert. The key fields are

   * **Computer** Enter the UNC name of the SQL Server you want to work with. Click the select computer button, shown with ellipses (...), to view a list of computers you have access to over the network.

   * **Object** Select the type of object you want to work with.

   * **Counter** Select one or more counters for the current object.

   * **Instance** Select one or more counter instances to monitor.

   * **Alert If Over/Under** Use the related option fields to specify when the alert occurs. The unit of measurement is whatever makes sense for the currently selected counter(s). For example, to alert if log space is under 20 percent, you would select the Under option button and then type **20**.

   * **Run Program On Alert** Set the complete file path of a program to run when the alert occurs.

Note You don't have to set a program to run on alert. But if you do, you should specify the full path to the program. Also, you can run any type of executable file set in the <%PATHEXT%> environment variable, including batch scripts with the .bat or .cmd extension and Windows scripts with the .vbs, .js, .pl, or .wsc extension.

   * **First Time** Send a notification message and log the alert only the first time it occurs.

   * **Every Time** Send a notification message and log the alert every time it occurs.

Figure 10-7. *You configure alerts much like you do counters, only you have a few different parameters to choose from.*

3. When you've selected all the necessary options, click Add to add the alert. Repeat this process as necessary to add other alerts. Choose Done when you're finished configuring alerts

4. After you configure alerts, you'll want to set alert options. Display the Alert Options dialog box shown in Figure 10-8 by going to the Options menu and selecting Alert.

5. You can log alerts in the application log by selecting the Log Event In Application Log check box.

6. To send network messages on alerts, select Send Network Message and then type a network name in the Net Name field. Network names can be computer names, such as Zeta, or user names, such as wrstanek.

 Note The Alerter and Messenger services must be running on the system that's generating alerts. The client receiving alerts must be running the Messenger service.

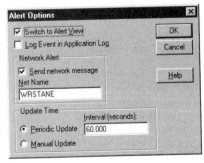

Figure 10-8. *Use the Alert Options dialog box to specify what happens when alerts occur and how often alerts are updated.*

7. You can update the alert log periodically or manually. For periodic updates, select the Periodic Update option button and specify an update interval. For manual updates, select the Manual Update option button and update alert data by clicking the Update Counter Data button on the toolbar.

Solving Performance Problems with Profiler

Whether you're trying to track user activity, troubleshoot connection problems, or optimize SQL Server, SQL Server Profiler is one of the best utilities available. Profiler enables you to trace events that occur in SQL Server. Events you can track in Profiler are similar to counters you can monitor in Performance Monitor. They're organized into groups called event classes, and you can track one or more events for any of the available event classes. Profiler's strength is in its advanced features and extensive customization capabilities.

Profiler traces can be recorded and replayed when you want to analyze the data—and this is one area where Profiler excels. You can

- Use the information to find slow-running queries and then determine what's causing the queries to run slowly
- Go through statements a step at a time to find the cause of a problem
- Track a series of statements that cause a particular problem and then replay the trace on a test server to determine the cause
- Use trace information to determine the cause of deadlocks
- Monitor user and application activity to determine actions that are using CPU time or queries that are taking a long time to process

Let's look at how you can work with Profiler. Afterward, I'll cover creating and managing traces.

Using Profiler

Profiler can be started in several different ways. You can

- Select the Profiler option from the Microsoft SQL Server 7.0 menu
- In Enterprise Manager, from the Tools menu, select SQL Server Profiler

Figure 10-9 shows Profiler in the process of running a trace. The columns shown for the trace, such as Event Class and Event SubClass, are completely configurable when you're setting up the trace, allowing you to select or clear columns as necessary. Two columns you'll want to pay particular attention to are Duration and CPU. The Duration column shows how long a particular event has been running in milliseconds. The CPU column shows the event's processing time in milliseconds by the CPU.

Figure 10-9. *Use the SQL Server Profiler dialog box to create traces of SQL Server events.*

Extended stored procedures provide an alternative to Profiler. Using these extended stored procedures gives you some options that you don't have with SQL Server Profiler. You can

- Store traces in the Windows NT application log.
- Autostart a trace when SQL Server starts.
- Forward event data to another computer running SQL Server (Windows NT or Windows 2000 only).

To create traces with stored procedures, complete the following steps:

1. Create a new trace queue using *xp_trace_addnewqueue.*
2. Set events to capture using *xp_trace_seteventclassrequired.*
3. Set event filters using any of the *xp_trace* stored procedures for filtering—there are nearly 30 of them.
4. Set the destination for the captured event data using *xp_trace_setqueue-destination.*

Creating New Traces

With Profiler, you can create shared traces or private traces. Shared traces are available to anyone who has permission to log on to the system. Private traces are only available to the user currently logged onto the system. You can use both

Figure 10-10. *Configure the trace using the tabs and fields available in the Trace Properties dialog box.*

shared traces and private traces to record events generated by local and remote SQL Servers. You can run these traces in the Profiler window and store them for later analysis.

You start a new trace by completing the following steps:

1. Start SQL Server Profiler and then click the New Trace button, or select File, then New, and then Trace. This opens the Trace Properties dialog box with the General tab selected, as shown in Figure 10-10.

2. In the Trace Name field enter a name for the trace, such as Data Trace or Deadlock Track For CustomerDB.

3. Select a trace type. For a shared trace, select the Shared option button. For a private trace, select the Private option button.

4. Using the SQL Server selection list, select the SQL Server that you want to trace. If you choose the <New Server> entry, you can register and configure a connection to a new server.

5. To the right of the SQL Server selection list is the server source options button. Click this button to configure the following advanced trace options for the source server:

   - **Number Of Rows To Buffer On Server** Sets the maximum number of rows to buffer or store in the trace queue. The recommended value is 1,000, but you can set any value from 0 to 20,000.

   - **Server Time-Out (Seconds)** Sets a time-out interval for the event queue. When a queue reaches its maximum size, event queuing is paused for this time-out period. The default time-out period is five seconds.

Note The trace queue is cleared out as events are processed, but it can get backed up if a lot of events are being triggered (or if you're performing multiple traces at the same time). Sometimes the queue may get flooded, and if this happens, the server time-out setting is used to allow the queue to catch up. As a result of the time-out, some events may get missed. To prevent this from happening, you can increase the size of the trace queue or boost the thread priority for the threads processing the trace queue, or both.

- **Boost Priority (%)** Determines when a thread processing the trace queue is boosted in priority, which helps to clear out the queue before it gets flooded. The value set represents the percentage of the buffer limit in the trace queue that must be reached before the priority boost occurs. The default value is 95 percent. You can set any value from 0 to 100.

- **Reduce Priority (%)** Determines when threads processing the trace queue are lowered in priority, which helps to reduce the amount of system resources being used to handle the trace queue. The value set represents the percentage of the buffer limit in the trace queue that must be reached before the priority is lowered. The default value is 90 percent. You can set any value from 0 to 99.

6. The Profiler window displays traces automatically. You can store traces as they are being created by setting the Capture To File or the Capture To Table option, or both. Or you can store the trace later by selecting File, then selecting Save As, and then choosing either the Trace File option or the Trace Table option.

 Tip As you might imagine, there are advantages and disadvantages to using trace files and trace tables. With trace files, you can store traces quickly and efficiently while using minimal system resources. With trace tables, you get ease of use by being able to store the trace directly in a table on another server, but you use many more system resources and usually have slower response times. Note also that storing a trace only saves the trace data. It doesn't save the trace definition. To reuse the trace definition, you'll have to export the trace definition.

7. Click the Events tab, as shown in Figure 10-11. Over 75 individual events are available. Available Events lists all events available to trace. Selected Events lists all events selected to trace. The best way to learn the types of events you can trace is to select each event or event class and read its description in the lower portion of the Events tab.

8. Select events to add to the trace. Use the Add button to add event classes or individual events to a trace definition. Use the Remove button to remove event classes or individual events from a trace definition. Remember, the more

Figure 10-11. *Use the Events tab to select event classes or individual events to add to the trace.*

events you trace, the more events will be generated on the source server, which can use up system resources and bog down the trace queue.

9. Click the Data Columns tab, as shown in Figure 10-12. Then select data columns to collect in the trace. The data columns you select determine the columns of information displayed with the trace. For example, if you select the Application Name column, you'll see the corresponding column in the trace data.

Figure 10-12. *Use the Data Columns tab to choose data columns to display for traced events. Most of the time the default settings are fine.*

Tip The default column selections usually work just fine. If you're tracking distributed queries, be sure to add the Server Name column. For transactions, be sure to add the Transaction ID column. Also, if you plan to replay the trace for troubleshooting, look for specific event classes and data columns that must be selected in the section of this chapter entitled "Replaying Traces."

10. To focus the trace on specific types of data, you may want to set criteria that exclude certain types of events. If so, select the Filters tab and then set filter criteria. For each event category, you can use different filtering criteria. These criteria are used as follows:

- **Minimum and maximum** Set the minimum or maximum value that triggers the event. Events with values outside the range are excluded. For example, with the CPU event category you can set a minimum or maximum milliseconds of CPU time, or both, for logged events. If the events use less CPU time than the minimum or more than the maximum, they are excluded.

- **Value** Enter a specific identifier to trace. For example, with the Connection ID event category you can set a specific connection ID to trace. Then only events for that connection ID are traced.

- **Include and exclude** Enter strings to include or exclude for this event category. Use the wildcard character (%) to match a series of characters. Use the semicolon (;) to separate multiple strings. For example, with the Application Name category, you could exclude all application names that start with MS and SQL Server by typing **MS%;SQL Server%**

11. When you're finished configuring the trace, click OK to create the trace.

Using the Create Trace Wizard

While you'll usually configure traces manually, you can also use the Create Trace Wizard to quickly create traces for the most common types of traces. To create a trace using the wizard, complete the following steps:

1. In Profiler, click the Create Trace Wizard button on the toolbar or select the Create Trace Wizard option from the Tools menu. Then, in the Create Trace Wizard window, click Next after reading the welcome dialog box.

2. In the Identify The Problem window shown in Figure 10-13, select the server you want to trace and then choose the type of problem you want to look for. Traces the wizard can perform are

- Finding the worst performing queries
- Identifying scans of large tables
- Identifying the cause of deadlocks
- Profiling the performance of a stored procedure

Figure 10-13. *Select a server and problem to trace.*

* Tracing Transact-SQL activity by application
* Tracing Transact-SQL activity by user

3. The next window you see depends on the type of problem you're identifying. Fields you may see include

* **Database** Select the database you want to trace using the Database selection list. To trace all databases on the source system, select <All Databases>.

* **Minimum Duration** Sets the minimum duration for queries. Only queries that have a longer run time are traces.

* **Stored Procedure** Select the stored procedure you want to trace in the selected database. To trace all stored procedures, select <All Stored Procedures>.

* **Table** Select the table you want to trace in the selected database. To trace all tables, select <All Tables>.

4. In the Completing The Create Trace Wizard window, type a name for the trace and then click Finish. The wizard creates the trace and then runs it in a Profiler window.

Working with Traces

Profiler displays information for multiple traces in separate windows, which can be cascaded or tiled. You can use buttons on the Profiler toolbar to control all available traces. Buttons in individual windows control the trace in that window only.

Using the buttons on the Profiler toolbar, you can

* Create a new trace by clicking on the New Trace button and then configuring the trace using the New Trace dialog box.

- Start traces by clicking the Start Traces button and then selecting one or more available traces to start.

- Pause traces by clicking the Pause Traces button and then selecting one or more available traces to pause temporarily. You can then use the Start Traces button to resume the trace where it left off.

- Stop traces by clicking the Stop Traces button and then selecting one or more available traces to stop. If you start the trace again with the Start Traces button, the Profiler display starts over from the beginning of the trace process; new data is appended to the files or tables to which you're capturing data.

- Delete traces by clicking the Delete Traces button and then selecting one or more available traces to delete. You can't recover traces you delete.

- Edit trace properties by clicking the Edit Trace Properties button and then selecting the trace you want to reconfigure.

Buttons in the active window's toolbar have similar purposes but affect the current trace only. You can

- Start the trace by clicking the Start Trace button.
- Pause the trace by clicking the Pause Trace button.
- Stop the trace by clicking the Stop Trace button.
- Edit trace properties by clicking the Properties button.

Saving a Trace

When you create traces in Profiler, you create trace data and trace definitions. Trace data is displayed in the Profiler window and can also be stored in a file or a table, or both. The trace data records a history of events that you're tracking, and you can use this history to replay the events for later analysis. The trace definition is displayed in the Trace Properties dialog box. You can use the trace definition to create a new trace based on the existing trace.

To save trace data, complete the following steps:

1. Through the Window menu, access the Profiler window displaying the trace you want to save.
2. Select File and then choose Save As. You can now save the trace data to a file or a table in a SQL Server database.

To save a trace definition, complete the following steps:

1. From the File menu, select the Export option.
2. Choose the trace whose definition you want to save.
3. Later, when you want to use the trace definition, import it by going to the File menu and selecting the Import option.

Replaying Traces

One of the main reasons for creating traces is that it gives you the ability to save traces and replay them later. When replaying traces, Profiler can simulate user connections and authentication, which allows you to reproduce the activity recorded in the trace. To aid in troubleshooting, you can

- Execute traces step by step to closely monitor each step in the trace
- Execute traces using the original time line to simulate user loads
- Execute traces with a high replay rate to stress test servers

As you monitor the trace execution, you can look for problem areas. Then, when you identify the cause of problems you're trying to solve, you can correct them and then rerun the original trace definition. If you're still having problems, you'll need to reanalyze the trace data or look at other areas that may be causing problems. Keep in mind that you may need to specify different events to capture in the subsequent trace.

Requirements for Replaying Traces

Traces that you want to replay must contain a minimum set of events and data columns. If the trace doesn't contain the necessary elements, you won't be able to replay the trace. The required elements are in addition to any other elements that you want to monitor or display with traces. Events that you must capture in order to allow a trace to be replayed are

- Connect
- CursorExecute (required only when replaying server-side cursors)
- CursorOpen (required only when replaying server-side cursors)
- CursorPrepare (required only when replaying server-side cursors)
- Disconnect
- Exec Prepared SQL (required only when replaying server-side prepared SQL statements)
- ExistingConnection
- Prepare SQL (required only when replaying server-side prepared SQL statements)
- RPC:Starting
- SQL:BatchStarting

Data columns that you must capture to allow a trace to be replayed are

- Application Name
- Binary Data
- Connection ID or SPID
- Database ID

- Event Class
- Event Sub Class
- Host Name
- Integer Data
- Server Name
- SQL User Name
- Start Time
- Text

Replaying Traces on a Different Server

You can replay a trace on a server other than the server originally traced. This server is called the target system. When replaying traces on the target, you should ensure that all logins contained in the trace

- Are created on the target system and are in the same database as the source system
- Have the same permissions they had originally
- Have the same passwords they had originally
- Are set to use a default database that matches the database on the source system

If these settings aren't the same, you'll see errors, but the replay operation will continue. Also, database IDs on the target system must be the same as those on the source system. The easiest way to set up databases on the target is to complete the following steps:

1. Back up the master database on the source and any user databases used in the trace.
2. Restore the databases on the target as explained in the section of Chapter 6 entitled "Restoring a Database to a Different Location."

Replaying and Analyzing a Trace

Replaying a trace allows you to analyze problems. To get started, start Profiler and then select the Trace File or Trace Table option from the Open menu, as appropriate for the type of trace you want to replay. The trace is then loaded into the Profiler window. As Figure 10-14 shows, events and command records in the trace are summarized in the Profiler window. You can click the plus sign (+) next to a category name to see an expanded list of commands and events traced.

As Figure 10-14 also shows, the window toolbar for replay is different from the standard toolbar. The buttons provide just about everything that you need to debug traces, including

- **Start Execution** Starts executing the trace
- **Pause Execution**   Pauses execution of the trace
- **Stop Execution**   Stops execution of the trace

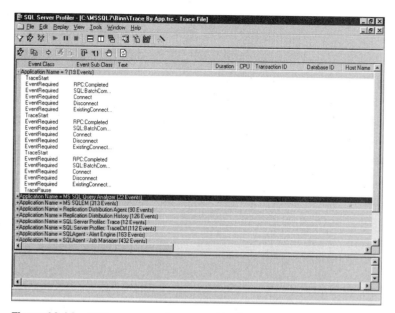

Figure 10-14. *All the commands executed in the trace and the events collected in the trace are displayed in the Profiler window.*

- **Execute Single Step** Allows you to move through the trace one step at a time

- **Execute To Cursor** Allows you to move through the trace using cursor sets

- **Toggle Breakpoint** Allows you to set breakpoints for the trace execution

When you start the replay, you'll get an initial dialog box that asks you to configure replay options (see Figure 10-15). You configure the options in the Replay SQL Server dialog box to control where and how the playback takes place. Start by setting the destination server for the replay operation. Then set the sync level and the replay rate.

The synchronization level determines how closely the replay mirrors the original event execution. You can choose

- **Full Synchronization** Events are started in the order in which they originally started. Full synchronization doesn't guarantee timing of event execution. Events may be executed sooner than their original start time or after their original time, depending on current activity levels, the current speed of connections, and other factors. This is the default sync level.

- **Partial Synchronization** Events are started at their expected start time, recorded in the trace, if possible. However, if there are excessive delays in waiting for other connections, event execution may be delayed as well.

Figure 10-15. *Replay options allow you to control where and how the play-back takes place.*

- **No Synchronization** Events using a particular connection are started as soon as the previous event on the same connection has completed. Otherwise, there is no synchronization between events on different connections.

The replay rate determines the timing SQL Server Profiler uses to replay events. You can choose

- **As Fast As Possible** Events are replayed as quickly as they can be processed. No timing is maintained between events. When one event completes, the next event is started. This is the default replay rate.

- **Maintain Interval Between Events** Events are replayed with the original time interval between them. Execution time for each event is variable and depends on current activity levels, the current speed of connections, and other factors.

- **Maintain Relationship To Start Time** Events are replayed at the same time they originally occurred. Because execution time may vary, SQL Server may need to adjust the interval between events to ensure that they are started at the correct time.

Other options you can set for replay are

- **Output File** Sets a file for the results of the replay, which you can view later
- **Progress** Displays the progress of replayed events
- **ODBC Errors** Displays ODBC errors
- **Internal Errors** Displays internal errors
- **Results** Displays result sets returned during replay

If you select an output file and choose the Progress option, you can replay the output file later—just as you would any other trace file.

Chapter 11

Creating Tables and Indexes

In Microsoft SQL Server 7.0, the structures of tables and indexes are just as important as the database itself, especially when it comes to performance. Tables are collections of data about a specific entity, such as a customer or an order. To describe the attributes of these entities, you use named columns. For example, to describe the attributes of a customer, you could use these columns: cust_name, cust_address, and cust_phone.

Each instance of data in a table is represented as a single data entry or row. Typically, rows are unique and have unique identifiers called *primary keys* associated with them. However, a primary key isn't mandatory in ANSI SQL, and it isn't required in SQL Server. The job of the primary key is to set a unique identifier for each row in the table and to allow SQL Server to create a unique index on this key. Indexes are user-defined data structures that provide fast access to data when you search on an indexed column. Indexes are separate from tables, and you can configure them automatically with the Index Tuning Wizard.

Most tables are related to other tables. For example, a Customers table may have a cust_account column that contains a customer's account number. The cust_account column may also appear in tables named Orders and Receivables. If the cust_account column is the primary key of the Customers table, a foreign key relationship can be established between Customers and Orders as well as between Customers and Receivables. The foreign key creates a link between the tables that you can use to preserve referential integrity in the database.

Once the link is established, you won't be able to delete a row in the Customers table if the cust_account identifier is referenced in the Orders or Receivables tables. This feature prevents you from invalidating references to information used in other tables. You would first need to delete or change the related references in the Orders or Receivables tables, or both, before deleting a primary key row in the Customers table. Foreign key relationships allow you to combine data from related tables in queries by matching the foreign key constraint of one table with the primary or unique key in another table. Combining tables in this manner is called a *table join*, and the keys allow SQL Server to optimize the query and quickly find related data.

Defining Tables

Tables consist of columns and rows of data, with each column having a native or user-defined data type. For all data types except *text*, *ntext*, and *image*, table data is stored in data pages that have a fixed size of 8 KB (8192 bytes). The page header uses the first 96 bytes of each page, leaving 8096 bytes for data and row offsets. Row offsets indicate the logical order of rows on a page, which means that offset 0 refers to the first row in the index, offset 1 refers to the second row, and so on. If a table contains text and image data, the text or image isn't stored with the rest of the data for a row. Instead, SQL Server stores a 16-byte pointer to the actual data, which is stored in a collection of 8-KB pages that aren't necessarily written contiguously.

Data rows can't span multiple pages (except for *text*, *ntext*, and *image* data, which are stored separately). The maximum size of a single data row is 8096 bytes (including any necessary overhead). Effectively, this means the maximum size of character columns is 8000 bytes and that columns can store up to 8000 ASCII characters or up to 4000 Unicode characters. As you can see, the 8-KB pages in SQL Server 7.0 offer a strong improvement over the 2-KB pages in SQL Server 6.5.

A table that has fixed-length rows always stores the same amount of rows per page. On the other hand, a table with variable-length rows stores as many rows as possible, based on the length of the data entered. As you might expect, there's a definite performance advantage to keeping rows compact and allowing more rows to fit on a page. With more rows per page, you'll have an improved cache-hit ratio and reduce input/output (I/O).

SQL Server provides several different ways to work with tables. You can

- Create new tables using the New Table window in Enterprise Manager or the CREATE TABLE command.
- Modify existing tables using the Design Table window in Enterprise Manager or the ALTER TABLE command. The syntax for ALTER TABLE is essentially the same as that for CREATE TABLE.

In Enterprise Manager, you create a new table or modify an existing table by completing the following steps:

1. Start Enterprise Manager and then work your way down to the database you want to work with. Click the plus sign (+) next to the database name to display a list of data objects and resources.

2. To create a new table, right-click the Tables node and, from the shortcut menu, select New Table. Enter a table name when prompted. You'll then access the New Table view in Enterprise Manager, which is similar to what you see in Figure 11-1.

3. To edit an existing table, right-click the table name in the right pane and, from the shortcut menu, select Design Table. This opens the Design Table view in Enterprise Manager, shown in Figure 11-1.

Figure 11-1. *Enterprise Manager makes it easy to create and modify tables. Work your way through the column properties from left to right.*

Tip Table names can be up to 128 characters long. Table names must begin with an alphabetic character but can contain underscores (_), at symbols (@), and pound signs (#). The exceptions to this rule are temporary tables. Private temporary tables begin with # and are only accessible to you during the current user session. Global temporary tables begin with ## and are accessible to anyone as long as your user session remains connected. Temporary tables are created in tempdb and are automatically deleted when your user session ends.

4. You can now create a new column by entering a column name and specifying its properties or by modifying an existing column by changing its name or its properties, or both. Rows and columns displayed in the Enterprise Manager window are used as follows:

- Rows in the New Table and Design Table views correspond to columns in the table you're working with. In Figure 11-1, columns listed include cust_id, cust_lname, cust_fname, phone, address, city, state, and zip.

- Columns in the New Table and Design Table views correspond to column properties in the table you're working with. In Figure 11-1, column properties listed include Column Name, Datatype, Length, Precision, and Scale.

The sections that follow examine key techniques and concepts for working with tables. Whether you want to create a new table or modify existing tables, the techniques you'll use and the concepts you'll need to understand are similar.

Using Native Data Types

Native data types are those built into SQL Server and supported directly. All data types have a length value, which is either fixed or variable. Length for a numeric or binary data type is the number of bytes used to store the number. Length for a character data type is the number of characters. Most numeric data types also have precision and scale. Precision is the total number of digits in a number. Scale is the number of digits to the right of the decimal point in a number. For example, the number 8714.235 has a precision of seven and a scale of three.

Table 11-1 summarizes native data types that work with numbers and money. The first column shows the general data type or data type synonym for SQL-92 compatibility. The second column shows the SQL Server data type.

Table 11-1. Native Data Types for Numbers and Money

SQL-92 Name–Type	SQL Server Name	Range–Description
Integers		
bit	bit	0 or 1
integer	int	-2^31 (-2,147,483,648) through 2^31-1 (2,147,483,647)
small integer	smallint	-2^15 (-32,768) through 2^15-1 (32,767)
tiny integer	tinyint	0 through 255
Money		
money	money	-922,337,203,685,477.5808 through +922,337,203,685,477.5807
small money	smallmoney	-214,748.3648 through +214,748.3647
Exact Numeric		
dec, decimal	decimal	-10^38-1 through 10^38-1
numeric	decimal	-10^38-1 through 10^38-1
Approximate Numeric		
double precision	float	-1.79E + 308 through 1.79E + 308
float	float	-1.79E + 308 through 1.79E + 308. float[(n)] for n = 1-53
float	real	-3.40E + 38 through 3.40E + 38. float[(n)] for n = 1-24

(continued)

Table 11-1. *(continued)*

SQL-92 Name–Type	SQL Server Name	Range–Description
Numerics		
cursor	cursor	A reference to a cursor
timestamp	timestamp	A database-wide unique number
uniqueidentifier	uniqueidentifier	A globally unique identifier (GUID)

Table 11-2 summarizes native data types for dates, characters, and binary data. Again, the first column shows the general data type or data type synonym for SQL-92 compatibility. The second column shows the SQL Server data type.

Table 11-2. Native Data Types for Dates, Characters, and Binary Values

SQL-92 Name–Type	SQL Server Name	Range–Description
Date		
datetime	datetime	January 1, 1753, to December 31, 9999; accuracy of 3/100 of a second
small datetime	smalldatetime	January 1, 1900, through June 6, 2079; accuracy of one minute
Character		
character	char	Fixed-length, non-Unicode character data with a maximum length of 8000 characters
character varying	varchar	Variable-length, non-Unicode data with a maximum of 8000 characters
text	text	Variable-length, non-Unicode data with a maximum length of $2^{31}-1$ (2,147,483,647) characters
national character	nchar	Fixed-length, Unicode data with a maximum length of 4000 characters
national char varying	nvarchar	Variable-length, Unicode data with a maximum length of 4000 characters
national text	ntext	Variable-length, Unicode data with a maximum length of $2^{30}-1$ (1,073,741,823) characters
Binary		
binary	binary	Fixed-length, binary data with a maximum length of 8000 bytes
binary varying	varbinary	Variable-length, binary data with a maximum length of 8000 bytes
image	image	Variable-length, binary data with a maximum length of $2^{31}-1$ (2,147,483,647) bytes

When you create or modify a table in Enterprise Manager, you assign a native data type by clicking in the Datatype column and using the selection list to choose a data type. In Transact-SQL, you set the data type when you create the table and populate its columns or when you alter a table and add or change columns. Listing 11-1 shows how you could create the table shown previously in Figure 11-1.

Listing 11-1. Creating a Table and Its Columns

```
USE CUSTOMER
CREATE TABLE Customers
    (cust_id varchar(11) NOT NULL,
    cust_lname varchar(40) NOT NULL,
    cust_fname varchar(20) NOT NULL,
    phone char(12) NOT NULL,
    address varchar(40) NULL,
    city varchar(20) NULL,
    state varchar(2) NULL,
    zip char(5) NULL,
    contract varchar(11) NOT NULL,
    rowguid uniqueidentifier NOT NULL DEFAULT newid())
```

Using Fixed-Length and Variable-Length Fields

Binary and character data types can be created as fixed-length or variable-length fields. When you use fixed-length data types, the column size you specify is reserved in the database and can be written to without having to manipulate the data around the column. This makes updates to the database quicker than with variable-length fields. When you use variable-length data types, you allow SQL Server to squeeze more rows into data pages, if possible. Generally, more rows per data page allows for more efficient reading of data, which can translate into improved performance for read operations.

To gain a better understanding of the performance implications, consider the following scenario. With fixed-length columns of 80, 120, 40, and 500 bytes each, rows would always be written using 750 bytes of storage (740 bytes for data plus 10 bytes of overhead for each row). Here, you could fit 10 rows per data page (8096/750, without the remainder). If you used variable-length columns, however, the number of bytes used per row and the amount of rows stored per page would vary. As an example, let's say that on average the variable-length rows use 400 bytes. This includes 380 bytes of data and 20 bytes of overhead (12 bytes of overhead for rows that use variable length data plus 2 bytes of overhead per variable-length column). Here, you could fit 20 rows per data page (8096/400, without the remainder), which would make data reads more efficient than the fixed-length example.

Using User-Defined Data Types

User-defined data types are special data types that are based on a native data type. You'll want to use user-defined data types when two or more tables store the same type of data in a column, and these columns must have exactly the same data type, length, and nullability. Either you or SQL Server can create user-defined data types. For example, *sysname* is a user-defined data type that's used to reference database object names. The data type is defined as a variable Unicode character type of 128 characters, which is why object names are limited to 128 characters throughout SQL Server. You can apply this same concept to ensure that a particular tidbit of data is used exactly as you want it to be used.

Creating User-Defined Data Types

You create user-defined data types at the database level rather than at the table level, which is why user-defined data types are static and immutable (unchangeable). This ensures that there is no performance penalty associated with user-defined data types. User-defined data types do have some limitations, however. You cannot declare a default value or CHECK constraint as part of the user-defined data type. You cannot create a user-defined data type based on a user-defined data type either.

Tip When user-defined data types are created in a user-defined database, they apply only to that database. If you want user-defined data types to apply to multiple databases, define the data type in the model database. After that, the user-defined data type will exist in all new user-defined databases.

In Enterprise Manager, you create a user-defined data type by completing the following steps:

1. Start Enterprise Manager and then work your way down to the database you want to work with.

2. Right-click the database name and select New. From the shortcut menu, select User Defined Data Type. This opens the User-Defined Data Type Properties dialog box shown in Figure 11-2.

3. Enter a name for the new data type.

4. In the Data Type list, select the data type on which you want to base the user-defined data type.

5. If the data type has a variable length, set the number of bytes or characters for the data type. For fixed-length variables, such as *int*, you won't be able to set a length.

6. To allow the data type to accept null values, select Allow Nulls.

7. Optionally, use the Rule and Default lists to select a rule or default to bind to the user-defined data type.

8. Click OK. If you open a new table or edit an existing table, you'll see the new data type as one of the last entries in the DataType selection list.

Figure 11-2. *Configure the new data type using the User-Defined Data Type Properties dialog box.*

You can also create user-defined data types with the *sp_addtype* stored procedure. Listing 11-2 shows the syntax and usage of this procedure.

Listing 11-2. *sp_addtype* **Syntax and Usage**

Syntax

```
sp_addtype [@typename =] type,
  [@phystype =] system_data_type
  [, [@nulltype =] 'null_type']
```

Usage

```
USE master
EXEC sp_addtype USPhoneNumber, 'char(12)', 'NOT NULL'
```

Managing User-Defined Data Types

Once you create user-defined data types, you'll often need to manage their properties. To manage user-defined data types, complete the following steps:

1. Start Enterprise Manager and then work your way down to the database you want to work with.

2. Select the User Defined Data Types node in the left pane. This displays current user-defined data types in the right pane.

3. Right-click the user-defined data type you want to manage and then select

   - Properties, to view the data type's properties and set dependencies
   - Delete, to delete the data type
   - Rename, to rename the data type

4. To see where the data type is used in the database, right-click the user-defined data type and then, from the shortcut menu, select Properties. Next, in the User-Defined Data Type Properties dialog box, click Where Used.

Allowing and Disallowing Nulls

When you create columns in a table, you can specify whether nulls are allowed or not. A null means there is no entry in the column for that row; it isn't the same as zero or an empty string. Columns defined with a primary key constraint or identity property can't allow null values.

If you add a row but don't set a value for a column that allows null values, SQL Server inserts the value NULL—unless a default value is set for the column. Additionally, if the column allows nulls, you can explicitly set a column to null using the NULL keyword. Don't use quotation marks when setting null explicitly.

In Enterprise Manager's New Table and Design Table views, you

- Allow nulls in a column by selecting the Allow Nulls column.
- Disallow nulls in a column by clearing the Allow Nulls column.

For a Transact-SQL example of allowing and disallowing nulls for a new table, see Listing 11-1.

Default Values

Null values are useful when you don't know the value or the value is missing. The use of null is controversial, though, and a better alternative is to set a default value. The default value is used when no value is set for a column you're inserting into a table. For example, you may want a character-based column to have the value N/A rather than NULL. Here, you would set the default value as N/A.

As Table 11-3 summarizes, combinations of default values and nullability are handled in different ways. The key thing to remember is that if you set a default value, the default is used whenever a value isn't specified for the column entry. This is true even if you allow nulls.

Table 11-3. Default Values and Nullability

Column Definition	No Entry, No DEFAULT Definition	No Entry, DEFAULT Definition	Enter a Null Value
Allows null values	Sets NULL	Sets default value	Sets NULL
Disallows null values	Error occurs	Sets default value	Error occurs

Using Identities and Globally Unique Identifiers

When you design tables, you'll often need to think about unique identifiers that can be used as primary keys or to ensure that merged data don't conflict with existing data. Unique identifiers for primary keys could include customer account numbers or social security numbers. However, if a unique identifier isn't available, you may want to use the identity property to generate sequential values that are unique for each row in a table. You could also use this unique identifier to automatically generate a customer account number, an order number, or whatever other unique value you need.

While the identity property provides a local solution for a specific table, it doesn't guarantee that the value will be unique throughout the database. Other tables in the database may have identity columns with the same values. In most cases, this isn't a problem because the identity values are usually used only within the context of a single table and don't relate to other tables. However, there are times when you'll need a value that's unique throughout one or more databases, and this is where globally unique identifiers come into the picture.

Globally unique identifiers are guaranteed to be unique across all networked computers in the world, which is extremely useful in merge replication. When you're merging data from multiple databases, globally unique identifiers ensure that records aren't inadvertently associated with each other. For example, the company's New York, Chicago, and San Francisco offices may have customer account numbers that are unique at local offices but not at the national level. Here, globally unique identifiers would ensure that account XYZ from New York and account XYZ from Chicago aren't merged as the same account.

Identities and globally unique identities aren't mutually exclusive. Each table can have one identifier column and one globally unique identity property. These values are often used together. For example, all clustered indexes in SQL Server should be unique, but they do not have to be unique.

In Enterprise Manager's New Table and Design Table views, you set identity values for a table by completing the following steps:

1. Create or modify other columns in the table, as appropriate, then start a new column for the identity value.

2. Give the identify column a name and then select a data type. Identifier columns must use the data type *tinyint*, *smallint*, *int*, *decimal*, or *numeric*. Globally unique identifier columns must have a data type of *uniqueidentifier*.

 Tip When you set the data type for an identifier column, be sure to consider how many rows are in the table as well as how many rows may be added in the future. A *tinyint* identifier would allow for only 256 unique values (0 to 255). A *smallint* identifier would allow for 32,768 values (0 to 32,767).

3. Clear the Allow Nulls check box for the identity column.

4. To assign a globally unique identifier, select the Is RowGuid check box for the identity column. A default value of *newid()* is created automatically for you.

Note The *newid()* function is used to generate new uniqueidentifier values. These values are obtained by combining the identification number of a network card with a unique number from the CPU clock. If a server process generates the identifier, the network card used is the server's. If the identifier is returned by application API function calls, the network card used is the client's. Network card manufacturers guarantee that no other network card in the next 100 years will have the same number.

5. To assign a unique identifier:

   - Select the Identify check box for the identity column.

   - Type a value in the Identity Seed cell. This value is assigned to the first row in the table. If you leave this cell blank, the value 1 is assigned by default.

   - Type a value in the Identity Increment cell. This value is the increment that is added to the Identity Seed for each subsequent row. If you leave this cell blank, the value 1 is assigned by default.

Note The identity seed and increment are used to determine the identifier for rows. If you entered a seed value of 100 and an increment of 10, the first row would have a value of 100, the second would have a value of 110, and so on.

When you create a table in Transact-SQL, globally unique identifiers aren't generated automatically. You must reference the *newid()* function as the default value for the identifier column, such as:

```
USE CUSTOMER
CREATE TABLE Customers
  (cust_lname varchar(40) NOT NULL,
  cust_fname varchar(20) NOT NULL,
  phone char(12) NOT NULL,
  uid uniqueidentifier NOT NULL DEFAULT newid())
```

Now, when you insert a new row into the table, SQL Server adds the globally unique identifier by default, such as:

```
INSERT INTO Customers
Values ('Stanek', 'William', '123-555-1212')
```

Or, when you explicitly call the *newid()* function, such as:

```
INSERT INTO Customers
Values ('Stanek', 'William', '123-555-1212', newid())
```

Working with Tables

As you can on other SQL Server resources, you can perform many tasks on tables. These tasks are examined in the sections that follow.

Viewing Table Row and Size Information

In Enterprise Manager you can view table row and size information by completing the following steps:

1. Start Enterprise Manager and then work your way down to the database you want to work with.

2. With the Taskpad enabled, select the database entry in the left pane and then, in the right pane, click the Tables & Indexes tab, as shown in Figure 11-3.

You can also view row, size, and space statistics for individual tables using the *sp_spaceused* stored procedure. The following accesses the Customer database and then checks the statistics for the Customers table:

```
USE CUSTOMER
EXEC sp_spaceused Customers
```

Figure 11-3. *The Tables & Indexes view provides a summary of tables and indexes used in the database, which includes the number of rows used and the table size.*

Displaying Table Properties and Permissions

In Enterprise Manager you can display table properties and permissions by completing the following steps:

1. Start Enterprise Manager and then work your way down to the database you want to work with.
2. Select the Tables node to display a table list in the right pane.
3. Double-click the table whose properties you want to examine.
4. Once the Properties dialog box is open, you can click Permissions to display and change table permissions.

Copying Tables

The easiest way to create a copy of a table is to use Transact-SQL. To do that, complete the following steps:

1. Make sure that the Select Into/Bulk Copy database option is selected as specified in the section of Chapter 4 entitled "Database Options for Enterprise Manager and Transact-SQL."
2. Use SELECT INTO to extract all the rows from an existing table into the new table. The new table must not exist already. For example, if you wanted to copy the Customers table to a new table called Customers2, you could use

```
SELECT * INTO Customers2 FROM Customers
```

Renaming and Deleting Tables

In Enterprise Manager, the easiest way to rename or delete a table is to complete the following steps:

1. Start Enterprise Manager, and then work your way down to the database you want to work with.
2. Select the Tables node to display a table list in the right pane.
3. To rename a table, right-click the table and then, from the shortcut menu, select Rename. You can now type a new name for the table.
4. To delete a table, right-click the table and then, from the shortcut menu, select Delete. When prompted to confirm the action, choose Yes.

You can also rename tables using *sp_rename,* such as:

```
USE CUSTOMER
EXEC sp_rename Customers, Customers2
```

You can remove a table from the database using the DROP TABLE command, such as:

```
USE CUSTOMER
DROP TABLE Customers2
```

If you'd rather delete the rows in a table but leave its structure intact, you can use DELETE. The following DELETE command deletes all the rows in a table but doesn't remove the table structure:

```
USE CUSTOMER
DELETE Customers
```

Adding and Removing Columns in a Table

In Enterprise Manager you add or remove columns in a table as described in the section of this chapter entitled "Defining Tables." In Transact-SQL, you modify table columns using the ALTER TABLE command.

Adding Columns

The following example adds a unique identifier column to the Customers table:

```
USE CUSTOMER
ALTER TABLE Customers
   ADD uid uniqueidentifier NOT NULL DEFAULT newid()
```

Modifying Columns

To change the characteristics of an existing column, use the ALTER COLUMN option, such as:

```
USE CUSTOMER
ALTER TABLE Customers
   ALTER COLUMN cust_fname CHAR(10) NOT NULL
```

Removing Columns

The following example removes the Address2 column from the Customers table:

```
USE CUSTOMER
ALTER TABLE Customers
   DROP Address2
```

Scripting Tables

All the SQL commands that go into creating tables in a database can be re-created and stored in a .sql file for later use. To do this, complete the following steps:

1. Start Enterprise Manager and then work your way down to the database you want to work with.

2. Select the Tables node to display a table list in the right pane.

3. Right-click the table you want to work with and then select All Tasks. Now choose Generate SQL Scripts to open the dialog box shown in Figure 11-4.

4. By default, the table you clicked is listed in the Object To Be Scripted list box. You can add other objects by selecting them and using the Add >> button.

5. Use the Formatting tab fields to add formatting information that details how the objects are to be scripted.

Figure 11-4. *Generate SQL commands needed to re-create tables using the Generate SQL Scripts dialog box.*

6. Use the Options tab fields to script additional information, such as roles, logons, and permissions.

7. Click OK when you're ready to save the .sql script. When prompted, set a folder and file path for the script.

Using Views

Views represent data in existing tables in an alternate way, and you can think of views as virtual tables. To create a view, you use a SELECT statement to select the data in one or more tables and display it as a view. For example, you could create a view that gets the customer's first name, last name, and account number from the Customers table and the order information from the Orders table, which makes the information more manageable for your company's sales representatives. As you can with tables, you can assign permissions to views. These permissions are specific to the view and separate from the table permissions.

Creating Views

Once you understand tables, creating views is a fairly straightforward process. You can create a view in Enterprise Manager by completing the following steps:

1. Start Enterprise Manager and then work your way down to the database you want to work with.

2. Select the Views node to display a view list in the right pane. As you'll see, two types of views are available: system and user. System views provide summary information about key database information, such as table constraints and table privileges. User views are defined by you or by other database users.

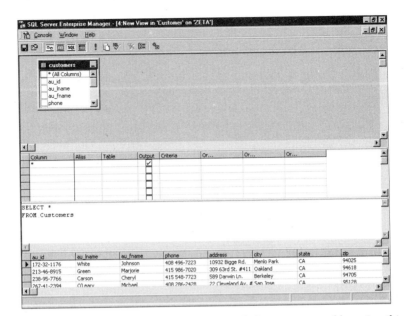

Figure 11-5. *Generate SQL commands needed to re-create tables using this dialog box.*

3. To create a new view, right-click the Views node and, from the shortcut menu, select New View. This displays the New View window shown in Figure 11-5.

4. To modify an existing view, right-click the view name and, from the shortcut menu, select Design View. This displays the Design View window, which is similar to the window shown in Figure 11-5.

5. To add tables to the pane, right-click and select Add Table. Then, in the Add Table dialog box, select the table(s) you want to add. This displays view panes for each selected table, which you can use to select table columns. Afterward, use the fields and options provided to manipulate the selection. Your actions create a SELECT statement that can be used to generate the view. When you are ready, click the Run button on the toolbar to create the view.

Tip In the example, I entered *Select ∗ From Customer2* to create an initial view. This loaded all the column data, which I then used to set limiting criteria, as shown in Figure 11-5.

6. To set view properties, click Properties. Then use the Properties dialog box to set view properties. Key properties you'll want to set include

   • **DISTINCT Values** Ensures that rows returned are unique by filtering out duplicates

- **Encrypt View** Encrypts the view so it's stored in an encoded format that can't be read using Enterprise Manager tools

7. After you run the view to update it for the latest changes, save the view. Click the Save button on the toolbar. If this is a new view, you'll be prompted for a view name. Enter the view name and then click OK.

You can also create views using the CREATE VIEW command. A simple view can be created by selecting all the values in a table, such as:

```
CREATE VIEW [Sales Custom View] As
SELECT *
FROM Customers2
```

You can then work directly with the view, such as:

```
SELECT * FROM [Sales Custom View]
```

To create the view shown previously in Figure 11-5, you would use the following command:

```
CREATE VIEW [Sales Custom View] As
SELECT cust_id AS Account, cust_lname AS [Last Name],
   cust_fname AS [First Name], state AS Region
FROM Customers2
WHERE (state = 'WA') OR
   (state = 'HI') OR
   (state = 'CA')
```

To change an existing view without having to reset its permissions and other properties, you use ALTER VIEW. The following example changes the definition of the Sales Custom view used in previous examples:

```
CREATE VIEW [Sales Custom View] As
SELECT cust_id AS Account, cust_lname AS [Customer Last Name],
   cust_fname AS [Customer First Name], state AS Region
FROM Customers2
WHERE (state = 'WA') OR
   (state = 'CA')
```

The full syntax for CREATE VIEW is shown as Listing 11-3.

Listing 11-3. CREATE VIEW Syntax

Syntax

```
CREATE VIEW view_name [(column [,...n])]
[WITH ENCRYPTION]
AS
   select_statement
[WITH CHECK OPTION]
```

Using Updateable Views

SQL Server supports updateable views as well. With an updateable view, you can change the information in the view using INSERT, UPDATE, and DELETE statements. You can create updateable views with one or more tables, provided the tables don't contain aggregate functions.

With updateable views, you'll usually want to set WITH CHECK OPTION. If you don't do this, changes to the view may result in rows not being displayed in the view anymore. To see how, consider the case of the view created in Figure 11-5. Here, you're selecting customer information for Washington, Hawaii, and California. If you change a state value to OR, the row would disappear from the view. The reason for this is that Oregon-based customers aren't displayed in the view.

Managing Views

As with tables, you can examine view properties, set view permissions, and perform other key management tasks. To get started, complete the following steps:

1. Start Enterprise Manager and then work your way down to the database you want to work with.

2. Select the Views node to display a view list in the right pane. Right-click the view you want to work with and then select

   * Rename, to rename the view
   * Delete, to delete the view
   * Properties, to examine view properties

3. To set view permissions or generate a script to re-create the view, right-click the view you want to work with and then select All Tasks. Afterward, select Manage Permissions or Generate SQL Scripts, as appropriate.

Creating and Managing Indexes

Indexes provide quick access to data when you search on an indexed column. Indexes are separate from tables, and you can configure them automatically using the Index Tuning Wizard. The sections that follow examine techniques you'll use to work with indexes.

Understanding Indexes

Indexes, like tables, use pages. Index pages are structured much like table data pages. They are 8 KB (8192 bytes) in size and have a 96-byte header. But unlike data pages, they don't have row offsets. Each index has a corresponding row in the *sysindexes* table with an index ID value (indid) of 1 for clustered indexes or 2–250 for nonclustered indexes. An index ID value of 255 indicates *text, ntext,* or *image* data.

SQL Server maintains indexes using a B-Tree structure, which is a basic tree structure consisting of a root node, intermediate level nodes, and leaf nodes. The wonderful thing about trees is that you can search them quickly and efficiently. Without the tree structure, SQL Server would need to read each table data page in the database in turn, searching for the correct record.

To put this in perspective, let's consider the limited situation where each data page contains a single row. In this case, if SQL Server searches for data in row 800 and there isn't an index, SQL Server may have to search 799 other rows before finding the right row. With a tree structure, SQL Server navigates the nodes down the index searching for the row that matches the corresponding index key. In the best case scenario, where the index keys have been arranged in a full tree, the number of nodes that need to be searched is proportional to the height of the tree. For example, 27,000 rows may be represented with 30 levels of nodes, and if so, SQL Server would have to navigate 15 nodes on average to find the matching row.

Note If you were paying particular attention, you know I streamlined the example to demonstrate the power of indexing. The point is that indexing can improve performance by orders of magnitude, and a database without it can seem extremely slow. By the same token, if you index the wrong information, you can make the database equally slow, which is why it's so important to select the most referenced/used column to index.

Clustered and Nonclustered Indexes

SQL Server supports two types of indexing:

- Clustered indexes
- Nonclustered indexes

You can create indexes on just about any column. The key exceptions are for columns that contain the text, ntext, image, and bit data types. You can't create indexes on these data types. You should always select the index column carefully. Selecting the correct column to index improves response time dramatically. Selecting the wrong column to index could actually degrade response time. For pointers on which column to index, use the Index Tuning Wizard.

Using Clustered Indexes

A clustered index stores the actual table data pages at the leaf level, and the table data is physically ordered around the key. A table can have only one clustered index and when this index is created,

- Table data is rearranged
- New index pages are created
- All nonclustered indexes within the database are deleted

The result is a lot of disk I/O operations and extensive use of system and memory resources. When creating a clustered index, it's a good idea to have free space that is at least 1.5 times the amount of data in the table. The extra free space ensures that you have enough space to complete the operation and do it efficiently.

Normally, you create a clustered index on a primary key. You can, however, create a clustered index on any named column, such as cust_lname or cust_id. With clustered indexes, the values you are indexing should be unique. If the values aren't unique, SQL Server creates secondary sort keys on rows that have duplicates of their primary sort keys.

Using Nonclustered Indexes

In a nonclustered index, pages on the leaf level contain a bookmark that tells SQL Server where to find the data row corresponding to the key in the index. If the table has a clustered index, the bookmark indicates the clustered index key. If the table doesn't have a clustered index, the bookmark is an actual row locator.

When you create a nonclustered index, SQL Server creates the required index pages but doesn't rearrange table data. SQL Server doesn't delete other indexes either. Each table can have up to 249 nonclustered indexes.

What Columns Should Be Indexed?

Now that you know how indexes work, you can focus on what columns you should index. Ideally, you'll select columns for indexing based on the type of queries executed against the database. A real help in determining the types of queries being run is SQL Server Profiler. You use SQL Profiler to create a trace that contains a good snapshot of activities performed by users on the database. You can then manually examine this trace to see what types of queries are executed, or you can use the trace file as a saved workload file in the Index Tuning Wizard. Regardless of which technique you use, keep in mind that the maximum length of all columns that comprise an index is 900 bytes. This means that the total byte size of all columns must be 900 or less.

Table 11-4 provides suggestions for the types of tables and columns you should and shouldn't index.

Table 11-4. What to Index or Not to Index

Index	Don't Index
Tables with lots of rows	Tables with few rows
Columns that are often used in queries	Columns that are rarely used in queries
Columns with strong selectivity, meaning that they have a narrow range of values	Columns with poor selectivity, meaning that they have a very wide range of values
Columns used in aggregate functions	Columns that have a large byte size
Columns used in group by queries	Tables with lots of modifications but few actual queries
Columns used in order by queries	
Columns used in table joins	

Table 11-5 provides suggestions for the types of columns that should use clustered or nonclustered indexes.

Table 11-5. When to Use Clustered or Nonclustered Indexes

Use Clustered Index	Use Nonclustered Index
Primary keys that are searched for extensively, such as account numbers	Columns frequently used in a *where* clause that return exact matches
Queries that return large result sets	Queries that return small result sets
Columns used in lots of queries	Columns used in aggregate functions
Columns with strong selectivity	Foreign keys
Columns used in order by or group by queries	
Columns used in table joins	

Viewing Indexes

In Enterprise Manager you can view indexes by completing the following steps:

1. Start Enterprise Manager and then work your way down to the database you want to work with.

2. With the Taskpad enabled, select the database entry in the left pane and then, in the right pane, click the Tables & Indexes tab.

3. Tables and indexes in the database are now listed in the right pane.

You can also view indexes using the *sp_helpindex* and *sp_statistics* stored procedures, such as:

```
use customer
exec sp_help_index Customers
exec sp_statistics Customers
```

Creating Indexes

The primary ways to create indexes are to use the Create Index Wizard or the Transact-SQL CREATE INDEX command. To create indexes with the wizard, complete the following steps:

1. Start Enterprise Manager and then work your way down to the database you want to work with.

2. Choose the Wizards button on the toolbar or, from the Tools menu, select Wizards. You'll see the Select Wizard dialog box. Expand the Database option by clicking the plus sign (+).

3. Select Create Index Wizard and click OK. Or double-click Create Index Wizard. This starts the Create Index Wizard.

4. Read the welcome message and then click Next to access the Select Database And Table dialog box shown in Figure 11-6.

Figure 11-6. *Use the Select Database And Table dialog box to select a database and table to work with.*

5. Select the database and table on which you want to add the index. Click Next.

6. Any indexes that already exist are summarized in the Current Index Information dialog box. Click Next.

7. Select the column(s) you want to include in the index, as shown in Figure 11-7. You can only select columns that have valid data types for indexing. Any columns that aren't available for indexing are shown with a red X.

8. Next, set the following indexing options:

   * **Make This A Clustered Index**   Select this option to create a clustered index on the columns selected. Otherwise, a nonclustered index is created. Keep in mind that you can only have one clustered index per table, so if the table already has a clustered index, this option is shaded and can't be selected.

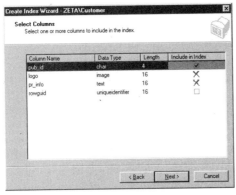

Figure 11-7. *Use the Select Columns dialog box to select columns for indexing.*

- **Make This A Unique Index** Select this option to enforce the uniqueness of column values.

- **Optimal Fill Factor** Select this option to let SQL Server use an optimized fill, as described in the section of Chapter 2 entitled "Setting the Index Fill."

- **Fixed Fill Factor** Select this option and then set a fill factor using the related field. For more information on index fill, see Chapter 2.

9. Click Next when you're ready to continue.

10. Type a name for the index in the Index Name field. You can use up to 128 characters for the index name. Ideally, the index name should be short and easy to associate with its purpose, such as Index For Cust ID.

11. Click Finish when you're ready to complete the process. The wizard then creates the index for you.

With the CREATE INDEX command, you create indexes using the syntax shown in Listing 11-4.

Listing 11-4. Creating Indexes on Existing Tables with Transact-SQL

Syntax

```
CREATE [UNIQUE] [CLUSTERED | NONCLUSTERED]
   INDEX index_name ON table (column [,...n])
[WITH
      [PAD_INDEX]
      [[,] FILLFACTOR = fillfactor]
      [[,] IGNORE_DUP_KEY]
      [[,] DROP_EXISTING]
      [[,] STATISTICS_NORECOMPUTE]
]
[ON filegroup]
```

Usage

```
CREATE CLUSTERED INDEX [Cust ID Index]
   ON Customers(cust_id)
```

Managing Indexes

After you create an index, you may need to change its properties, rename it, or delete it. You handle these tasks in Enterprise Manager by completing the following steps:

1. Start Enterprise Manager and then work your way down to the database you want to work with. Click the plus sign (+) next to the database name to display a list of data objects and resources.

Figure 11-8. *Manage indexes using the Indexes/Keys tab of the Properties dialog box.*

2. Right-click the table name whose indexes you want to manage and then, from the shortcut menu, select Design Table. This opens the Design Table view in Enterprise Manager.

3. On the toolbar, click Table And Index Properties. This opens the Properties dialog box shown in Figure 11-8.

4. Select the Indexes/Keys tab.

5. Use the Selected Index selection list to choose the index you want to manage. With the index selected, you can now

   • Rename the index by entering a new index name in the Index Name field.

   • Delete the index by clicking Delete.

   • Change the index properties by selecting new options.

You can also manage indexes with stored procedures and Transact-SQL commands, namely *sp_rename* and DROP INDEX. Unfortunately, a lot of caveats go with these commands. For example, you can't drop an index that was created by defining a primary key or unique constraints. You must instead drop the constraint with ALTER TABLE.

Using the Index Tuning Wizard

The Index Tuning Wizard is one of the best tools a database administrator has in the indexing and optimization process. As discussed earlier in the chapter, before you start this wizard, you should create a trace containing a representative snapshot of database activity. You'll use this snapshot as the workload file in the Index Tuning Wizard. For specific pointers on creating a trace file, see the section of Chapter 10 entitled "Solving Performance Problems with Profiler."

To use the Index Tuning Wizard, complete the following steps:

1. Start Enterprise Manager and then work your way down to the database you want to work with.

2. Choose the Wizards button on the toolbar or, from the Tools menu, select Wizards. You'll see the Select Wizard dialog box. Expand the Management option by clicking the plus sign (+).

3. Select Index Tuning Wizard and click OK. Or double-click Index Tuning Wizard. This starts the Index Tuning Wizard.

4. Read the welcome message and then click Next to access the Select Server And Database dialog box shown in Figure 11-9.

5. Select the server and database you wish to analyze.

6. To ensure that existing indexes aren't dropped, select Keep Existing Indexes. Otherwise, clear this option.

Tip If you've selected a strong, representative snapshot of database activity in the trace, you'll probably want to clear the Keep Existing Indexes option and let the Index Tuning Wizard make the appropriate suggestions for you. This ensures that existing indexes don't conflict with the recommendations the wizard may make.

7. To perform a thorough analysis of the trace activity, select Perform Thorough Analysis. Otherwise, clear this option. Again, if you created a good snapshot, you should select this option and give the wizard the opportunity to make recommendations.

8. Next, on the Identify Workload dialog box, make sure that the I Have A Saved Workload File option button is selected. You set this option because you're using an existing trace data.

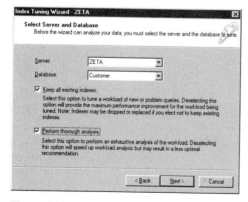

Figure 11-9. *Use the Select Server And Database dialog box to select a server, database, and indexing options.*

Figure 11-10. *Setting advanced options for the analysis.*

9. If you saved the trace data to a file, select My Workload File and then use the Open dialog box to find the trace file.

10. If you saved the trace data to a table, select SQL Server Table and then use the Source Table dialog box to specify which table to use.

11. Choose the Advanced Options button to set advanced options, as shown in Figure 11-10. The advanced options are

- **Maximum Queries To Tune**   Sets the maximum number of queries to tune. By default, this is set to 32,767.

- **Maximum Space For The Recommended Indexes (MB)**   Sets the maximum space that can be used by index pages. The default is 2 MB, which may not be sufficient for a large or complex database.

- **Maximum Columns Per Index**   Sets the maximum number of columns that can be used in a single index. The default is 16, which is a high value for an average-sized database.

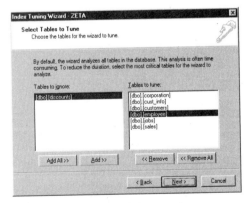

Figure 11-11. *Select tables to tune.*

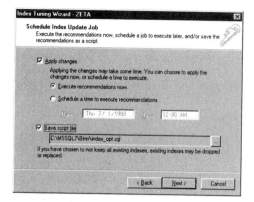

Figure 11-12. *Apply the changes, if desired. Otherwise, clear the Apply Changes option.*

12. Next, select tables whose indexes you want to optimize, as shown in Figure 11-11. By default, all tables are selected. You can remove tables by selecting them and clicking << Remove.

13. Click Next and the Index Tuning Wizard will begin analyzing your workload file. You can click End to stop the analysis at any time.

14. When finished with the analysis, the wizard will make recommendations and display them in the Index Recommendations dialog box. To see detailed analysis information, click the Analysis button.

15. Next, specify whether and when the index changes should be applied, as shown in Figure 11-12. If you want to apply the changes, select the Apply Changes box and then choose either the Execute Recommendations Now or the Schedule A Time To Execute Recommendations option button. If you schedule the changes, enter a date and time to make them.

16. Optionally, save the recommended changes as a SQL script file by selecting the Save Script File box and then setting a file path.

17. Click Next and then click Finish.

Column Constraints and Rules

Column constraints and rules are important parts of database administration. You use constraints to control the way column values are used, such as whether a value must be unique or whether it must have a specific format. While you usually apply constraints directly to a specific column, you can use rules to create constraints that can be applied to multiple tables in a database.

Using Constraints

SQL Server enforces the uniqueness of column values using unique and primary key constraints. You'll often use unique constraints to create secondary keys (for nonclustered indexes) that can be used in conjunction with the primary key. Another type of constraint you may want to use is a CHECK constraint. CHECK constraints restrict the format or range of acceptable values for columns.

Setting Uniqueness Constraints

When you set a UNIQUE constraint on a column or columns, SQL Server automatically creates a unique index and then checks for duplicate values. If duplicate key values exist, the index creation operation is cancelled, and an error message is displayed. SQL Server also checks the data each time data is added to the table. If the new data contain duplicate keys, the insert or update is rolled back and an error message is generated. You can specify that duplicate keys should be ignored using the IGNORE_DUP_KEY option.

In Enterprise Manager you set the uniqueness constraint with the Make This A Unique Index option, as described in the "Creating Indexes" section of this chapter. In Transact-SQL you can set the unique constraint when you create the index, such as:

```
USE Customer
CREATE UNIQUE INDEX [Cust ID Index]
   ON Customers(cust_id)
```

A nonclustered index is created unless a clustered index is explicitly specified, such as:

```
USE Customer
CREATE UNIQUE CLUSTERED INDEX [Cust ID Index]
   ON Customers(cust_id)
```

Primary Key Constraints

SQL Server also allows you to designate any column or group of columns as a primary key, but primary keys are often defined for identity columns. A table can have only one primary key and, because unique values are required, no primary key column can accept null values. Additionally, when you use multiple columns, the values of all the columns are combined to determine uniqueness.

As with unique constraints, SQL Server creates a unique index for the primary key columns. With primary key constraints, however, the index is created as a clustered index—unless a clustered index already exists on the table or a nonclustered index is explicitly specified.

In Enterprise Manager, you set the primary key in the New Table view or the Design Table view by completing the following steps:

1. Clear Allow Nulls for any columns that will be used in the primary key.

2. Select the column or columns that you want to use as the primary key by holding down Shift and clicking the shaded box to the left of the column name.

3. Click the Set Primary Key button on the toolbar.

You can also set the primary key when you create or alter tables. Examples are shown in Listing 11-5.

Listing 11-5. Creating a Table and Its Columns

```
USE CUSTOMER
CREATE TABLE Customers
   (cust_id varchar(11) NOT NULL,
      cust_lname varchar(40) NOT NULL,
      cust_fname varchar(20) NOT NULL,
      phone char(12) NOT NULL,
      CONSTRAINT PK_Cust PRIMARY KEY (cust_id))

      USE CUSTOMER
      ALTER TABLE Customers
   (ADD CONSTRAINT PK_Cust PRIMARY KEY (cust_id))
```

Using *CHECK* Constraints

CHECK constraints allow you to control the format or range of values, or both, that are associated with tables and columns. You could use this type of constraint to specify that zip codes must be entered in the format 99999-9999 or that phone numbers must be entered as 999-999-9999.

In Enterprise Manager, you set CHECK constraints in the New Table or Design Table view by completing the following steps:

1. Click the Table And Index Properties button on the toolbar. Then, as shown in Figure 11-13, select the Tables tab.

2. To create a new constraint, click New and then type a name in the Constraint Name field. Then type a constraint expression in the Constraint Expression text box.

3. To edit an existing constraint, choose it in the Selected Constraint selection list. Then modify the existing constraint expression in the Constraint Expression text box.

4. To delete a constraint, choose it in the Selected Constraint selection list and then click Delete. When prompted to confirm the deletion, choose Yes.

You can also add and remove constraints using the CREATE TABLE or ALTER TABLE command, such as:

```
USE CUSTOMER
ALTER TABLE Customer3
  ADD CONSTRAINT CheckZipFormat
  CHECK (([zip] like '[0-9][0-9][0-9][0-9][0-9]-[0-9][0-9][0-9][0-9]'))
```

Figure 11-13. *Set constraints in the Tables tab.*

Creating Rules

A rule is a constraint that you can apply to multiple tables. To create a rule in Enterprise Manager, complete the following steps:

1. Start Enterprise Manager and then work your way down to the database you want to work with. Click the plus sign (+) next to the database name to display a list of data objects and resources.

2. To create a new rule, right-click the Rules node and, from the shortcut menu, select New Rule. This opens the dialog box shown in Figure 11-14.

Figure 11-14. *Type a rule name and set the text of the constraint.*

3. In the Name field type a name for the rule. Although the name can be up to 128 characters long, you should use a fairly short name so that it can be easily referenced.

4. In the Text field, enter the constraint to set as a database rule. Substitute the *@value* function in the place of a specific column reference.

Once you create a rule, it's displayed in the Rules view, and you can manage it much as you would any other database resource. The corresponding Transact-SQL commands for creating and managing rules are CREATE RULE and DROP RULE. You can use create rule as follows:

```
CREATE RULE CheckFormatZip
    AS @value LIKE '[0-9][0-9][0-9][0-9][0-9]-[0-9][0-9][0-9][0-9]'
```

Chapter 12

Database Automation and Maintenance

Automation and maintenance go hand in hand. You can automate many routine database administration tasks, most of which have to do with maintenance issues, such as backing up databases or running consistency checks. Automation allows you to increase productivity, complete tasks while away from your computer, and more. You can configure the server to monitor processes and user activities, to check for errors, and to alert you when related events occur. If alerts are configured properly, Microsoft SQL Server 7.0 can monitor itself and you can focus on other areas of administration. You can also schedule jobs to automate routine administration tasks. You can configure these jobs to run on a one-time basis or on a recurring basis, such as once a week or, say, every third Tuesday of the month.

Using SQL Server Agent

SQL Server Agent is the driving force behind database automation. It's responsible for processing alerts and running scheduled jobs. When alerts are triggered and when scheduled jobs fail, succeed, or complete, you can notify SQL Server operators. Operator notifications are also processed through SQL Server Agent.

Accessing Alerts, Operators, and Jobs

You can use Enterprise Manager to access resources related to SQL Server Agent by completing the following steps:

1. In Enterprise Manager, access the Management folder on the server running SQL Server Agent.

2. Select the SQL Server Agent entry in the left pane.

3. You should see entries for Alerts, Operators, and Jobs. Select one of these entries in the left pane to display its properties in the right pane, as shown in Figure 12-1.

4. Double-click an alert, job, or operator entry to access its associated properties dialog box.

Figure 12-1. *Summary entries for alerts provide an overview of each individual alert. You can also access summaries for operators and jobs.*

 Note If you've configured replication on the server, you'll see many alerts and jobs that you configure to make it easier to monitor replication. To start these alerts or jobs, you need to set the appropriate property settings.

Configuring the SQLServerAgent Service

For SQL Server Agent to work properly, you should configure the SQLServerAgent service to run automatically. Start SQL Server Service Manager by double-clicking the SQL Server shortcut on the taskbar or by selecting Start, then Programs, then Microsoft SQL Server 7.0, and finally Service Manager. You can then configure the SQLServerAgent service with Service Manager by completing the following steps:

1. Use the Server selection list to choose an available server or enter the server name.

2. From the Services selection list, choose SQLServerAgent.

3. Choose Start to start the service, if necessary.

4. Choose Auto-Start Service When OS Starts. This will cause SQLServerAgent service to start automatically when the system boots.

Figure 12-2. *Configure SQL Server Agent properties using the available tabs and fields.*

Configuring the SQL Server Agent

The SQL Server Agent has different properties that you can configure to control how the service works. You configure Agent properties through the SQL Server Agent Properties dialog box shown in Figure 12-2. To access this dialog box, right-click the SQL Server Agent entry in Enterprise Manager's Management folder and then select Properties. The following sections of this chapter use a task-oriented approach to explore the most frequently used configuration options.

Configuring the SQL Server Agent Startup Account

The startup account used by the SQLServerAgent service determines SQL Server Agent's access permissions. If the startup account doesn't have appropriate permissions, SQL Server Agent won't run properly. In most cases, you'll want to use a Microsoft Windows NT user account that is a member of the sysadmin role. This ensures that SQL Server Agent can generate alerts, run jobs, and restart services, as necessary.

You set the startup account by completing the following steps:

1. Select the General tab of the SQL Server Agent Properties dialog box.

2. Choose System Account to use the built-in system account as the startup account. Otherwise, select the This Account option button and then type the username and password of a Windows NT account.

3. If the startup account doesn't have appropriate permissions for making connections to SQL Server, access the Connection tab and then select an authentication method. With SQL Server authentication, you'll also need to specify a login account and password.

4. Choose Apply.

Setting the SQL Server Agent Mail Profile

SQL Server Agent sends e-mail and pager notifications through the SQLServer-Agent service. In order for mail to work properly, you must set the name of the mail profile you want to use for sending these notifications. Type this profile name in the Mail Profile field of the SQL Server Agent Properties dialog box's General tab. For more information on configuring mail, see the section of Chapter 3 entitled "Managing SQL Mail and SQLServerAgent Mail."

Using SQL Server Agent to Restart Services Automatically

You can configure SQL Server Agent to automatically restart the MSSQLServer and SQLServerAgent services if they stop unexpectedly. Configuring automatic restart of these services is a good idea that'll keep you from getting paged at 3:00 A.M. on a Tuesday morning.

To configure automatic service restart, complete the following steps:

1. Access the Advanced tab of the SQL Server Agent Properties dialog box.

2. Select Auto Restart SQL Server If It Stops Unexpectedly. Select Auto Restart SQL Server Agent If It Stops Unexpectedly.

3. Choose Apply.

Viewing SQL Server Agent Logs

SQL Server Agent writes output to a separate log file. You can access this log file by completing the following steps:

1. In Enterprise Manager, access the Management folder on the server running SQL Server Agent.

2. Right-click SQL Server Agent and then, from the shortcut menu, select Display Error Log.

Managing Alerts

Using alerts, you can send e-mail, pager, or Net Send alerts when errors occur or when performance conditions are reached. For example, you can configure an alert to send a message when a Log File Is Full error occurs, or when the number of deadlocks per second is more than five. You can also execute a job on an alert event.

Default Alerts

Default alerts are configured when you install SQL Server and when you configure key features, such as replication. The names of alerts configured for a new installation of SQL Server begin with Demo: and include

- **Demo: Full tempdb** An example alert triggered for a full log file in the tempdb database.

- **Demo: Full msdb log** An example alert triggered for a full log file in the msdb database.

- **Demo: Sev. 19 errors** An example alert triggered for an error with a severity of 19, which is the first level of fatal errors. Other alerts handle severity levels 20–25.

The demo alerts are enabled for use but don't have operators configured to receive the alerts. Because the alerts for fatal errors are the most useful, you'll probably want to edit their properties and configure them for use on the server.

The names of alerts configured when you set up replication begin with Replication:. The replication alerts include

- **Replication: Agent Success** Tells you that the replication agent was successful

- **Replication: Agent Failure** Tells you that the replication agent failed

- **Replication: Agent Retry** Tells you that the replication agent failed and is retrying

- **Replication: Expired Subscription Dropped** Tells you that an expired subscription was dropped, which means the subscriber won't be updated anymore

- **Replication: Subscriber Has Failed Data Validation** Tells you that data in the subscriber's subscription couldn't be validated

- **Replication: Subscriber Has Passed Data Validation** Tells you that data in the subscriber's subscription was validated

- **Replication: Subscriber Reinitialized After Validation Failure** Tells you that data in the subscriber's subscription was reinitialized with a new snapshot

The replication alerts are disabled and don't have operators assigned either. So if you want to use these alerts, you'll need to enable them and assign operators.

Creating Error Message Alerts

Error message alerts are triggered when SQL Server generates an error message. You can create an error message alert by completing the following steps:

1. In Enterprise Manager, access the Management folder on the server running SQL Server Agent.

2. Select the SQL Server Agent entry in the left pane.

3. Right-click Alerts and then, from the shortcut menu, select New Alert. This opens the New Alert Properties dialog box.

4. Type a short but descriptive name for the alert in the Name field, as shown in Figure 12-3.

5. In the Type selection list, choose SQL Server Event Alert. You can now set alerts according to the number or severity level of error messages.

6. To set alerts by error number, choose Error Number and then type an error number in the related field. To search for an error number, click the build button (...) and then use the Manager SQL Server Messages dialog box to find an appropriate message.

Figure 12-3. *Configure new alerts for error messages.*

7. To set alerts by severity level, choose Severity and then use the related selection list to choose a severity level that triggers the alert. You'll usually want to configure alerts for severity levels 19–25.

8. Use the Database Name selection list to choose the database in which the error must occur to trigger the alert. To specify all databases on the server, select the (All Databases) option.

9. To restrict alerts to messages containing specific text strings, type the filter text in the Error Message Contains This Text field.

10. Choose Apply and then configure the alert response as specified in the section of this chapter entitled "Handling Alert Responses."

Creating Performance Condition Alerts

Performance condition alerts are triggered when a certain performance parameter is met, such as when the total server memory available falls below 2 MB. You configure performance condition alerts in much the same was as you configure alerts in Performance Monitor. Complete the following steps:

1. In Enterprise Manager, access the Management folder on the server running SQL Server Agent.

2. Select the SQL Server Agent entry in the left pane.

3. Right-click Alerts and then, from the shortcut menu, select New Alert. This opens the New Alert Properties dialog box.

4. Type a short but descriptive name for the alert in the Name field, as shown in Figure 12-4.

5. In the Type selection list, choose SQL Server Performance Condition Alert.

6. Use the Object, Counter, and Instance selection lists to configure the performance condition you want to check for.

Figure 12-4. *Configure new alerts for performance conditions.*

7. Use the Alert If Counter selection list to set when the condition occurs. Select Falls Below, Becomes Equal To, or Rises Above, and then enter a value to check for.

8. Choose Apply and then configure the alert response as described in the following "Handling Alert Responses" section.

Handling Alert Responses

In response to an alert, you can execute SQL Server jobs or notify operators of the alert, or both. To configure the alert response, complete the following steps:

1. In Enterprise Manager, access the Management folder on the server running SQL Server Agent.

2. Select the SQL Server Agent entry in the left pane.

3. Select the Alerts entry in the left pane and then double-click the alert you want to configure. Then choose the Response tab, as shown in Figure 12-5.

4. To execute a job in response to the alert, select Execute Job and then use the related selection list to select a job to execute. If you want to create a new job, choose the (New Job) entry and then configure the job as discussed in the section of this chapter entitled "Scheduling Jobs."

5. Operators configured to handle alerts and schedule jobs are shown in the Operators To Notify area. The available notification methods depend on how the operator account is configured. You can select E-mail, Pager, or Net Send notification, or all three.

6. Use the Include Alert Error Text In check boxes to specify whether error text is sent with the notification message. By default, error text is sent only with E-mail and Net Send notifications.

Figure 12-5. *You can respond to alerts by executing jobs or notifying operators of the alert, or both.*

7. Set an additional message to operators using the Additional Notification Message To Send To Operator text box.

8. Set the delay between responses for subsequent alert notifications using the Delay Between Responses fields labeled Minutes and Seconds.

 Tip To limit the amount of alert responses triggered, you'll probably want to set a delay response value of five minutes or more.

9. Click OK to complete the configuration.

Deleting, Enabling, and Disabling Alerts

Deleting an alert removes its entry from the alerts list. Because old alerts may be useful to you (or another DBA) in the future, you may want to disable them instead of deleting them. When an alert is disabled, no alerts are triggered if the related event occurs.

To delete, enable, or disable an alert, complete the following steps:

1. In Enterprise Manager, access the Management folder on the server running SQL Server Agent.

2. Select the SQL Server Agent entry in the left pane and then select Alerts.

3. To enable or disable an alert, double-click its entry in the Alerts list to open the related properties dialog box. Then, in the General tab, select or clear the Enabled check box to enable or disable the alert.

4. To delete an alert, click it and then press Delete. When prompted to confirm the deletion, choose Yes.

Managing Operators

Operators are special accounts that can be notified when alerts are triggered and when scheduled jobs fail, succeed, or complete. Before operators become available, you need to register them. After you register operators, you can enable or disable them for notifications.

Registering Operators

You register operators by completing the following steps:

1. In Enterprise Manager, access the Management folder on the server running SQL Server Agent.
2. Select the SQL Server Agent entry in the left pane.
3. Right-click the Operators entry in the left pane and then, from the shortcut menu, select New Operator. This opens the New Operator Properties dialog box shown in Figure 12-6.
4. Type a name for the operator in the Name field.
5. Specify E-mail, Pager, or Net Send accounts (or all three) to notify. If you can't remember the account you want to use, click the build button (...) to display the Contacts list from your address book, then select the account to use.
6. Click the Notifications tab to specify existing alerts that the operator should receive (if any). Existing alerts are listed in the Alert Name column. If you find an alert that the operator should receive, select the corresponding checkboxes in the E-mail, Pager, and Net Send columns as appropriate.
7. Once you've configured the Notifications tab, you can click Send E-mail to send the operator an e-mail listing his or her alert responsibilities.

Figure 12-6. *Operators can receive alert and job notifications. To associate the operator with multiple users, reference a group e-mail account.*

Tip If you specify a pager account for the operator, you can set a duty schedule for the pager using the Pager On Duty Schedule area's fields and check boxes. This option is helpful if you have operators who should only be notified during working hours. To set default configuration settings for pagers, access the Alert System tab of the SQL Server Agent Properties dialog box.

8. Click OK to register the operator.

Deleting and Disabling Notification for Operators

When DBAs leave the organization or go on vacation, you may want to delete or disable their associated operator accounts. To do this, complete the following steps:

1. In Enterprise Manager, access the Management folder on the server running SQL Server Agent.

2. Select the SQL Server Agent entry in the left pane and then select Operators.

3. To disable an operator, double-click the operator entry in the right pane. This opens the Operator Properties dialog box. Now select the Notifications tab and then cancel Operator Is Available To Receive Notifications.

4. To delete an operator, click its entry in the right pane and then press Delete. If the operator has been selected to receive alert or job notifications, you'll see the Delete Operator dialog box shown in Figure 12-7. To reassign notification duty, select a different operator using the Re-assign To selection list and then click Re-assign.

Figure 12-7. *You can reassign notification duties when deleting an operator registration.*

Configuring a Fail-Safe Operator

When things go wrong with notification, operators don't get notified and problems may not be corrected in a timely manner. To prevent this, you may want to designate a fail-safe operator. The fail-safe operator is notified when

- SQL Server Agent can't access system tables in the msdb database, which is where operator definitions and notification lists are stored.

- All pager notifications to designated operators have failed or the designated operators are off-duty (as defined in the pager schedule).

Note Using the fail-safe operator on pager notification failure may seem strange, but it's the way to go. E-mail and Net Send messages almost always reach their destination—whether someone is watching their mail or sitting at their computer to receive Net Send messages is another matter altogether.

To configure a fail-safe operator, complete the following steps:

1. Right-click the SQL Server Agent entry in Enterprise Manager's Management folder and then select Properties.

2. In the SQL Server Agent Properties dialog box, select the Alert System tab and then use the Operator selection list to choose an operator to designate as the fail-safe operator. You can reassign the fail-safe duty by selecting a different operator or disable the feature by selecting (No Fail-Safe Operator).

3. Use the Notify Using check boxes to determine how the fail-safe operator is notified.

4. Choose Apply.

Scheduling Jobs

Job scheduling is a key part of database automation. You can configure SQL Server jobs to handle just about any database task.

Creating Jobs

Jobs are created as a series of steps that contain actions in the sequence you want to execute them. When you schedule jobs in conjunction with other SQL Server facilities, such as database backups or DTS, the necessary commands are configured for you. Normally, these commands are set as step 1, and all you need to do is set a run schedule for the job. You can add extra steps to these jobs and thus perform other tasks. For example, after importing data through DTS, you may want to back up the related database. In the DTS Wizard, you would schedule the import, and then you would edit the associated job in Enterprise Manager to add an additional step for backing up the database. By coordinating the two processes, you ensure that the import operation is completed before starting the backup.

Another reason for editing a job created by another SQL Server facility is to add notifications based on success, failure, and completion of the job. In this way, you can notify operators of certain conditions, and you don't have to search through logs to determine whether the job executed properly.

When you schedule jobs to execute for alerts, you configure the entire job process from start to finish. You

- Create a job definition
- Set steps to execute
- Configure a job schedule
- Handle completion, success, and failure notification messages

Assigning or Changing Job Definitions

Whether you're creating a new job or editing an existing job, the steps for working with job definitions are the same. Complete the following steps:

1. In Enterprise Manager, access the Management folder on the server running SQL Server Agent.

2. Select the SQL Server Agent entry in the left pane and then double-click Jobs.

3. Existing jobs are shown in the right pane. Double-click a job to access its related properties dialog box, which is essentially the same as the New Job Properties dialog box shown in Figure 12-8.

4. To create a new job, right-click the Jobs entry and, from the shortcut menu, select New Job. This displays the New Job Properties dialog box shown in Figure 12-8.

5. In the Name field, type a descriptive name for the job. The name can be up to 128 characters long. If you change the name of an existing job, the job is displayed with the new name. Any references to the old job name in logs or history files remain the same and aren't modified.

Figure 12-8. *Use the General tab of the New Job Properties dialog box to name, describe, and categorize the job.*

6. If job scheduling across multiple servers is configured, select the target server. The target server is the server on which the job runs. To run on the currently selected server, select Target Local Server. To run on multiple servers, select Target Multiple Servers and then choose the target servers.

7. Job categories help to organize jobs so they can be easily searched and differentiated. The default category is Uncategorized (Local). Use the Category selection list to choose a different category for the job.

Note Job categories are created and managed through a separate process. To create a new job category or update an existing category, use the techniques described under "Managing Job Categories."

8. By default, the job is owned by the current user. Administrators can reassign jobs to other users. To do this, use the Owner selection list. Only predefined logons can be used. If the logon you want to use isn't available, you'll need to create a logon for the account.

9. Type a description of the job in the Description text box. You can use up to 512 characters.

10. Choose Apply to create the job definition. Then set Steps, Schedules, and Notifications as detailed in the sections that follow.

Setting Steps to Execute

Jobs can have one or more steps. While the SQL Server Agent always attempts to execute the Start step, additional steps can be executed conditionally, such as only when the Start step succeeds or fails. You work with steps using the Steps tab in the job property dialog box, as shown in Figure 12-9. Any existing steps for the job are displayed. You can use the fields and buttons in this dialog box as follows:

- **New** Creates a new step.
- **Insert** Inserts a step before the currently selected step.

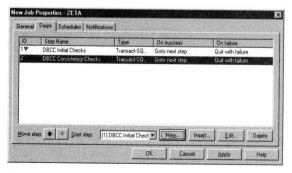

Figure 12-9. *Steps can be executed conditionally and in any sequence you specify.*

- **Edit** Allows edits to the selected step.
- **Delete** Deletes the selected step.
- **Move Step Up/Down** Changes the order of the selected step.
- **Start Step** Sets which step is executed first. The green flag icon highlights the start step in the step list.

When you create or edit a step, you see a dialog box similar to the one shown in Figure 12-10. To configure this dialog box, complete the following steps:

1. Type a short but descriptive name for the step in the Step Name field.
2. Use the Type selection list to choose a step type. Each step can

- **Execute Transact-SQL commands** Type Transact-SQL commands in the Command area or load the statements from a Transact-SQL script. To load commands from a script, choose Open and then select the Transact-SQL script you want to use. The entire contents of the script are then stored with this step.

- **Run active scripts** Active scripts can be written in VBScript, JScript, or another active scripting language configured for use on the system. Enter script statements directly into the Command area or load the statements from a script file. Again, the entire contents of the script are then stored with this step, and later changes to the script file aren't updated automatically.

- **Execute operating system commands** Enter the operating system commands on a separate line, making sure that you specify the full path to commands and in command parameters. Commands can run batch scripts, Microsoft Windows scripts, command-line utilities, or applications.

- **Pass Transact-SQL commands to replication agents** The Distributor, Snapshot, Merge, and Transaction Log-Reader agents can

Figure 12-10. *Set summary information and commands to execute for the step you're configuring, using the fields in the General tab of the New Job Step dialog box.*

be scripted with Transact-SQL commands. To see examples, refer to the existing jobs that are configured to handle replication, distribution, and subscription processes on the server (if available).

Tip Subsequent changes to scripts aren't updated automatically. You'll need to edit the step properties and reload the script file. Additionally, you shouldn't edit existing replication jobs. Instead, modify the replication process as described in Chapter 9, "Data Replication."

3. When executing Transact-SQL commands, use the Database selection list to set the database on which the commands are executed.

4. Select the Advanced tab as shown in Figure 12-11.

5. In the On Success Action selection list, set the action to take when the step succeeds. You can

- Go to the next step to continue sequential execution of the job
- Go to a different step to continue execution of the job on a different step
- Quit the job and report success or failure

6. By default, Retry Attempts is set to zero and SQL Server Agent doesn't try to execute steps again. You can change this behavior by setting the number of retry attempts and a retry interval. You do this by using the Retry Attempts and Retry Interval fields, respectively. The retry interval is the delay in minutes between retries.

7. If the job fails on all retry attempts (if any), the action set in the On Failure Action selection list is executed. The available options are the same as those for success.

8. If desired, configure a file for logging output from Transact-SQL and CmdExec commands. Enter the filename and path in the Output File field or use the

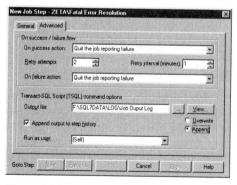

Figure 12-11. *Control the behavior and logging of the step using the fields of the Advanced tab.*

find file button (…) to search for an existing file. An alternative is to append output to the step history.

 Tip You may want to create a central log file for the output of all jobs or only all jobs in a particular category. If you do this, be sure to select the Append option button rather than the Overwrite option button. This ensures that the output file doesn't get overwritten.

9. Set the logon to use when executing commands using the Run As User selection list. By default, commands are run using the current login ID.

10. Choose Apply to complete the step configuration.

Configuring Job Schedules

You track schedules in the Schedules tab of the job properties dialog box, as shown in Figure 12-12. Jobs can have one or more schedules associated with them, and just as you can enable or disable jobs and their individual steps, you can enable or disable individual schedules. This makes the job scheduling process very flexible. For example, you could set one schedule to execute the job on weekdays at 2 A.M., another to execute the job on Saturday and Sunday at 8 A.M., and another for ad hoc execution at 12 P.M.

Whether you're creating a new job or editing an existing job, you work with schedules in the Schedules tab as follows:

- **Create a new schedule**   Click New Schedule to configure a new schedule.

- **Edit a schedule**   Select an existing schedule and then click Edit to view or modify its properties.

- **Delete a schedule**   Select an existing schedule and then click Delete to remove the schedule.

You create or edit schedules by completing the following steps:

1. Click New Schedule to open the New Job Schedule dialog box, or click Edit to open the Edit Job Schedule dialog box. These dialog boxes are essentially

Figure 12-12. *Jobs can have multiple schedules associated with them.*

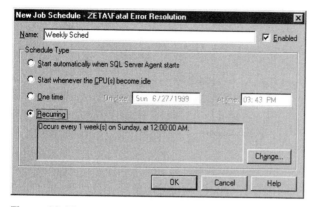

Figure 12-13. *Set the schedule name and type.*

the same except for the title. Figure 12-13 shows the New Job Schedule dialog box.

2. Type a name for the schedule and then select one of the following schedule types:

* **Start Automatically When SQL Server Agent Starts**   Runs the job automatically whenever SQL Server Agent starts.

* **Start Whenever The CPU(s) Become Idle**   Runs the job whenever the CPU is idle. CPU idle time is specified on the Advanced tab of the SQL Server Agent Properties dialog box.

* **One Time**   Runs the job once at the date and time specified in the On Date and At Time fields.

* **Recurring**   Runs the job according to the recurring schedule displayed.

3. Recurring jobs are the ones that need the most explanation. When you click Change, you'll see the Edit Recurring Job Schedule dialog box shown in Figure 12-14. Recurring jobs can be scheduled to run on a daily, weekly, or monthly basis.

4. To run the job on a daily basis, select the Daily option button. Then use the Every Day field to set when the job runs. Daily recurring jobs can run every day, every other day, or every Nth day.

5. To run the job on a weekly basis, select the Weekly option button. Then configure the job using these fields:

* **Every Nth Week (s)**   Allows you to run the task every week, every other week, or every Nth week

* **Day Of Week**   Sets the day(s) of the week when the task runs, such as on Monday, or on Monday, Wednesday, and Friday

Figure 12-14. *Configure a recurring schedule.*

6. To run the job on a monthly basis, select the Monthly option button. Then configure the job using these fields:

- **Day N Of Every Nth Month** Sets the day of the month and on which months the job runs. For example, if you select Day 15 of every 2nd month, the job runs on the 15th day of alternating months.

- **The Nth Day Of Every Nth Month** Sets the job to run on the Nth occurrence of a day in a given month, such as the 2nd Monday of every month or the 3rd Sunday of every other month.

7. Set the Daily Frequency for the daily, weekly, or monthly job. Jobs can be configured to run one or more times on their scheduled run date. To run the job once on a given date, select Occurs Once At and then set a time. To run the job several times on a given date, select Occurs Every and then set a time interval in hours or minutes. Afterward, set a start and end time, such as from 7:30 A.M. to 5:30 P.M.

8. By default, schedules begin on the current date and don't have a designated end date. To change this behavior, select the End Date option button and then use the Start Date and End Date fields to set a new duration for the schedule.

9. Double-click OK to complete the schedule process.

Handling Notification Messages

Notification messages are generated when a job succeeds, fails, or completes. You can handle these messages in several ways. You can notify operators, log the related event, automatically delete the job, or do all three. To configure notification, complete the following steps:

1. Access the Notifications tab of the job you want to configure. This tab is shown in Figure 12-15.

2. You can notify operators by e-mail, pager, or Net Send message. Select the check box for the technique you want to use. Choose an operator to handle

Figure 12-15. *Notification messages can be sent to operators, logged in the event log, or used to automatically delete a job.*

the notification. Then choose a notification type. Repeat this process to configure other notification methods.

3. To log a particular type of notification message in the event log, select Write To Windows NT Application Event Log and then select the notification type to log. Usually, you'll want to log failure, so select When The Job Fails.

4. To delete a job upon notification, select Automatically Delete Job and then choose the notification type that triggers the deletion.

5. Choose Apply.

Managing Existing Jobs

In Enterprise Manager, you manage jobs with the SQL Server Agent. To do that, complete the following steps:

1. Access the SQL Server Agent window in the console root. You'll see an entry labeled Jobs.

2. Select Jobs in the left pane and you'll see existing jobs in the right pane.

3. You can now double-click a job entry to access its related properties dialog box or right-click a job entry to display a shortcut menu. Key options on the shortcut menu are

- **Delete** Deletes the job definition. Before deleting a complex job, you may want to create a script that can be used to re-create the job.

- **Disable Job** Disables the job so it won't run.

- **Download** If you've configured multiserver administration, use this option to post scheduled job instructions to a target server. Downloading jobs to a target allows you to immediately start execution of a job or to use the job on the target at a later date.

- **Script Job** Select All Tasks and then choose Script Job to access the Generate SQL Script dialog box. This dialog box enables you to generate a Transact-SQL script that can be used to re-create the job.

- **Start Job**   Starts the selected job if it's not already running.
- **Stop Job**   Stops the selected job if it's running.
- **View Job History**   Displays the Job History dialog box. This dialog box enables you to view summary or detail information on the job execution.

Managing Job Categories

Job categories are used to organize jobs into topical folders. When you install SQL Server, default job categories are created automatically. You can add new job categories and change the existing categories at any time.

Working with Job Categories

To create a new job category or update an existing category, complete the following steps:

1. In Enterprise Manager, access the SQL Server Agent window in the console root.
2. Right-click the Jobs node. Select All Tasks, then choose Manage Job Categories. This displays the Job Categories dialog box.
3. You can delete a category by selecting it and then clicking Delete.
4. You can view the properties of a category by selecting it and then clicking Properties.
5. To add categories or change the properties of a category, follow the steps outlined under "Creating Job Categories" or "Updating Job Categories," respectively.

Creating Job Categories

You can create a new job category by completing the following steps:

1. Access the Job Categories dialog box as detailed previously. Click Add to display the New Job Categories dialog box.
2. Enter a name for the category in the Name field, then select Show All Jobs.
3. All jobs defined on the current server should now be listed. Add a job to the new category by selecting the corresponding check box in the Member column. Remove a job from the new category by clearing the corresponding check box in the Member column.
4. Click OK when finished.

Updating Job Categories

You can update an existing job category as follows:

1. Access the Job Categories dialog box as detailed previously. Click Properties to display a properties dialog box.
2. Select Show All Jobs. All jobs defined on the current server should now be listed.

3. Add a job to a new category by selecting the corresponding check box in the Member column. Remove a job from the category by clearing the corresponding check box in the Member column.

4. Click OK when finished.

Multiserver Administration

A new feature for SQL Server 7.0 is the ability to use SQL Server Agent to perform multiserver administration tasks. With multiserver administration, you can use one server to centrally manage alerts and job scheduling for other servers. You centrally manage alerts through event forwarding. You centrally manage job scheduling by designating master and target servers.

Event Forwarding

If you have multiple installations of SQL Server running on systems throughout the network, event forwarding is a time and resource saver. With event forwarding, you can forward application log events to a central server and then process those events on this server. Thus, rather than having to configure alerts on 12 different servers, you configure event forwarding on 11 servers and have one server handle all the incoming events. You could then use the application log's Computer field to determine the system on which the event occurred and take corrective actions as appropriate using scripts or remote procedure calls.

To configure event forwarding, complete the following steps:

1. Access the Advanced tab of the SQL Server Agent Properties dialog box, as shown in Figure 12-16.

Figure 12-16. *Event forwarding can be helpful in reducing the time you spend configuring alerts on individual servers.*

2. Select Forward Events To A Different Server.

3. Use the Server selection list to choose the server that will handle the events. Choose <New Forwarding Server> to register a new server.

4. Set the type of events to forward by selecting Unhandled Events or All Events. An unhandled event is one that you haven't configured alerts for on the current server.

5. In the If Event Has Severity Of Or Above selection list, determine the severity threshold for events that are forwarded.

 Tip To reduce network traffic caused by event forwarding, set the severity threshold to a fairly high value. Fatal errors have a severity level of 19–25.

6. Choose Apply.

Multiserver Job Scheduling

When you want to centrally manage job scheduling, you'll need to create a master server and one or more target servers. The SQL Server Agent running on the master server

- Centrally manages jobs for the target servers. Then you create jobs on the master that runs on the targets. For details, see the section of this chapter entitled "Assigning or Changing Job Definitions."

- Can also download jobs to a target. For details, see the "Managing Existing Jobs" section of this chapter.

Multiserver Scheduling Requirements

For the master/target relationship to work correctly, you must

- Make sure that the master server and all target servers are running SQL Server 7.0.

- Use domain accounts, not local accounts, when configuring the master and target.

- Make sure that SQL Server Agent is running on the master server and all target servers.

Configuring Master Servers

To create a master server, complete the following steps:

1. In Enterprise Manager, access the SQL Server Agent window on the server you want to configure as the target.

2. Right-click SQL Server Agent and then select the Multiserver Administration option. From the shortcut menu, select Make This A Master. This starts the Make MSX Wizard.

3. Read the welcome dialog box and then click Next.

Figure 12-17. *Configure the MSXOperator to handle multiserver job notifications.*

4. As shown in Figure 12-17, create a special operator to handle multiserver job notifications. This operator, called MSXOperator, is created on the master and all target servers that use this master. Set an e-mail, pager, and Net Send address, as appropriate. You can change this information later by editing the MSXOperator properties on the master server.

5. Next, select the target servers to associate with this master server. The process of associating target servers with a master is called *enlisting*. Later, you can remove the association by right-clicking the server's entry in Enterprise Manager and selecting Defect.

6. Click Next and then click Finish. The wizard performs the necessary tasks and reports its progress. You'll be notified of any errors and can click Pause to stop the operation.

Configuring Target Servers

You can configure one or more target servers for each master server. You create target servers by completing the following steps:

1. In Enterprise Manager, access the SQL Server Agent window on the server you want to configure as the target.

2. Right-click SQL Server Agent and then select the Multiserver Administration option. From the shortcut menu, select Make This A Target. This starts the Make TSX Wizard.

3. Read the welcome dialog box and then click Next.

4. Set a valid Windows NT account that can be used to access network resources. As shown in Figure 12-18, type an account name and a password.

5. In the next dialog box, type the name of the master server for this target.

6. Click Next and then click Finish. The wizard performs the necessary tasks and reports its progress. You'll be notified of any errors and can click Pause to stop the operation.

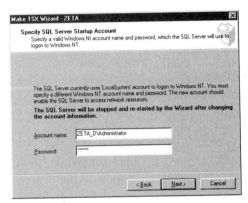

Figure 12-18. *When you configure a target, you'll need to specify a domain account to use for making network connections and accessing network resources.*

Database Maintenance

Database maintenance involves different tasks. Because most of these tasks have been discussed in previous chapters, this section doesn't go into detail on the tasks already covered. Instead, it provides a checklist that you can use as a starting point for your maintenance efforts. Then it explains how to set up maintenance plans and run database consistency checks.

Database Maintenance Checklist

The following is a checklist for daily, weekly, and monthly maintenance tasks:

Daily

Monitor application, server, and agent logs. Configure alerts for important errors that aren't configured for alert notification.

Check for performance and error alert messages.

Monitor job status, particularly jobs that back up databases and perform replication.

Review the output from jobs in the job history or output file, or both.

Back up databases and logs (as necessary and if not configured as automatic jobs).

Weekly

Monitor available disk space on drives.

Monitor the status of linked, remote, master, and target servers.

Check the maintenance plan reports and history to determine the status of maintenance plan operations.

Generate an updated record of configuration information by executing *sp_configure*.

Monthly

Monitor server performance, tweaking performance parameters as necessary to improve response time.

Manage logins and server roles.

Audit server, database, and object permissions to ensure that only authorized users have access.

Review alert, job, and operator configurations.

As Needed

Back up the SQL Server Registry data.

Update the Emergency Repair Disk.

Run database integrity checks and update database statistics. (SQL Server 7.0 handles this automatically in most cases.)

Using Maintenance Plans

Maintenance plans provide an automated way to optimize databases, check database integrity, and create backups. A maintenance plan can be run against a single database or multiple databases. You can also generate report histories for maintenance plan execution.

You create maintenance plans with the Database Maintenance Plan Wizard. The wizard generates jobs to handle the maintenance tasks you select. These jobs should be managed through the Database Maintenance Plan dialog box, as discussed in "Viewing, Editing, and Deleting Maintenance Plans."

Creating a Maintenance Plan

You can create a maintenance plan by completing the following steps:

1. In Enterprise Manager, access the Management folder on the server you want to work with.

2. Right-click Database Maintenance Plans and then select New Maintenance Plan. This starts the Database Maintenance Plan Wizard.

3. Read the welcome dialog box and then click Next.

4. As shown in Figure 12-19, select the databases that'll use this maintenance plan. The maintenance plan can be used with all databases, all system databases, all user databases, or a combination of one or more individual databases.

Tip For most installations, I recommend configuring separate mainte- nance plans for system and user databases. This gives you greater flexibility when it comes to how and when maintenance operations are performed. For large installations, on the other hand, you may want to have separate maintenance plans for each database. This way you can work with different databases on different days or at different times of the day.

Figure 12-19. *Select the database(s) that'll use this maintenance plan.*

5. Select database optimization operations to perform and then set a schedule for these operations, as shown in Figure 12-20.

6. If you prefer, select the Reorganize Data And Index Pages check box to drop and re-create current table indexes with a new fill factor. Then select one of the following options:

- **Reorganize Pages With The Original Amount Of Free Space** Re-creates indexes with the original fill factor that was specified when the indexes were created.

- **Change Free Space Per Page Percentage To** Specifies a new fill factor. The higher the percentage, the more free space is reserved on the index pages and the larger the index grows. The default is 10 percent. Valid values are from 0 to 100.

Note Fill factors are discussed in Chapter 2 in the section entitled "Setting the Index Fill." Reorganizing pages changes table indexes and thus invalidates existing statistics. You can't reorganize data and update statistics in the same plan, and you may want to create separate maintenance plans for handling each of these important tasks.

7. If you prefer, select the Update Statistics Used By Query Optimizer check box to resample the distribution statistics of each index created on user tables. Distribution statistics are used by SQL Server to optimize performance when executing statements on tables. Then set a percentage of the database to sample using the Sample % Of The Database field. A higher percentage generates more accurate statistics than a lower percentage. The default value is 10 percent. Valid values are from 1 through 100.

Note If you set the sample value to low, SQL Server automatically adjusts the sample size as necessary to ensure that a sufficient sample is collected.

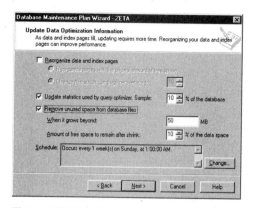

Figure 12-20. *Choose optimization options and then set a schedule for execution.*

8. If you prefer, select the Remove Unused Space From Database Files check box to remove any unused space from the database. Then set values for these fields:

• **When It Grows Beyond** Free space is only removed when its size exceeds this value. The default value is 50 MB, which means that if there is more than 50 MB of free space, SQL Server should shrink the database to the size specified in the next field.

• **Amount Of Free Space To Remain After Shrink** Sets the amount of unused space to remain after the database is reduced in size. The value is based on the percentage of the actual data in the database. The default value is 10 percent. Valid values are from 0 through 100.

9. Click Change and then set a schedule for the optimization operations you've selected. This schedule can be different from other schedules in the maintenance plan.

10. Next, as shown in Figure 12-21, determine whether you want to perform integrity checks. Integrity checks can detect inconsistencies and errors in databases by running DBCC CHECKDB.

11. To run database integrity checks, select Check Database Integrity and then configure additional options as follows:

• **Include Indexes** Checks the data and index pages in the database during the integrity tests.

• **Attempt To Repair Any Minor Problems** Attempts to correct minor problems detected during the database integrity checks automatically. This option is recommended and is only available when you include indexes in the checks.

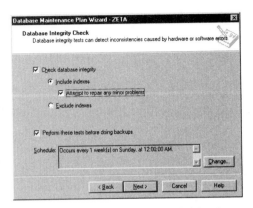

Figure 12-21. *Check and repair the database according to the integrity check schedule.*

- **Exclude Indexes** Checks data pages only during integrity tests and doesn't check indexes. Because fewer database pages are tested, this option executes faster than the Include Indexes option.

 Note If you exclude indexes, you can't repair minor problems automatically; you'll need to handle this manually instead.

12. If you prefer, select the Perform These Tests Before Doing Backups check box to perform consistency checks before backing up databases or logs. This ensures that the databases or logs are only backed up if the integrity checks are normal. Otherwise, if the integrity tests detect inconsistencies, the affected databases or logs aren't backed up.

13. Click Change and then set a schedule for the integrity operations you've selected. This schedule can be different from other schedules in the maintenance plan.

14. Next, specify a database backup plan for the selected databases, as shown in Figure 12-22. If you select Backup The Database As Part Of The Maintenance Plan, complete backups are performed at the scheduled times. You can also verify the backup after completion.

15. Select the location of the backup as Tape or Disk. Then click Change to set a backup schedule.

16. After you configure the backup plan, you need to set storage options for the backups, as shown in Figure 12-23. With disk-based backups, you can set a specific backup directory and create subdirectories for each database being backed up. You can also set the file extension for the backups. The default extension is .bak.

Figure 12-22. *Configure when complete backups of the database are performed.*

17. An interesting option for backups is the ability to automatically remove old backups. Select the Remove Files Older Than check box and then set a specific time period in minutes, hours, days, weeks, or months. For example, you could remove backups more than three weeks or two months old.

18. Next, set backup options for the transaction logs associated with the selected databases. These options are basically the same as those shown in Figure 12-22.

19. Afterward, set storage options for transactions logs. These options are basically the same as those shown in Figure 12-23.

20. The remaining dialog box lets you generate maintenance reports and a maintenance history. Maintenance reports are stored in a directory you designate,

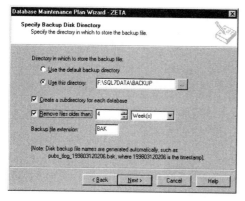

Figure 12-23. *Configure the backup location and storage options.*

and you can specify that old reports should be automatically deleted. Maintenance history information is stored in msdb and by default is limited to 1000 rows of data. If you increase this value or create several plans, make sure that msdb is sized appropriately to handle this data.

21. After you've configured reporting and history, click Finish to complete the process and generate jobs to handle the designated maintenance tasks. These jobs are labeled

- Optimizations Job for DB Maintenance Plan <Plan Name>
- Integrity Checks Job for DB Maintenance Plan <Plan Name>
- DB Backup Job for DB Maintenance Plan <Plan Name>
- Transaction Log Backup Job for DB Maintenance Plan <Plan Name>

Checking Maintenance Reports and History

Creating a maintenance plan is only the beginning. After you create the plan, you'll need to check the maintenance reports and history periodically. Maintenance reports are stored as text files in the designated directory. You can view these reports in a standard text editor or word processor. To access the maintenance history through Enterprise Manager, complete the following steps:

1. In Enterprise Manager, access the Management folder on the server you want to work with.

2. Right-click Database Maintenance Plans and then select Maintenance Plan History. This displays the Database Maintenance Plan History dialog box shown in Figure 12-24.

3. Use the Status selection list to view all jobs, only successful jobs, or only failed jobs.

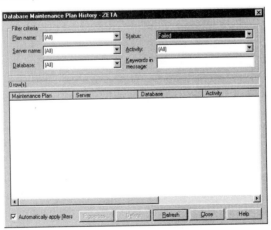

Figure 12-24. *Periodically check the Database Maintenance Plan History dialog box to ensure that maintenance jobs are successfully executing.*

Figure 12-25. *Options in the Database Maintenance Plan dialog box are almost identical to those available in the Database Maintenance Plan Wizard.*

Viewing, Editing, and Deleting Maintenance Plans

You can view, edit, or delete maintenance plans by completing the following steps:

1. In Enterprise Manager, access the Management folder on the server you want to work with.

2. Select Database Maintenance Plans in the left pane. You'll see the existing maintenance plans in the right pane.

3. To view or edit a maintenance plan, double-click the maintenance plan entry in the right pane. This displays the Database Maintenance Plan dialog box shown in Figure 12-25. The options of this dialog box are almost identical to those provided by the Database Maintenance Plan Wizard.

4. To delete a maintenance plan, select its entry and then press Delete. When prompted to confirm the deletion, choose Yes.

Checking and Maintaining Database Integrity

With SQL Server 6.5 you had to perform database consistency checks frequently to ensure that databases didn't get corrupted. With the improved architecture of SQL Server 7.0, you rarely have to perform database integrity checks, and when you do, you can use maintenance plans to handle most of the work for you. On those rare occasions when you perform consistency checks manually, you'll use the DBCC command. DBCC stands for database consistency check. While there are many different DBCC commands, the ones you'll use most often to maintain a database are covered in the sections that follow.

Using DBCC CHECKDB

The DBCC CHECKDB command checks the consistency of the entire database and is the primary technique you'll use to check for database corruption. The command ensures that

- Index and data pages are linked correctly
- Indexes are up to date and sorted properly
- Pointers are consistent
- The data on each page is up to date
- Page offsets are up to date

Listing 12-1 shows the syntax and usage for the DBCC CHECKDB command. When you run the command without a repair option, errors are reported but not corrected. To correct errors, you need to put the database in single-user mode and then set a repair option. After you repair the database, create a backup.

Listing 12-1. DBCC CHECKDB Syntax and Usage

Syntax

```
DBCC CHECKDB
   ( 'database_name'
      [, NOINDEX
         | { REPAIR_ALLOW_DATA_LOSS
            | REPAIR_FAST
            | REPAIR_REBUILD
            }]
   ) [WITH {ALL_ERRORMSGS | NO_INFOMSGS}]
```

Usage

```
DBCC CHECKDB ('customer', NOINDEX)
DBCC CHECKDB ('customer', REPAIR_REBUILD)
```

The REPAIR_FAST option performs minor repairs that don't consume a lot of time and won't result in data loss. The REPAIR_REBUILD option performs comprehensive error checking and correction that requires more time to complete but doesn't result in data loss. The REPAIR_ALLOW_DATA_LOSS option performs all the actions of REPAIR_REBUILD and adds new tasks that may result in data loss. These tasks include allocating and deallocating rows to correct structural problems and page errors as well as deleting corrupt text objects.

 Tip When trying to fix database problems, start with REPAIR_FAST or REPAIR_REBUILD. If these options don't resolve the problem, use REPAIR_ALLOW_DATA_LOSS. Keep in mind that running the REPAIR_ALLOW_DATA_LOSS option may result in unacceptable loss of important data. To ensure that you can recover the database in its original state, place the DBCC command in a transaction. This way you can inspect the results and roll back the transaction, if necessary.

Using DBCC CHECKTABLE

To correct problems with individual tables, you can use the DBCC CHECKTABLE command. As Listing 12-2 shows, the syntax and usage for this command is almost the same as DBCC CHECKDB.

Listing 12-2. DBCC CHECKTABLE Syntax and Usage

Syntax

```
DBCC CHECKTABLE
  ( 'table_name'
    [, NOINDEX
       | index_id
       | { REPAIR_ALLOW_DATA_LOSS
         | REPAIR_FAST
         | REPAIR_REBUILD
         }]
  ) [WITH {ALL_ERRORMSGS | NO_INFOMSGS}]
```

Usage

```
DBCC CHECKTABLE ('receipts')
DBCC CHECKTABLE ('receipts', REPAIR_REBUILD)
```

Using DBCC CHECKALLOC

To check the consistency of database pages, you can use DBCC CHECKALLOC. Again, the syntax for this command is nearly identical to the previous DBCC commands. One item worth noting is that although Listing 12-3 shows a NOINDEX option, it's maintained only for backward compatibility with previous SQL Server versions. The command always checks the consistency of page indexes.

Listing 12-3. DBCC CHECKALLOC Syntax and Usage

Syntax

```
DBCC CHECKALLOC
  ( 'database_name'
    [, NOINDEX
       |
       { REPAIR_ALLOW_DATA_LOSS
         | REPAIR_FAST
         | REPAIR_REBUILD
         }]
  ) [WITH {ALL_ERRORMSGS | NO_INFOMSGS}]
```

Usage

```
DBCC CHECKALLOC ('customer')
DBCC CHECKALLOC ('customer', REPAIR_REBUILD)
```

Using DBCC CHECKCATALOG

Another useful DBCC command is CHECKCATALOG. You use this command to check the consistency of a database's systems tables. Listing 12-4 shows the syntax and usage of the command.

Listing 12-4. DBCC CHECKCATALOG Syntax and Usage

Syntax

```
DBCC CHECKCATALOG
   ( 'database_name'
   ) [WITH NO_INFOMSGS]
```

Usage

```
DBCC CHECKCATALOG ('customer')
```

Using DBCC DBREINDEX

To rebuild one or more indexes on a database, you can use DBCC DBREINDEX. Listing 12-5 shows the syntax and usage of the command.

Listing 12-5. DBCC DBREINDEX Syntax and Usage

Syntax

```
DBCC DBREINDEX
   ( ['database.owner.table_name' [, index_name [, fillfactor ]]]
   ) [WITH NO_INFOMSGS]
```

Usage

```
DBCC DBREINDEX ('customer.dbo.customers', PK_cust, 75)
DBCC DBREINDEX (customers, '', 85)
```

Index

About the Author

William R. Stanek has a master of science in information systems degree and 15 years of hands-on experience in advanced programming and development. He is a leading network technology expert and an award-winning author. Over the years, his practical advise has helped programmers, developers, and network engineers throughout the world. He is also a regular contributor to such publications as *PC Magazine*, where you'll often find his articles in the "Solutions" section. He has written, coauthored, or contributed to more than 20 computer books. Current or forthcoming titles include *Microsoft Windows NT Server 4.0 Administrator's Pocket Consultant, Microsoft Windows 2000 Administrator's Pocket Consultant, FrontPage 2000 Unleashed 4th Edition, Windows NT Scripting Administrator's Guide,* and *Peter Norton's Guide to Java Programming.*

William has been involved in the commercial Internet community since 1991 and has worked with SQL Server since 1990. Before that he worked mostly with Unix networks and Sybase. Lately, he has been doing advanced research and development for Windows 2000 and SQL Server 7.0. In 1998 and 1999 he was a senior member of the technical staff at Intel Corporation's iCat e-commerce division. William's core networking experience comes from over 11 years of military service. He is proud to have served in the Persian Gulf War as a combat crew member on an electronic warfare aircraft. He flew on numerous combat missions into Iraq and was awarded nine medals for his wartime service, including one of the highest flying honors awarded by the United States, the Air Force Distinguished Flying Cross. He lives in the Pacific Northwest with his wife and four children.

The manuscript for this book was prepared and submitted to Microsoft Press in electronic form. Text files were prepared using Microsoft Word 97 for Windows. Pages were composed by nSight, Inc., using Adobe Pagemaker 6.5 for Windows, with text in Garamond Light and display type in ITC Franklin Gothic. Composed pages were delivered to the printer as electronic prepress files.

Cover Designer
Girvin Design

Layout Artist
Tara L. Murray

Project Manager
Sarah Kimnach

Tech Editor
Piotr Prussak

Copy Editor
Joseph Gustaitis

Proofreaders
Joanne Crerand and Rebecca Merz

Indexer
James Minkin